Praise for Developing Knowledge-Based Client ~~~

"This fresh new edition of **Developing Knowledge-Based Client** ~~~ has Ross Dawson's revolutionary view of the future been realized, ~~~ ~~~ practices and methods he laid out so beautifully in the first edition have been expanded, fine tuned, chiseled and polished into a truly masterful guide and tool set. From simple but powerful strategic frameworks to comprehensive principles of knowledge-value creation this book converts the "big ideas" of the knowledge economy into practical assessments, heuristics and processes for making intelligent choices about professional service offerings and strategic relationships. Insightful, practical and beautifully straightforward — this should be essential reading for anyone offering professional or creative services."

— **Verna Allee,**
author, *The Future of Knowledge: Increasing Prosperity through Value Networks*

"The first time I read **Developing Knowledge Based Client Relationships**, it provided me with a fantastic understanding of the powerful role knowledge and technology play in client relationships. I knew it was a book that was ahead of its time. This second edition of the book brings forth a much further developed vision of knowledge-based relationships that really brings into focus all of the potential and promise a knowledge enabled business world would deliver. As we venture forward into the idea and information age, this book provides a valuable guide to what we can hope to expect in the future."

— **Guy Alvarez,**
Founder, Business Development Institute, LLC

"Law, accountancy and other professional firms have long recognized that acquiring, creating and developing knowledge and relationships is critical in providing value. As knowledge and relationships become the only sustainable escape from global commoditization, Dawson uses a wide range of relevant examples to show how professional firms really work, and urges public and private sector leaders everywhere to adopt the professional firm model. Required reading."

— **Richard Chaplin,**
Founder & Executive Director, Managing Partners' Forum

"Ross Dawson is the closest student I know of knowledge-based client relationships. From his perch in Australia, his frequent fact finding world tours and his wide reading he keeps as close a watch as possible of the pell-mell networking developments in this field and he writes about them in a simple uncluttered way which make it easy to understand what is actually happening and who is involved."

— **Napier Collyns,**
Co-founder, Global Business Network

"Ross Dawson was the first among the world's business thought leaders to pursue the intersection of knowledge and client relationships in professional services. No matter what your business, if you want to know more about your clients or customers, you'll find this book useful."

— **Thomas H. Davenport,**
Professor and Director of Research, Babson College and Accenture Fellow

"Dawson has pulled off the nigh-impossible: improved on what was already a terrific book. Even more than before, this is essential reading for professional service firms."

— **David Maister,**
author, *Managing the Professional Service Firm* and *The Trusted Advisor*

"Dawson really cuts through with the book, highlighting the essential ingredient for establishing strong client relationships. His perspectives on how knowledge catalyzes relationships should be read by industry professionals and users alike. It is a penetrating, yet practical guide."

— **Martin L. North,**
General Manager, Strategic Consulting, Fujitsu Australia

# DEVELOPING KNOWLEDGE-BASED CLIENT RELATIONSHIPS

## Leadership in Professional Services, Second Edition

BY ROSS DAWSON

ELSEVIER
BUTTERWORTH
HEINEMANN

AMSTERDAM · BOSTON · HEIDELBERG · LONDON
NEW YORK · OXFORD · PARIS · SAN DIEGO
SAN FRANCISCO · SINGAPORE · SYDNEY · TOKYO

Project Manager: Carl M. Soares

Elsevier Butterworth–Heinemann
30 Corporate Drive, Suite 400, Burlington, MA 01803, USA
Linacre House, Jordan Hill, Oxford OX2 8DP, UK

Recognizing the importance of preserving what has been written, Elsevier prints its books on acid-free paper whenever possible.

**Library of Congress Cataloging-in-Publication Data**
Dawson, Ross, 1962-
  Developing knowledge-based client relationships : leadership in professional services / Ross
    Dawson.—[2nd ed.]
    p. cm.
  Includes bibliographical references and index.
  ISBN 0-7506-7871-2
  1. Business consultants.  I. Title.
  HD69.C6D39 2005
  001'.068'8—dc22
                          2005009797

**British Library Cataloguing-in-Publication Data**
A catalogue record for this book is available from the British Library.

ISBN: 0-7506-7871-2

For information on all Elsevier Butterworth–Heinemann publications visit our Web site at www.books.elsevier.com

Printed in the United States of America
05  06  07  08  09  10    10 9 8 7 6 5 4 3 2 1

# Working together to grow libraries in developing countries

www.elsevier.com | www.bookaid.org | www.sabre.org

ELSEVIER     BOOK AID International     Sabre Foundation

# Contents

# Preface to the Second Edition

As I write these words it is almost exactly five and a half years since I finished writing the first edition of this book. The release of the book in January 2000 helped launch a powerful wave of interest in the topic. Immediately after its release, the book was ranked #1 on *Amazon.com* from Australia for over two months, and since then has spent time on a range of *Amazon.com* bestseller lists, including the Deloitte & Touche bestseller list for over two years. Not long ago the book went into its fifth printing. The concept of knowledge-based relationships has now become a broadly acknowledged aspect of leading business thinking and practice. Many other threads came together to create this momentum. However, I hope the detailed treatment of the topic in the first edition of this book helped to crystallize this emerging domain.

Much has happened since the first edition came out, certainly in terms of changes in the business environment, notably in the professional services landscape and in how communication technologies are changing business relationships. However, during this period my thinking has evolved even more. Over many years of putting the ideas into practice, helping leading organizations to implement knowledge-based relationships, running workshops all over the world for some of the smartest people around, and speaking widely, I have learned a great deal on what works and does not work. I also recognized that I needed to broaden the ambit of my work from the core concept of knowledge-based client relationships to everything a professional firm must do to be successful in its client relationships.

The first key lesson is that even if you are brilliant at engaging in knowledge-based relationships with your clients that does not help you if your clients do not recognize the value you can create for them through this deeper level of engagement. Professionals must *lead* their clients into knowledge-based relationships by demonstrating the value of collaboration. On every front, the future success of professional services firms will depend absolutely on the leadership capabilities within the firm. They must lead their clients into new ways of working, they must lead their professionals into combining their expertise collaboratively, and they must lead their industries by showing that new business models and approaches to value creation are possible and desirable. Thus, the new subtitle of this book is "Leadership in Professional Services." The subtitle of the original edition, "The Future of Professional Services," still applies, as knowledge-based relationships are indeed the future of the professions. However, the essence of this second edition is how to develop the leadership that will bring these types of professional relationships into reality.

One of the major shifts in the second edition is to focus far more on the immediate issues of professional services firms than on the broader issues of knowledge in business. The first edition brought many of the lessons of knowledge management into professional services and organizational relationships, in a way combining the domains. However, the real value of the book is in its relevance to its core readership of practicing professionals. It is intended to help them enhance their client relationships, and build practices and firms that will prosper enormously in our burgeoning knowledge economy.

Since writing this book I have written a quite different book, *Living Networks*, on the implications for business of the connected economy. My work today falls into two domains. I am a specialist in professional services client relationships, and I am a generalist in helping executives understand how to create success in our swiftly evolving global network economy. These two seemingly disparate themes in fact mesh into a perfect unity. A networked world is nothing more than a set of relationships. In an intensely commoditized global economy, value creation will be increasingly concentrated in trusting, collaborative, knowledge-based relationships. Professional services, as the quintessential knowledge business, provide a perfect template and model for developing and implementing these types of relationships on a broad scale.

The changes to this second edition have resulted in a book that is almost half new material. In some ways I would have liked to have changed more, almost rewritten the entire book. However, I also wanted to maintain the integrity of a book that has clearly struck a chord, and has sold consistently very well for five years. With two entirely new chapters, and half the remainder of the book heavily reworked, this second edition has truly been brought up to date and will be of great value to professional services and knowledge practitioners in a rapidly evolving business environment. There are certainly many challenges ahead for every professional, but looking through the lens of knowledge-based relationships I believe there are massive opportunities for those that can successfully implement deep, collaborative approaches to value creation with their clients. I wish you all success on that path.

# Preface to the First Edition

I believe that the future of professional services — which is itself much of the future of differentiated business — is all about people, knowledge, and relationships. In my various careers in systems sales and product management, international stockbroking, financial market analysis and reporting, and management consulting, it has always seemed obvious to me that the greatest value provided to clients has been in making them more knowledgeable. The task for my team and me has always been to help clients to know more, to make better decisions, to have greater capabilities. I have experienced developing relationships and the fruits of building mutual trust while working in a number of different countries and cultures. I observed in practice that adding value to corporate and institutional clients is deeply tied to knowledge, relationships, and developing ongoing rich interaction. At the heart of each of the industries in which I have worked the same basic issues existed, and each one was ultimately centered on interactions among people.

Since my youth I have been profoundly interested in the nature of knowledge, including how the mind works, and how it can function more effectively. Fairly early on I came across the field of neuro-linguistic programming (NLP), which draws on the principles of cognitive and behavioral psychology. However, it is eminently practical in that it is framed to answer the question, "Is this useful?" For more than a dozen years I have engaged in extensive study and training in the field, and have had the good fortune to study with some of the founders and leading thinkers in the field. From there I extended my study to the more academically accepted field of cognitive psychology, and also found that extremely practical in its business applications.

When I started to develop my ideas on knowledge and relationships, I came across the nascent field of knowledge management. Here were people who recognized that valuable knowledge is about people and interactions among people, and that technology is an enabler for that process rather than an end in itself. But somehow everyone always seemed to be talking about knowledge inside organizations. Knowledge is the primary asset of the organization, so if it is made more productive, it will provide better products and services to clients. This way of thinking appears to me to be substantially missing the point, as it seems to be implicitly based on holding clients in low esteem, and thinking of them as consumers. I have sought those who had thought or written about enhanced knowledge as the source of value to clients, and found just a few scattered allusions to the idea as something important, but with no further development of the theme. It strikes me that this represents an enormous gap in current thinking about knowledge in business, and about the whole nature and future of professional services, so with this book I am hoping to begin to remedy this oversight. Perhaps others will build further on what I have begun.

The book is intended primarily for practitioners — professionals in all industries who are in the frontline of adding value to clients. Professional services are more a way of doing business than a group of industries. Therefore, while I expect consultants, investment bankers, accountants, lawyers, and the like to see immediately the relevance and value of these ideas, I hope professionals — that is, all knowledge specialists — in every sphere of business recognize that these issues are also directly applicable to their industries.

The book is designed around the theme of client relationships. However, knowledge sharing and transfer is equally important inside and outside organizations, and this book is intended for everyone interested in the issues of dealing effectively with knowledge in business. I also anticipate that graduate students of business and related disciplines, especially those who intend to work in the field of professional services, will find this book extremely useful in understanding the underlying nature of these businesses.

# Acknowledgments

This second edition of *Developing Knowledge-Based Client Relationships* exists only because Karen Maloney of Elsevier was persistent, thoughtful, and understanding in encouraging me to undertake the task. Originally I had intended to take the new content that is contained in this edition and use it as a foundation for an entirely new book. I now believe that it was definitely the right thing to reshape the original book rather than start again from scratch. Thank you Karen for being such a pleasure to work with as I develop my ideas and work.

A work such as this stems from research, deep thinking, sophisticated clients, workshops, conversations, interviews, and more. Deep thanks to everyone who I have interacted with over the years who has helped me to develop my understanding, and particularly to those who have generously shared with me details of their organizations' innovative practices, and the lessons they have learned along the way. For their input into both the first and second editions of this book, I would especially like to thank Fred Abbey, Verna Allee, Sally Andrews, Margareta Barchan, Chuck Bartels, Andy Bellass, Gregg Berman, Eric Best, Mark Boggis, Geoff Brehaut, Liz Broderick, Lesley Brydon, Mark Bunke, Chrissy Burns, Richard Chaplin, Stewart Clegg, Ken Clements, Napier Collyns, Martin Crabb, Ken Creighton, David Dawes, Don Derosby, Margaret Douglas, Kate Ehrlich, Bill Ford, Oliver Freeman, Chris Galanek, Mike Gilpin, Michael Go, Dan Goldstone, Kris Gopalakrishnan, John Grinder, Vic Gulas, Sridar

Iyengar, Tim Jenkins, Greg Joffe, Sally Jones, Michael Katz, Julia Kirby, Marcel Kreis, Bruno Laporte, Andy Law, Peter Leonard, Laurie Lock Lee, Terje Lovik, David Maister, Doug McDavid, Iain McGregor, Tony Morriss, Nancy Murphy, Matt Nolker, Martin North, Mark O'Brien, Peggy Parskey, John Peetz, Jr., M. T. Rainey, Keith Reinhard, Greg Reid, Greg Rippon, Göran Roos, Michael Ross, Rudy Ruggles, Melissie Rumizen, Mark Runnalls, John Scott, Linda Scott, David Shannon, Reid Smith, Tom Stewart, J. K. Suresh, Richard Susskind, Carol Thomas, Kees van der Heijden, Stuart Westgarth, Steve Weber, and Mark Zoeckler. Please forgive me, those I have overlooked!

It has been a delight working with Dennis McGonagle, Carl Soares, Jennifer Pursley Jones, and all the other highly dedicated staff at Elsevier — thank you for helping make it a reality. Thanks for your love and support to Mum, Dad, Graham, Janet, and the ever-delightful Amy. Most of all, thank you Victoria, for being there and supporting me through the travails of book writing. There is nothing better than being with you.

# Introduction

Knowledge and relationships are where almost all value resides in today's economy. Together they are the only true sources of sustainable competitive advantage.[1] Moreover, knowledge itself is all about relationships. New knowledge is created by combining different people's knowledge, and then only has value when it is applied within relationships. Being excellent at implementing knowledge-based relationships — in which knowledge flows are a critical aspect of the relationship — is a bedrock foundation for success as the pace of change in business accelerates.

Nowhere is this more evident than in the world of professional services. The job of professionals is to apply deep specialist knowledge within client relationships. Their expertise is becoming ever more valuable as business, technology, and society grow more complex. Yet they still face intense pressures of commoditization. Client sophistication, price pressures, global sourcing, and easy access to information are just some of the forces making professional services more competitive. In today's economy the distinction between commoditized offerings (which are driven by price and cost) and differentiated offerings (which are driven by greater value to the client) is becoming ever clearer, and differentiation is ever more fleeting and tenuous as the undertow of commoditization pulls down. The only way out of this trap is to engage in knowledge-based relationships, which not only create superior value for clients but also enable the development of deeply entrenched relationships. The powerful and accelerating forces of commoditization mean that those who are not prepared to work with, rather than for, their clients will find that the fees and margins they are able to command will gradually wither away.

An entire management discipline — knowledge management — has arisen to understand how to leverage the value of knowledge in organizations. The field has many problems, not least its name.[2] Yet knowledge management has a strong future, as over the years it has shifted to be based more on relationships than using technology as a store of knowledge. There is, however, still a primary emphasis on managing knowledge within organizations. There has been much talk of the extended enterprise, which includes not only clients but also suppliers, partners, and alliance members. Yet organizations still often fail to consider knowledge as something that connects them with their clients and other stakeholders. Knowledge is not just an internal issue. Every facet of it is deeply tied to external relationships.

It is important to remember that both knowledge and relationships are ultimately about people. Only people have knowledge, and all high-value relationships are based on individuals interacting. As such, developing knowledge-based client relationships must be based on understanding how people acquire and create knowledge, and how people can learn to exchange and develop knowledge together more effectively. Technology is an increasingly critical driver in professional services. One key aspect is that communications technologies — if used well — enable broader, deeper relationships between people, and for people and companies to work together across boundaries.

This book is intended to be eminently useful — a practitioner's manual. It begins by establishing key foundations, goes on to examine some of the primary approaches used, and then the majority of the book covers implementation — the realities of making it happen in organizations. Case studies of excellent, innovative, and instructive practice are strewn throughout the book to illustrate key themes, and to provoke thinking about how to implement similar approaches in your own firms.

In Part I I examine the foundations of developing knowledge-based client relationships. Chapter 1 gives an overview of the ideas of knowledge-based relationships and client leadership. Chapter 2 examines the current state and forces of change in professional services industries, along with selected strategic frameworks.

Part II addresses adding value to clients with knowledge. Chapter 3 examines the processes of adding value to information that will be used by clients, and how to develop organizational information and knowledge capabilities. Chapter 4 covers adding value to client decision making, while Chapter 5 discusses adding value to client capabilities.

Part III is about implementation — making it happen. Chapter 6 looks at enhancing client relationship capabilities, especially through implementing key client programs. Chapter 7 examines how to manage client communication channels, including applying technology in client relationships. Chapter 8 builds on this to look at effective approaches to structuring client contact in firm-wide relationship management. Chapter 9 explores how to create and lead effective client relationship teams. Chapter 10 deals with issues involved in co-creating value and knowledge with clients, while Chapter 11 examines new pricing models that can be used for knowledge-based services. Chapter 12 draws together the various strands developed throughout the book to look at how to take action. The Appendix draws on the field of cognitive psychology and related disciplines to provide a practical framework for understanding how knowledge is acquired.

For those who have already read the first edition and are looking for what is new in this edition, definitely start with the first two chapters, which have been largely rewritten, and cover the core of the development of my thinking on these topics over the last few years. Chapter 6 (on implementing key client programs) and Chapter 9 (on leading relationship teams) are completely new. Chapters 7, 8, and 12 are substantially rewritten. In addition, all of the original case studies have been rewritten, and there are many new case studies scattered through the book that reflect current practice in the field. Dare I say that the rest of the book probably bears rereading as well, and has also been moderately reworked to bring it up to date.

This book covers all aspects of professional services. It is your responsibility to adapt the specific ideas, examples, and case studies you find here to make them directly relevant to your own situation. Beyond that, you should regard what is offered in this book as a platform on which you can develop new, innovative, and practical approaches that lead your company and industry forward. I am always keen to hear about effective approaches to high-value client relationships. I look forward to hearing about your innovative practices as you put the book's ideas into action, and the lessons you have learned along the way.

## Notes

[1]  See Richard Normann and Rafael Ramírez, "From Value Chain to Value Constellation: Designing Interactive Strategy," *Harvard Business Review*, July/August 1993, pp. 65–77.

[2]  See Ross Dawson, "The Five Key Frames for the Future of KM," *KM Review*, vol. 7, Issue 4, September/October 2004, p. 3.

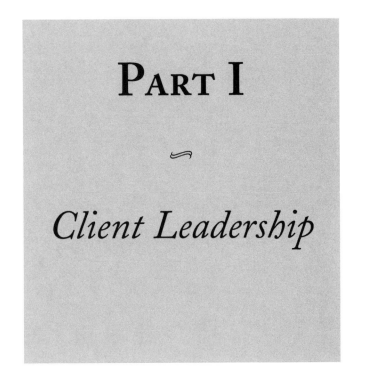

# PART I

*Client Leadership*

# 1

# Leading Your Clients
## Developing Knowledge-Based
## Client Relationships

In 1980, the U.S. economy was worth $4.9 trillion, producing 1.3 billion tons of goods. Fast forward 20 years to 2000, and the U.S. economy had almost doubled in size to $9.3 trillion, yet the weight of goods produced had only edged up by a few percent to 1.37 billion tons.[1] The economic activity that accounted for this near doubling in size of the economy was associated with almost nothing of substance, nothing that you could see. This massive growth in the economy was driven by information, ideas, services, and knowledge — things that weighed nothing. The value is in knowledge.

At the same time, the most powerful trend in business today is commoditization. This is apparent across every industry in every country, as our connected world enables global search and availability. The one element that really makes a difference is the relationship. Without a relationship you become a commodity. With a relationship, everything is possible. You can create far greater value for your clients than your competitors can, and as a result lock your clients into longstanding, mutually profitable, collaboration.

The heart of being able to create this extremely high level of differentiation is what I call *knowledge-based relationships*. These are

3

relationships founded on knowledge — knowledge of your clients, your clients' knowledge of you, and the ability to create knowledge together. In our increasingly virtualized world, knowledge is the primary source of value.

Professional services provide a sound foundational model for our knowledge-intensive economy. They are based purely on the application of highly specialized knowledge. In Chapter 2 I will explore in detail the nature of professional services, and how the professional services model is applicable across all aspects of the global economy. The key issue is that this deep specialist knowledge is applied to create value for a client. That client can be either inside or outside the organization. Either way, the knowledge is applied within a relationship.

Knowledge and relationships are inextricably linked in today's economy. Understanding that fully and acting on it is essential for success in every aspect of business. Some of the key issues of knowledge-based relationships I examine in this book are

- Why it is an imperative to engage in knowledge-based relationships
- How to add the greatest value with knowledge in client engagements
- How to structure your firm and professionals to develop deeper, more loyal, and more profitable client relationships
- How to shift clients to partners and create maximum shared value

Since the first edition of this book was published in January 2000, there has been substantial progress in the practice of knowledge-based relationships. Professionals have become more externally focused, firms have recognized that they need to transfer knowledge to clients, and most professional firms have invested in shifting their structures, processes, and skills to support more effective client relationships. I hope that these trends will accelerate.

## KNOWLEDGE-BASED RELATIONSHIPS

The guilds of yesteryear are the predecessors of today's professions. Their role was largely to protect the commercial privileges of those who held valuable skills or knowledge. Among the rules protecting elite professionals, who gained their mastery through a long process of apprenticeship, were regulations — sometimes commanding very harsh penalties — against disclosing knowledge to any non-guild members. Although regulations often prohibited anyone outside a guild from practicing a particular profession, the focus was on protecting the specialist knowledge at the core of privileged social positions. Some of the same attitudes have lasted over the centuries, where professionals want to protect their knowledge. However, in a world in which vast amounts of information flow freely this can no longer be the case. Approaches to delivering professional services can be divided into two categories: *black box* and *knowledge based*.

- *Black box:* Many professional service firms deliver services in such a way that the client receives an outcome, but does not see the process involved, and is literally none the wiser as a result of the engagement. These black-box services are opaque to the client. Since the only reference point the client has is the result, it is relatively easy for other firms to replicate that result and then compete primarily on price. In other words, they are commoditizing the service. In addition, the only opportunities for interaction with the client in a black-box engagement are during the briefing and the presentation of outcomes, leaving little scope for personal or organizational relationships to develop.
- *Knowledge based:* All professional services are based on specialized knowledge. When professionals engage with their clients to make them more knowledgeable, they are implementing knowledge-based services. The outcome is that clients are more knowledgeable, are able to make better

decisions, and have enhanced capabilities. In short, the client is different as a result of the engagement. Professional firms and clients are pooling their capabilities to create results they could not achieve individually. This makes it impossible for competitors to replicate these outcomes. The entire engagement is based on rich interaction, meaning there are many opportunities to develop a valuable and lasting relationship.

An example of the distinction between these two types of relationships we are all familiar with is how your doctor relates to you. When I lived in Japan, I found doctors stuck firmly to the black-box style of interacting with their patients. The culture was one of great respect and deference to doctors, who told their patients what to do but gave no background or information on what was wrong. I was repeatedly dispensed unlabelled drugs without being told what they were or what was wrong with me. I found it a great relief to visit a doctor during a brief return home, who treated me to a long discussion on current medical knowledge on the background and cause of my ailment, and asked if I had any questions for clarification on what I should be doing to get better and how to avoid similar issues happening again. However, in Western medical centers as well (where doctors are rewarded for high throughput), patients end up with prescriptions but no greater knowledge of what is wrong or how to prevent the ailment from happening in the future. The black-box model often prevails, but the ready availability of medical information on the Internet is starting to shift doctors to a more knowledge-based style of interaction. A very similar dynamic is at play in most professions.

Some professions are more compatible with a black-box style of engagement. For example, litigation is often an issue of getting the best courtroom representation. Yet even in this case there can be strategy implications of the process of litigation, and certainly the litigators will be most effective with deep knowledge of their client. More to the point, one of the most valuable services a law firm can deliver to its clients is enabling them to avoid expensive and risky litigation. This requires ongoing knowledge-based interaction with the client in order to shift processes and skills and add knowledge.

More often professional services can be delivered in a variety of ways along the spectrum from black-box to knowledge-based services. The strategy consulting industry exemplifies this. On the one hand you still find firms that quietly gather and digest information about the client's situation, and then deliver their recommendations with great ceremony, leaving the client with the options of either following or rejecting the loftily priced recommendation. Yet there are also firms that engage with their clients purely with the intention of assisting their clients to develop the most effective strategies for themselves, and that design and implement analytical work to provide input to the client's decision making rather than their own.

In every industry across the globe, clients have increasing access to information, are getting smarter, and are more demanding with their professional service providers. The old paradigm of deferring to the superiority of the professional now rarely holds. Clients seek real value to be added.[2]

## The Virtuous Circle of Knowledge-Based Relationships

Developing effective knowledge-based relationships with clients is not a one-shot effort. There is no magic wand, no single action you can take, that will transform your relationship, enabling the deeper client knowledge, superior value creation, intimacy, loyalty, and profitability you seek. Rather, it is a process where efforts build on themselves over time to create ever-improving results.

One of the single most important aspects of developing relationships is understanding that it is a process. There is no such thing as a static relationship. In Chapter Two I will examine some of the industry forces that are continually tending to erode relationships. The result is that if a key client relationship is not moving forward it is going backward. You need to keep building, gradually creating a

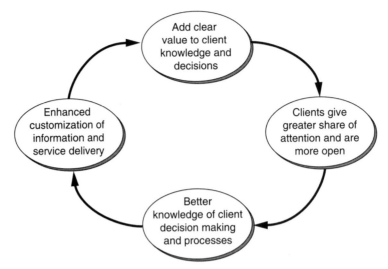

FIGURE 1–1    *The virtuous circle of knowledge-based relationships.* Copyright © 2004 Advanced Human Technologies. Reprinted with permission.

deeper, more mutually valuable, relationship. This is done through a "virtuous circle," in which you cycle through continuously in deepening the client relationship, as illustrated in Figure 1–1.[3]

The four key components of this virtuous circle are:

- *Adding value with knowledge:* Increasingly, clients value knowledge-based outcomes. They seek to gain greater knowledge, be able to make better business decisions, and to have enhanced capabilities.
- *Client openness:* Demonstrating the ability to add value with knowledge means that clients are willing to give you more of their scarce attention, listen to what you have to say, take your calls, and spend time with you. They are also more open in telling you about themselves, their operations, and their issues and concerns, because you have proven to them the benefits of doing so.
- *Greater client knowledge:* It is critical to use greater client openness not just to sell more projects but to gain a deeper

understanding of their internal processes, how key executives think, and how they use information regarding changes in the business environment to adjust their strategies. You want to understand how they engage with knowledge and the external world in making business decisions.

- *Enhanced customization:* One of the most challenging aspects of the virtuous circle of knowledge-based relationships is applying the deep client knowledge you have gained to customize how you communicate with key clients, how you provide information about projects and issues that are relevant to them, and how you tailor service delivery so that it integrates smoothly into their internal processes. This is at the heart of creating true knowledge-based relationships, closing the loop by demonstrating the ability to create vastly more value with knowledge than your competitors can.

To progress, you must be engaged in the virtuous circle of knowledge-based relationships, gaining deeper client knowledge, and applying it to creating greater value. If you fail to continuously enhance your relationships in this way, increasing competition and transparency will gradually erode them, leaving you struggling as a commoditized provider.

## Locking In Your Clients

Wouldn't it be wonderful if you could lock in your clients, making them yours forever? It is a nice idea. However, the reality is that we live in an increasingly open world. Back in the early 1980s, when you purchased a computer application to run your business it was certainly based on a proprietary operating system, which in turn only ran on one company's computer system. If you wanted to keep the same application, you were locked in to that computer vendor. Changing vendors often meant having to reengineer your business around a new application. Today, it is almost impossible to get clients to buy closed systems that would mean substantial switching costs if they choose to move to another supplier. Given a choice, clients will always go for the option that gives them more flexibility. The trick is to create lock-in in a business environment in which systems and standards are more and more open.

In this world, the only way to lock in clients is by consistently being able to create more value for them than your competitors can. This is a positive form of lock-in, in contrast to the negative lock-in of trying to make it expensive for clients to leave you. There are three key foundations for how professional service firms can keep clients coming back through positive lock-in.

- *You know your client better.* It is nothing new for professionals to have to know their clients well. It is just that these days doing this better than your competitors is the primary field of competition. Today, it is important not just to know your client better but to apply this knowledge in customizing your communication and service delivery, as discussed above. If you do, this creates a very powerful form of lock-in through the unique value you can create.
- *Your client knows you better.* If your clients understand the way you work, your people, your processes, and your capabilities, they can get more value from you. They can align their processes with yours, and more easily apply your services internally. In order to switch suppliers, they would have to start from scratch in learning about how another company works to achieve these benefits.
- *You are embedded in your clients' processes.* The fact that business processes can now be readily allocated across organizational boundaries has uncovered a whole new domain for professional service firms to embed themselves in their clients' workflow. Once you have put in the effort required to become an intrinsic part of your clients' work processes, they can experience how much more value you can create for them.

It is not enough to generate these three foundations of lock-in, however. You must take each one that critical step further in creating greater value for clients. For example, some professionals know their clients very well, yet they fail on two scores: first in effectively applying that deep client knowledge to tailoring absolutely every aspect of client interaction and service delivery, and second in continuously working to enhance that client knowledge. As such, their knowledge can have little practical value.

Through this decade, the field of play in professional services will be largely about gaining and applying ever-deeper mutual knowledge with clients. However, now that online technologies increasingly allow professional firms to embed themselves in their clients' processes entirely new ways of creating lock-in and superior value for clients are unfolding. These issues are examined in detail in Chapter 7.

## CLIENT LEADERSHIP

Knowledge-based relationships are at the heart of being able to create powerful, differentiated relationships with high-value clients. Yet unless your clients recognize the value of this style of working and interaction it has little value. You need to *lead* your clients into these rich, highly interactive, collaborative styles of working.

### Relationship Styles

What do you do when a highly desirable client presents you with a tender document, with every issue specified in excruciating detail, and announces that they will engage the firm that offers them the lowest price? At that point there is little you can do other than choose whether or not you want to play on those terms, and if you do go for the business, sharpen your pencil and put in a frighteningly low price. This increasingly common situation represents a commoditized relationship style on the part of the client. It intrinsically believes that the service it is seeking is a commodity, essentially the same from each vendor, and that the lower the price the better.

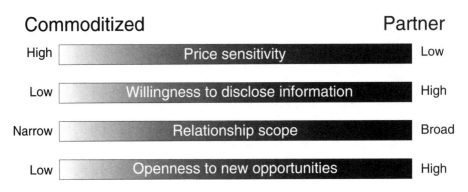

FIGURE 1–2  *The spectrum of relationship styles.* Copyright © 2004 Advanced Human Technologies. Reprinted with permission.

Other firms actively seek to build partnership-style relationships with their suppliers. Shell's Clyde Refinery in Australia chose to consolidate its many service suppliers to one firm, Transfield, and built a relationship based on shared value creation. On one key performance indicator, the refinery moved from lowest quartile among major oil refineries to number two in the world, with Shell executives pointing to their collaborative supplier relationship with Transfield as a major driver.[4] Figure 1–2 shows the spectrum of relationship styles that exist between service providers and their clients.

Organizations will demonstrate a certain relationship style with regard to their suppliers, ranging from treating suppliers as replaceable commodities to trying to build true partnerships. This will vary depending on the situation and the supplier, and can change over time. Indeed, organizations are very rarely monolithic, and different people or instances can reflect quite different stances. Yet you can generalize about where organizations stand in any particular context on the spectrum of relationship styles.

Similarly, professional service firms will tend to deal with their clients with a range of relationship styles. All too often, and far more than they believe they are, firms present themselves to their clients as commoditized suppliers. They offer black-box services, and do not seek partnering opportunities and ways of creating value together. Sometimes with a few long-established clients they find themselves in deep partner relationships, while with others they still effectively work as commoditized providers.

## The Path of Client Leadership

In 1992, DuPont, tired of dealing with a plethora of legal firms that did not understand its business, established what it calls the DuPont Legal Model. This consolidated its legal firm relationships from several hundred to 35, and provided clear guidelines as to how it would work with them and remunerate them. This single example typifies what has been happening for the last decade: clients are leading professional service firms into new ways of working. Professional firms must turn the tables, and lead their clients.

How the relationship styles of clients and professionals mesh is shown in Figure 1–3. If your client wants a partner relationship and you are acting as a commoditized provider, not actively seeking to collaborate with them, at best you will lose opportunities, and most likely you will lose the client. If your client treats its professional service providers as commodities and you are spending all of your energy trying to work with them as a partner, it will probably be an unprofitable relationship, as you are getting minimal return on a large effort. What professional service firms must do is to *lead* their clients into partner relationships, by over time demonstrating the value of greater interaction and collaboration, where both parties share in the value creation process.

Think of your key contacts at one of your significant clients. Consider where they currently stand in their relationship style relative to your firm, on the spectrum from treating you as a commoditized provider to a partner. Also consider your firm's relationship style with regard to your client. It is important to be honest, because the reality is that the way many firms interact with their clients in fact positions them more as commodities than as partners. If you are not currently

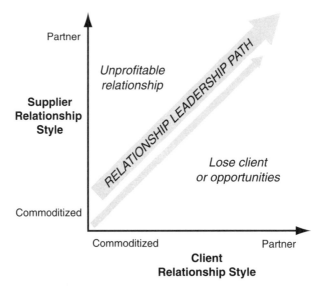

FIGURE 1-3 *The path of client leadership.* Copyright © 2004 Advanced Human Technologies. Reprinted with permission.

in a true partnership with this client, and would like to be, there are three questions you have to consider.

- Is it possible to lead the client into a partner-style relationship?
- If yes, how much investment of energy, time, and resources is it likely to take to shift the client to a partner relationship style?
- Are the potential rewards of leading the client to a partner-style relationship worth the likely investment?

These are some of the most important questions you can ask in relationship development. The bulk of the rewards is in building true partnerships with your clients, which give you the opportunity to create massive value for you and your clients. However, your client has to be open to this for it to be possible. If your client is likely to continue treating you as a commoditized provider, however much effort you put into demonstrating the value of a more collaborative relationship, there is no point in trying. It is possible to have a worthwhile relationship when being treated as a commoditized provider, but what is critical is recognizing when this is the case, and not wasting a significant investment of resources when there is likely to be no or little payback.

Indeed, *return on relationship investment* is one of the most critical considerations at every level of the firm. From the chief executive to the individual relationship leaders, professionals must consider where their investment of relationship effort will bear the richest fruit. The reality is that relationship investment should not be focused solely on the largest clients who spend the most. If they do not respond to your efforts to lead the relationship into one that is more mutually beneficial, and insist on maintaining you as a commodity, it is preferable to concentrate your efforts on firms that may not be as large or prestigious but are open to giving you greater scope to create value.

A key implication is that clients are often not doing themselves a favor by indiscriminately treating their providers as commodities, for example by using standard procurement procedures across all services. If you are able to create substantially greater value for clients in a more open relationship and they do not respond, both sides lose. Organizations need the flexibility to shift their relationship style, when warranted, to allow collaborative approaches to engagements. Those that do not will find that some of the best providers are not investing themselves fully in developing and exploring those opportunities with them. Although the balance of power usually rests firmly with the client, professional firms should be seeking to position themselves to be able to select their clients.

In the bigger picture, one of the key issues for professional firms is how to balance and integrate commoditized and partner aspects into their portfolio of client relationships. I will cover issues regarding business strategy relative to client relationships in Chapters 6 and 12.

## CHARACTERISTICS OF KNOWLEDGE

Over the last decade the concepts of knowledge and knowledge management in business have been up and down the sinuous curves of the hype cycle. Now they have settled into an accepted place in business. We have been through the era of generating definitions of knowledge to the point of nausea, appending it to every other term in the business lexicon from *knowledge worker* to *knowledge economy*, and of technology vendors proclaiming themselves to be knowledge management specialists. Now with a more balanced view of where the global economy is going, we can recognize that knowledge as a management theme is a fundamental part of our present and future.

Yet we still need to gain clarity on the import of knowledge to business, and as importantly on its characteristics in a pragmatic business environment. The hype and confusion surrounding these topics have muddied the waters, and so it is useful to step back for a moment and see the big picture.

### Information and Knowledge

One of the best ways of understanding knowledge is to bring out the distinctions between information and knowledge. The most useful distinction is to note that information is *anything that can be digitized*. As such, if you can store it in a database or attach it to an e-mail it is information.

In contrast, knowledge is *the capacity to act effectively*. In the world of business, knowledge only has any value or meaning if it results in action. Knowledge pioneer Karl-Erik Sveiby offers a working definition of knowledge as "a capacity to act."[5] Similarly, Tom Davenport and Larry Prusak contend that "knowledge can and should be evaluated by the decisions or actions to which it leads,"[6] while Donald Schön notes of professionals that "our knowledge is *in* our action."[7]

This capacity to act effectively in complex and uncertain environments requires the understanding and consideration of a broad array of factors, making effective decisions, and acting on them. For the time being, we can usefully consider this to be the exclusive domain of human beings. As artificial intelligence efforts gain further ground, we may have to readjust this perception, but for now it holds.

## Tacit and Explicit Knowledge

Michael Polanyi, previously a fairly obscure philosopher of science, has been rediscovered by the business community over the last years. In 1967, Polanyi offered a distinction between *tacit knowledge* and *explicit knowledge*. Polanyi pointed out that we can know more than we can tell or explain to others.[8] Explicit knowledge is what we can express to others, while tacit knowledge comprises the rest of our knowledge — that which we cannot communicate in words or symbols.

Much of our knowledge is tacit. That is, we do not even necessarily know what we know, and what we do know can be very difficult to explain or communicate to others. I always like using the example of surfing. A surfer's ability to watch the patterns of swells in the ocean, to see where and how the waves are likely to break, and to catch and ride one into shore is based on long experience. Little of that knowledge can be readily captured or communicated to others. Whatever that surfer can capture in a document, description, or demonstration is explicit knowledge. Reading a document titled *How to Surf* gives you information on how to ride waves, but it is completely different from knowledge, in the sense of having the ability to do it for yourself. That requires going out in the waves, experiencing it, and gaining your own skills in action.

The analogy of surfing is in fact very apt in business. Businesspeople endeavor to pick up on emerging trends, catch them as they break, and ride them to a successful outcome. In professional services, we try to help our clients be more effective at riding the rough and unpredictable waves of our business environment.

Explicit knowledge, conversely, can be put in a form that *can* be communicated to others through language, visuals, models, or other representations. Whatever the surfer could say, write, or draw about his knowledge of the wave patterns, or the businessperson could communicate about her ability to write letters, would be explicit knowledge. In most business situations, especially in the professions, the bulk of an individual's valuable and useful knowledge is tacit rather than explicit.

Polanyi's critical distinction was to frame explicit knowledge as that portion of a person's knowledge that *can* be communicated by being made explicit, and tacit knowledge as that which *cannot* be communicated directly. However, when knowledge is made explicit by putting it into words, diagrams, or other representations, it can then be digitized, copied, stored, and communicated electronically. In other words, it has become information. What is commonly termed explicit knowledge is nothing more nor less than information, while tacit knowledge is simply knowledge.

Knowledge Conversion

In the TV series *Star Trek*, Dr. Spock could simply touch someone's temples with his fingers to perform the "Vulcan Mind Meld," directly communicating their thoughts to each other. Until the day when we can all do this, we have to rely on less direct means of transferring our knowledge to others, including written and spoken words, diagrams, and demonstration.

In fact, even if we could transfer our thoughts directly that would not constitute a full transfer of knowledge. Our ability to act effectively in any particular circumstance is based on all of our experiences through our lifetime, and the way we have chosen to make sense of these. Anyone that has not been through the same experiences cannot have exactly the same knowledge and responses. When we acquire new knowledge, we have to relate it to our existing experience and ways of thinking, and integrate it into these models. No two people will understand an idea in exactly the same way, because they interpret it in relation to different sets of experience. The Appendix goes into more detail on how we acquire knowledge in relation to our existing models of understanding the world.

One way we can share our tacit knowledge with others is *socialization*, where we converse directly, share experiences, and together work toward enhancing another person's knowledge. We can also convert our personal knowledge into information through the process of *externalization* — by making it explicit and rendering it as information, as in the form of written documents or structured business processes. However, information in digital form in itself is often words or diagrams in a document. These are meaningless and valueless without a person to use it or make sense of it. This information must go through the process of *internalization* to become part of someone's knowledge, or "capacity to act effectively."[9] Having a document on your server or bookshelf does not make you knowledgeable, nor even does reading it. Rather, knowledge comes from understanding the document by integrating the ideas into existing experience and knowledge, thus providing the capacity to act usefully in new ways. In the case of written documents, language and diagrams are the media by which the knowledge is transferred. The information presented must be actively interpreted and internalized, however, before it becomes new knowledge to the reader.

This process of internalization is essentially that of knowledge acquisition, which is central to the entire field of knowledge management and knowledge transfer. Understanding the nature of this process is extremely valuable in implementing effective business initiatives and in adding greater value to clients. These issues are examined in detail in the Appendix.

Socialization refers to the transfer of one person's knowledge to another person, without being intermediated by captured information such as documents. It is the most powerful form of knowledge transfer. People learn from other people far more profoundly than they learn from books and documents, in both obvious and subtle ways. Despite technological advances that allow people to telecommute and work in different locations, organizations function effectively chiefly because people who work closely together have the opportunity for rich interaction and learning on an ongoing and often informal basis.

## The Knowledge Management Cycle

One of the classic ways of thinking about knowledge management is found in the dynamic cycle from tacit knowledge to explicit knowledge and back to tacit knowledge. In other words, people's knowledge is externalized into information, which to be useful must then be internalized by others to become part of their knowledge, as illustrated in Figure 1–4. This flow from knowledge to information and back to knowledge constitutes the heart of organizational knowledge management. Direct sharing of knowledge through socialization is also vital. However, in large organizations capturing whatever is possible in the form of documents and other digitized representations means that information can be stored, duplicated, shared, and made available to workers on whatever scale desired.

The field of knowledge management encompasses all of the human issues of effective externalization, internalization, and social-

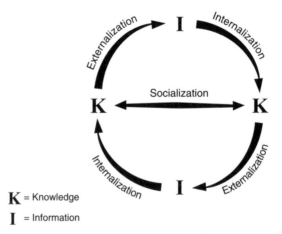

FIGURE 1–4    *The knowledge management cycle.* Copyright © 2004 Advanced Human Technologies. Reprinted with permission.

ization of knowledge. As subsets of that field, information management and document management address the middle part of the cycle, in which information is stored, disseminated, and made easily available on demand. It is a misnomer to refer to information-sharing technology, however advanced, as knowledge management. Effective implementation of those systems must address how people interact with technology in an organizational context, which only then is beginning to address the real issues of knowledge.

## Knowledge Transfer

The idea of knowledge transfer sounds fairly straightforward: knowledge is transferred from one person or organization to another. However, as we have seen, knowledge depends on its context. There are two key types of knowledge transfer.

- *Knowledge communication:* This refers to what most people think of as knowledge transfer. It suggests that a person or group has knowledge, and communicates that knowledge so that another person or group has the same or similar knowledge. We have already seen that because personal knowledge is necessarily intermediated by our communication and interaction, the knowledge received will never be the same as the knowledge transmitted.
- *Knowledge elicitation:* This describes assisting others in generating their own knowledge. It suggests that the potential for knowledge is inherent in clients, and that specific types of interaction can result in their creating their own knowledge and understanding its value. This happens more often than many people realize. Attempts to communicate knowledge often result in insights and learning, just not those that were intended! Increasingly, clients value suppliers that can help them generate their own knowledge and learning.

We acquire knowledge throughout our lives, both on the basis of reflecting on direct personal experience and by learning from others. Sir Isaac Newton did not acquire knowledge about gravity from outside when the proverbial apple fell on his head. He generated it by combining a new perspective with his existing understanding. It is not just through the communication of existing knowledge that we can add value.

Knowledge transfer is often considered an issue of sending documents. This is certainly one component of knowledge transfer. However, this means that the knowledge — the capacity to act effectively — has to go through the medium of information. For this *intermediated transfer* to work, it requires that the original knowledge be effectively and as completely as possible externalized into information, and on the other side that the information be internalized into more effective thinking and business processes. If either of these elements is not effective, knowledge transfer cannot be successful. When knowledge transfer is not intermediated through the medium of information, you are using *socialized transfer*, which requires direct personal contact and interaction.

Both methods of knowledge communication have advantages and disadvantages. I will cover these in more detail in chapters 3 and 7. Knowledge communication is necessarily mediated either by information or personal interaction, and any comprehensive strategy for knowledge communication will include both approaches. Effective communication must be based on a solid understanding of the dynamics of externalization, internalization, and socialization.

One illustration of this principle is found in management games, which are intended far more to get participants to gain insights and think in new ways about their particular situation than to impart specific knowledge or information. Another example is the tendency of fund managers to deliberately seek out research and opinions on financial markets that challenge their thinking. Even if they disagree with the conclusions of the research, they can find the logic or analysis behind it valuable in developing their own thinking, and they are usually more than willing to pay for stimulating ideas.

Effective knowledge communication and knowledge elicitation are based on rich two-way interaction and dialogue. Engaging in discussion — essentially a process of socialization — is central to the process of knowledge communication, which can rarely be accomplished effectively through the mere exchange of files or documents. Knowledge elicitation is even more dependent on interaction. People generate their own knowledge most effectively in a stimulating environment involving discussion of ideas and perspectives. To a great extent the value and quality of knowledge transfer is a function of the richness of interactions with clients. Alan Webber, founding editor of *Fast Company* magazine, writes in *Harvard Business Review* that knowledge workers create relationships with customers through conversations.[10]

In communications technology, bandwidth refers to the amount of information that can be communicated in a given period of time. The growth of the Internet, for example, is predicated on steadily increasing bandwidth, allowing the flow of richer forms of information (such as sound and video) rather than just text and pictures.

The concept of bandwidth is also applicable in interaction between people. Telephone conversations allow for the expression of subtleties of emphasis and emotion far exceeding that of the content and meaning of the words themselves, though this can be limited by the relatively low audio quality of the connection. Video conferencing, in turn, gives far greater bandwidth in interaction between people, by allowing visual as well as auditory information to be conveyed. Even so, the bandwidth achievable by any current technology — in terms of information flow between participants — is many orders of magnitude less than that of face-to-face meetings. Despite the very rapid growth in quality and uptake of videoconferencing, business travel is not likely to diminish. There is no substitute for being in the same room.

In practical terms, maximizing bandwidth means developing the greatest degree of interactivity with clients, by engaging in dialogue through all available means of communication. This principle is vital, not just in individual interactions with clients but in designing the overall structure of client relationships, as you will see in chapters 7 and 8.

## KNOWLEDGE IN RELATIONSHIPS

A large natural resources company drilling for offshore oil and gas was seeking a contractor to design, build, and operate platforms to exploit the large reserves under its control. However, there were a number of new and specific challenges in the project the company had not encountered before. In its request for tender for the contracting services, it specified knowledge transfer as a key element in the decision process. It wanted to be sure that the knowledge generated in the course of the project would be captured and available to be applied in future projects, and that the skills of its contractor would be effectively embedded in its organization at the end of the multi-year multi-billion-dollar project.

It is an increasing characteristic of professional services that clients are explicitly demanding knowledge transfer. Firms that wish to compete for this work have to respond. More generally, differentiation between competitors is frequently centered on effective knowledge transfer. As you have seen, black-box services are readily commoditized. Knowledge-based relationships enable and encourage the rich interaction out of which deeper, more valuable, and more profitable relationships emerge.

These issues of knowledge in relationships are increasingly important across every type of business-to-business relationship. Clients not only seek to maximize knowledge transfer from their suppliers but want to assess what knowledge they need to make available to suppliers to ensure best value and effectiveness.

The role of knowledge has come to the forefront in outsourcing. The first major wave of outsourcing business processes began in the mid 1990s. At this time, decisions were made to place business functions outside the company without considering the role of knowledge. In the process, many firms lost valuable people and their knowledge, and established systems in which they were not able to tap the knowledge generated in business functions close to their core processes. In all types of business-to-business relationships, there are five key aspects of knowledge flow that need to be considered.

- *Knowledge to:* Knowledge being transferred from your firm to another firm, often a client or alliance members
- *Knowledge from:* Importing knowledge from other parties, such as suppliers or research and development partners
- *Knowledge about:* Gaining deeper knowledge about clients and other partners that enables more effective service and interaction
- *Knowledge blending:* Bringing together existing knowledge from your firm and other firms to create business value
- *Knowledge cocreation:* Creating new knowledge in collaboration with others that has value in tangible intellectual property or enhancing capabilities

Each of these issues will be addressed through this book. The primary focus of this book is on client relationships, which means that the most important of these five aspects of knowledge flows are *knowledge to*, *knowledge about*, and *knowledge cocreation*. However, all five issues are potentially relevant in all relationships. As such, executives dealing with supplier, alliance, and outsourcing relationships need only slightly adapt the content of this book for it to be directly relevant to their situations.

## Adding Value with Knowledge

Professional services firms, by their very nature, add value to clients through their knowledge. The central issue for these firms is how to apply this knowledge to create the greatest value for clients and to build the deepest, most differentiated, relationships in the process. There are three key ways to apply knowledge to add value to a client.

- Providing high-value information
- Enabling the client to make better business decisions
- Enhancing the client's business capabilities

These topics are dealt with in depth in Chapters 3 through 5 respectively. However, I will introduce them here to provide a preliminary frame for these ideas.

### High-Value Information

When the Internet grew to become a standard medium for business communication by the mid 1990s, people proclaimed that information would no longer have any value. It would flow freely, and no one would be prepared to pay for it anymore. The last decade has given the lie to that idea. Certainly many classes of information have become highly commoditized, and that trend will continue. However, there remain many types of information that retain very high prices. The critical issue is identifying information that is relevant to the user.[11] If information is highly relevant to an individual's or organization's pressing concerns and issues, and can be readily internalized as useful knowledge, it will be valuable, and price will not be an issue. This is primarily generated through the process of customization. Information must be customized to individual clients, both in content and delivery. These issues are covered in more detail in Chapter 3.

### Better Decision Making

Making decisions and implementing them is where the greatest value is created in an organization. Information and knowledge have value only insofar as they result in better business decisions, in terms of increased shareholder or stakeholder value, or alternatively increased profitability with lower risk. Decisions are the final and critical step in the chain of adding value to information and knowledge. For the purposes of a service provider adding value from outside, decisions in an organization can most usefully be classified into strategic, line, and portfolio decisions.

- *Strategic decisions:* Strategic decisions are those that determine the direction and positioning of the organization. Unless prescribed by the organization's charter, there are no boundaries on strategic decision making. Although there is often input from many levels of the organization, these decisions are usually made by the board of directors or most senior managers, and are based on the broadest scope of information and knowledge about the organization, its business environment, and the relationship between them.
- *Line decisions:* Line decisions can be made at any level of the organization, from top executives to production workers. They are distinguished from strategic decisions in that they are made within a bounded scope, determined at the strategic level by the allocation of responsibility within the organizational structure. All knowledge workers make line decisions in performing their functions.
- *Portfolio decisions:* Portfolio decisions are those made in the ongoing management of a portfolio of assets, liabilities, or risks. This set of decisions most obviously applies to financial markets, though it is also relevant to a host of corporate-level functions.

## Enhanced Capabilities

An organization's competitiveness is based on its business capabilities. That is, how well it performs the activities that impact its performance. Those capabilities are based on a fusion of effective business processes and skills, both of which are forms of knowledge. An organization's processes are an institutionalized form of knowledge, sometimes partially documented but more typically simply "the way things are done." Individual skills are also critical in effectively implementing processes, and developing specific skills within the context of an organization's capabilities can add substantial value. Firms that can effectively contribute to enhanced capabilities in their clients are in a prime competitive position.

The concept of knowledge transfer to clients can be expressed in many ways, and is by no means a new idea. In 1982, Arthur Turner of the Harvard Business School identified eight levels of value in consulting engagements. The top two levels were permanently improving organizational effectiveness and facilitating client learning.[12] Another formulation is found in differentiating between prescriptive and facilitative consulting. Prescriptive consulting is telling clients what to do, while facilitative consulting is helping them to do it for themselves. Demand for the latter is increasing.

## Internal Clients

While knowledge-based relationships are usually associated with external organizations, the concept is equally applicable internally. One of the strongest shifts in organizational practice over the last decade has been for the support divisions of companies — such as information technology, finance, human resources, and internal consulting — to be chartered with providing services to clients in other parts of the company. These relationships mimic external commercial relationships to varying degrees. These divisions usually charge or allocate costs to their clients, and it is common to implement service-level agreements (SLAs) that specify acceptable levels of service. Sometimes the divisions are profit centers, and also provide services to clients outside the firm. It is not at all unusual for company divisions to have the choice of using the internal service provider or going outside the firm.

As such, virtually all of the issues of knowledge-based relationships covered in this book apply equally to servicing internal clients. The key dynamic here is that clearly the internal service division should have significantly greater knowledge of its clients than external providers. The issue is applying this greater knowledge to create differentiated service. An internal service division will rarely have the breadth of expertise of a large external firm. However, if it uses its knowledge advantage effectively it can provide in most cases significantly greater value to its clients.

## THE FOUR STAGES OF RELATIONSHIP DEVELOPMENT

In my work with professional services relationship leaders, perhaps the most common problem I encounter is the mentality that a significant client relationship is going just fine and does not need further development. The reality is, if a relationship is not progressing it is going backward. To improve their client relationships, professionals need to understand that relationships are never static but are a process. Solid forward momentum is the only way to stop a client relationship eroding, driven by manifold pressures, including ever-stiffer competition.

Imagine a path leading over a hill, with a ball that has been rolled up the hill to be perched right on the crest. One way or another, it is not going to stay there, comfortably perched in stasis. Either it will start to roll forward along the path, picking up pace as it goes and gaining momentum, or it will start to roll back down the hill from where it came. Client relationships are the same. They will not remain static. They will always have some type of momentum, either positive or negative. The relationship leader's role is to ensure that relationship momentum is positive. In building positive relationship momentum, it is valuable to recognize the four stages in the client relationship development process, as shown in Figure 1–5.

- *Engaging:* In this stage the firm and client begin to engage and explore the potential benefits of a deeper relationship. This is usually characterized by initial contacts and

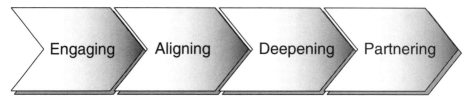

FIGURE 1–5   *The four stages of relationship development.* Copyright © 2004 Advanced Human Technologies. Reprinted with permission.

discussions, qualifying, proposals, and possibly small-scale engagements.

- *Aligning:* The next stage is for firms and clients to begin to align their objectives, relationship styles, processes, language, and culture. Knowledge about clients is applied to customizing interaction and service delivery. Discussion of high-level relationship objectives shifts the basis for the relationship.

- *Deepening:* Here firms focus on both deepening and broadening the relationship; gaining more client contacts across levels of seniority, functions, divisions, and locations; and introducing more of its executives to create a true organization-wide relationship.

- *Partnering:* A small proportion of business-to-business relationships move beyond the buy/sell relationship to one of partnership. This entails jointly creating and sharing value, and is characterized by value-sharing contracts, deep mutual disclosure of objectives, and joint initiatives that draw on the resources of both organizations.

Typical activities of each of the stages of relationship development are shown in Table 1–1. These activities will vary depending on the particular industry and type of relationship. Details regarding the variety of relationships are explored in Chapter 2. Relationship leaders must identify at which stage they are with any specific client, and how to take the relationship to the next stage. If you are not actively

TABLE 1–1   *Typical activities at each stage of the relationship development process.*

| Engaging | • Initial contact<br>• Explore compatibility/qualifying<br>• Proposal<br>• Provide ideas<br>• Small-scale engagements/transactions |
| --- | --- |
| Aligning | • Align technology<br>• Establish objectives, expectations, parameters<br>• Discuss relationship strategies<br>• Map a path forward<br>• Establish a trust development program |
| Deepening | • Develop deeper client knowledge<br>• Gain varied mutual experience<br>• More diverse projects and lines of business<br>• Broader contacts across both organizations<br>• Knowledge transfer and sharing |
| Partnering | • Process integration<br>• Value-based pricing<br>• Share exclusive information<br>• Joint development and marketing of intellectual property<br>• Joint ventures |

working to move the relationship to the next stage, it is in strong danger of moving backward.

These relationship stages can be applied equally to other types of business relationships, including supplier and alliance relationships. The alliance process is one of moving to partnership, where firms jointly create value. This is often not an immediate process. To unlock the potential of an alliance, trust and value creation need to build over time. It is only then that the greatest potential benefits of combining the firms' resources and assets come to light.

Indian technology services company Satyam Computer Services began working for equipment manufacturer Caterpillar in 1993. The following year Satyam executive Bipin Thomas was assigned full time to coordinate the many projects being run for the client. The relationship gradually developed, and by 1998 Satyam was performing $2 million of work annually for Caterpillar, and had 38 employees working on its projects. This is when Thomas began to apply in earnest the client knowledge and solid relationships he had developed over the years working with Caterpillar. Thomas approached Caterpillar to propose working more collaboratively, providing a sophisticated framework for how they could work together. The trust developed over five years of working together made Caterpillar very receptive.

A key platform for moving the relationship forward was a joint IT strategic planning process. Out of this came a framework that clearly identified the competencies required to assist Caterpillar to achieve competitive advantage, and a host of associated initiatives, including jointly established key performance indicators for the relationship. Over the next four years, Caterpillar's business with Satyam leaped to $16 million annually, with 230 Satyam employees working on the account and measures such as responsiveness and customer satisfaction reaching record levels.[13] Thomas never rested on his laurels, however, and continually pushed to take the relationship further.

## THE IMPERATIVE OF KNOWLEDGE-BASED RELATIONSHIPS

In my experience, the importance of knowledge-based relationships is by now fairly broadly accepted by professionals. There has been a strong shift in even the last five years, since the first edition of this book came out, and older styles of professional relationships are gradually eroding. However, there is still substantial push-back, and the reality is that stated acceptance of the ideas may bear little correlation to actual behaviors in client meetings and engagements. There remain some key issues that need to be understood and addressed in order to obtain traction within organizations.

### Doing Great Work Is Not Enough

"Do great work, and your clients will come back." Undoubtedly you have heard this axiom or some variation on it, as it is often repeated by professionals and their advisors. This is a half-truth. It is essential to do good or even outstanding work in order for your clients to come back. However, it is no longer enough. Clients' expectations have changed. They now want service providers that can create exceptional value, make them more knowledgeable, and be true partners.

When you examine the manifold surveys of how clients perceive their professional services providers, a pattern often emerges. There are many leading professional firms that are rated very highly by their clients in terms of technical expertise, but rather poorly in terms of their capabilities at relationships, including understanding their clients business, communicating effectively, being a pleasure to deal with, and creating broad business outcomes. These same clients indicate that the importance of these relationship factors is increasing. Even if they are seeking the professional with the best technical expertise, this is by no means the only criterion, and if they do not have the same knowledge of the client as their competitors or the ability or inclination to apply it to provide differentiated service they increasingly lose the business. In short, doing great work is not enough.

Professional Knowledge Cultures

In his novel *The Bonfire of the Vanities*, Tom Wolfe brought to life the "Master of the Universe" syndrome.[14] Professionals pride themselves on their knowledge, their talent, and their power of influence. Indeed, the advice and action of top professionals can sometimes change the shape of industries or entire economies in massive transactions. The result is that the leading professions are known as much for the massive egos of their key players as for the work they do.

Without underplaying the talent and value of the best professionals, it is important to see the trap. Clients want the best expertise applied to their situation, but they do not appreciate the attitude that often goes with it. Professionals sometimes think that their clients want them to be clever. They do, but this is not enough. They must be willing to engage with their clients in a way that can create mutual value. Chris Argyris' classic *Harvard Business Review* article

"Teaching Smart People How to Learn" is essential reading for professional services leaders.[15] It uncovers how incredibly bright and successful professionals very often have problems relating to clients and shifting to a position of joint engagement on an issue.

Knowledge-based relationships require an underlying attitude of client respect. Without respect for your clients, it is impossible to work collaboratively with them and to tap their knowledge of their business to create outcomes for them. The antithesis of client respect is arrogance. No client will seek out arrogant professionals. Not only is it an unpleasant experience to deal with them but it makes them incapable of moving beyond a black-box relationship. The essence of arrogance is an unwillingness to learn from others.

The other key cultural issue is that professionals see their knowledge as their source of wealth. They are very reluctant to part with it, and eager to promote themselves as experts for hire.[16] Knowledge management is largely about getting people to *want* to share knowledge. It is useless putting in elaborate intranets and other sharing technology and systems unless users are motivated to share their knowledge. Considering the difficulty in getting people to share their knowledge inside their organizations, it is not surprising that many professionals are reluctant to share knowledge with their clients.

## Why Should I Teach My Clients to Do What I Do?

The great fear of professionals is that if they make their clients more knowledgeable they are giving away their key productive asset from which they make money. In many instances this is a misunderstanding of the nature of knowledge-based relationships. This is often not about teaching your clients to do what you do but making them better at what they do, which is very far from doing yourself out of a job.[17]

In other cases, it is true that knowledge-based relationships result in clients becoming more self-sufficient. In some situations it is possible that this means they will rely less on you in the future. More often their increased self-sufficiency will allow you to move to higher value and more profitable types of engagements.

Either way, refusing to engage in knowledge-based relationships with clients is an unsustainable position. In professional services, the far greater risk is that competitors will offer more value to your clients than you do, so that you will lose all their business. In the past, most professions have effectively closed ranks to ensure none of their members revealed professional secrets, and they maintained their hermetic and privileged knowledge. Today's competitive pressures mean that there will always be participants who break ranks to make clients more knowledgeable, and win business away from others. Those are the firms that will build sustained client relationships. Black-box relationships are quickly commoditized, and increasingly mobile clients will gradually navigate their way to firms that engage in true knowledge-based relationships, based on transparency, development of mutual knowledge, and the uncovering of opportunities for superior value creation.

## SUMMARY: KNOWLEDGE AND CLIENT RELATIONSHIPS

Commoditization is a powerful driver in today's economy. For professional services firms, continuing to provide black-box relationships to clients, in which services are provided at arm's length, will simply aggravate this trend. The only sustainable way to escape commoditization is to engage in what I called knowledge-based relationships, in which knowledge exchange is the foundation of the relationship. Creating a self-reinforcing circle of knowledge-based relationships, involving deeper customer knowledge, greater openness, and service customization, can enable positive client lock-in through superior value creation.

While this approach can create greater value for clients as well as their service providers, clients need to have the benefits of these approaches shown to them. Professionals must demonstrate leadership to take their clients on the challenging journey into deep, knowledge-based relationships. It is critical to understand the distinction between information and knowledge in developing client relationships, including considering how knowledge is applied to create value for the client.

Professionals must focus on getting positive momentum in their client relationships. Those firms that do not successfully engage in knowledge-based relationships will find business very challenging moving forward. Building on the idea of the knowledge-based relationship, in Chapter 2 I will explore the quintessential knowledge organizations — professional service firms — and the challenges they are currently facing.

## NOTES

[1]   GDP figures in constant 1996 dollars. Based on information in Chris Meyer, "What's the Matter?," *Business 2.0*, pp. 88, April 1999, and from the U.S. Department of Commerce.

[2]   See G. C. Shelley, "Dealing with Smart Clients," *Ivey Business Quarterly*, Autumn 1997, pp. 50–55.

[3]   Liedtka et al. make a similar point that in professional service firms there is a "generative cycle" of employee and client development (i.e., knowledge and relationships), but they implicitly treat client relationships as black boxes. See Jeanne M. Liedtka, Mark E. Haskins, John W. Rosenblum, and Jack Weber, "The Generative Cycle: Linking Knowledge and Relationships," *Sloan Management Review*, Fall 1997, pp. 47–58.

[4]   Brian Cotterill, "*How Outsourcing Helped Shell Achieve World's Best Practice*," Competitive Advantage from Best Practice Outsourcing: The Untold Success Story Conference, University of Technology Sydney, Sydney, Australia, June 24, 2004.

[5]   Karl-Erik Sveiby, *The New Organizational Wealth: Managing and Measuring Knowledge-Based Assets*, San Francisco: Berrett-Koehler, 1997, pp. 29–38.

[6]   Thomas H. Davenport and Laurence Prusak, *Working Knowledge*, Boston: Harvard Business School Press, 1998, pp. 1–12.

[7]   Donald A. Schön, *The Reflective Practitioner: How Professionals Think in Action*, New York: Basic Books, 1983, pp. 49. Italics in original.

[8]   Michael Polanyi, *The Tacit Dimension*, London: Routledge & Kegan Paul, 1967, p. 4.

9  The concepts of socialization, externalization, and internalization are drawn from Ikujiro Nonaka and Hirotaka Takeuchi, *The Knowledge-Creating Company*, New York: Oxford University Press, 1995.

10  Alan M. Webber, "What's So New About the New Economy?," *Harvard Business Review*, January-February 1993.

11  See Lisa Galarneau's blog on relevancy at *www.oddwater.com/relevancy*.

12  Arthur N. Turner, "Consulting Is More Than Giving Advice," *Harvard Business Review*, September-October 1982.

13  Joseph Sperry, "Turning Innovative Account Management into Dollars: The Satyam-Caterpillar Story," *Velocity*, Q4 2003, pp. 31–34.

14  Tom Wolfe, *The Bonfire of the Vanities*, New York: Bantam, 1988.

15  Chris Argyris, "Teaching Smart People How to Learn," *Harvard Business Review*, May-June 1991, pp. 99–109.

16  Quinn et al. comment on the challenges of getting professionals to share knowledge, as well as the exponential benefits of companies learning from outsiders. See James Brian Quinn, Philip Anderson, and Sydney Finkelstein, "Managing Professional Intellect: Making the Most of the Best," *Harvard Business Review*, March-April 1996, pp. 71–80.

17  As Arthur Turner points out, consultants who facilitate client learning will have satisfied clients who will recommend them to others and invite them back the next time there is a need.

# 2

# The Future of Professional Services
## Differentiation in Rapidly Changing Industries

In a world dominated by knowledge, professional services represent a large and rapidly increasing proportion of the economy. The world is rapidly becoming more complex. This makes highly specialized knowledge the most valuable commodity, by enabling organizations to deal with this complexity and to create value in an intensely competitive world. The field of providing and selling services based on highly specialized knowledge is the domain of professional services.

Professional work is as old as civilization. The first craftspeople developed and applied their specialist knowledge to play a central role in burgeoning communities. In the Middle Ages, guilds formed so that people of a common profession could protect their knowledge, create barriers to entry, and garner respect. Today's professions have shifted primarily to pure knowledge work rather than physical crafts. Some professions, notably medicine and law, have managed to maintain exclusivity based on educational requirements. However, all business services require specialized knowledge, whether or not industry associations have grown to establish certification and parameters around the profession. Graphic designers or web site creators are certainly professionals, even though in terms of certification they need do nothing more than print a business card or set up a web site to go into business. It certainly includes the traditional professional services industries such as law, consulting, investment banking, and accounting. But it goes far beyond the traditional parameters to include firms in fields such as advertising, architecture, market research, engineering, public relations, software implementation, independent research and development, and many more. All of these provide services based on specialized knowledge.

Moreover, as you saw in Chapter 1, professional services are increasingly provided to internal clients. Modern organizations consist largely of what are in essence professional services units (in technology, finance, marketing, human resources, and so on) that are working for other parts of the firm. These functions absolutely fit the professional services model, because they consist of knowledge specialists applying their expertise to create value for clients. In this book I deal primarily with the dynamics of independent professional services firms. However, the same lessons can be applied to internal services provision with slight adaptation.

The unifying theme behind professional services — that of applying specialist knowledge — is very simple. However, it underscores the similarity between these businesses. Certainly the content of the specialist knowledge differs across industries, but it remains that each of these businesses has to deal with very similar dynamics. Professional services maven David Maister affirms that "in spite of many differences, businesses within the professional services sector face very similar issues, regardless of the specific professions they are in."[1]

This book focuses on professional services firms that work for corporate and institutional clients. This is where knowledge-based relationships are most relevant. It is not news for professional services firms that they are in the knowledge business. They have long focused on developing their abilities in leveraging knowledge. They also fully understand that their relationships with clients are the foundation of their current and future success. However, not so many have successfully brought all of these together to create true knowledge-based client relationships, as the dominant mentality has been to keep the knowledge and relationships separate.

This chapter explores the nature of professional services. This is valuable not only to professional services practitioners but also to any leader across the public and private sectors. Those that seek to achieve success in our knowledge-based economy need to study professional services as the quintessential knowledge business.

## KNOWLEDGE IN PROFESSIONAL SERVICES

As you have seen, professional services is founded on deep knowledge specialization. Corporate clients can perform many functions with their own capabilities and expertise, but increasingly need to access highly specialized knowledge from outside, both in outsourcing functions and enhancing their own processes. Professionals have the scope to focus their resources on very narrow fields of expertise, gain experience across a diverse range of clients, and innovate in the course of their engagements. As both individuals and organizations they are able to develop a far greater depth of knowledge and expertise within highly specialized areas than their clients can. As such, most corporations and institutions usually find that the most effective use of their resources is to seek out professional services firms when they require highly specialized expertise.

The other key aspect to professional services is that they are usually delivered in highly interactive relationships with clients. Services are usually specific to the client, and thus need to be customized based on knowledge of the client. In addition, service delivery often entails extensive client interaction. This is not always the case. For example, in business process outsourcing, once the outsourcing service has been established it may require minimal further interaction. However, designing the engagement in this way means that neither the professional firm nor the client can receive the benefits of engaging in knowledge-based relationships. As such, there are two defining aspects of implementing a professional services model, both based on knowledge.

- *Internal ways of working:* Firms work in project and client teams that form around specific opportunities and engagements. Active knowledge sharing within and beyond teams is critical to success.
- *Client interaction:* The value for clients is created through applying and delivering specialist knowledge in the engagement, with much of the value in the delivery and interaction itself.

Clearly, large professional services firms are able to bring together many experts in diverse fields in order to become in some sense "knowledge generalists" to their clients, though this capability is built on a legion of specialists.

## Professional Services Industries

Many of the traditional professional services industries have only relatively recently engaged in enhancing their business practices. What I refer to as the "professionalization of the professions" is finally well under way, and none too soon. The leaders of professional services firms usually rose from the ranks, promoted on the basis of their professional expertise and success, yet did not have the opportunities to expand their general managerial and leadership capabilities.

This has meant that — at their best — professional services firms in industries such as law, advertising, and engineering have started to look beyond the boundaries of their own professions for lessons on effective practices. Professional services firms are realizing not only that the fundamental nature of their businesses is the same as those in other professional industries but also that they are facing essentially the same competitive pressures, and sometimes even the same competitors. Given their common foundation, each professional services industry has a tremendous opportunity to learn from the methods of all other professional fields. From now on the greatest innovation in professional services firms will come from that cross-pollination, by adapting and implementing excellent practice from what are fundamentally similar businesses working in different industries.

This book treats the sphere of professional services as a unity, in order to assist practitioners in each industry to learn not only from commonalities across professional services but also from specific practices in other industries that can be applied in their own fields. Throughout the book I will draw on a wide variety of professional services industries for examples of innovative, excellent practice. Most of these provide lessons that can be adapted or directly implemented in other professional services companies. I strongly recommend that in reading each of the examples and case studies you endeavor to adapt and relate the approaches to the circumstances of your own industry.

## Applying the Professional Services Model

All organizations are becoming professional services firms, as Tom Peters contends.[2] The success of every company, whether it is in services, manufacturing, retailing, utilities, or any other industry sector, is increasingly based on applying knowledge effectively. Businesses are thus naturally evolving toward the ways of working that the professional services industries have pioneered. In studying professional services firms, we are also learning approaches that are applicable in almost any organization. Any sales organization whose products are not completely commoditized is seeking to build relationships and draw on its knowledge to service its clients. Often the objectives of government and not-for-profit organizations are to apply and make available valuable knowledge. One of the World Bank's primary aims is to provide enabling knowledge to governments, agencies, and individuals throughout the developing world, as described in Chapter 10.

Knowledge transfer can be a key differentiator in many product industries. Buckman Laboratories, a provider of specialty chemicals, is a great example of this. Many clients choose to buy from Buckman because of the access they get to deep experience on how to use the chemicals within their own manufacturing processes. Despite delivering products, it has become a services company. Some of Buckman's team processes are described in Chapter 6. My focus on corporate and institutional clients in no way suggests that knowledge transfer is not important for individual and retail clients. Certainly the degree of client sophistication impacts the most effective approaches to transferring knowledge, although many individuals make purchasing decisions based on the knowledge transfer component of offerings. An obvious example of this tendency is found in financial services, ranging across banking, insurance, and stockbroking. Although individuals are not usually as sophisticated as institutional clients, they have a strong desire to increase personal control by developing their knowledge underlying the financial decisions they make, and will tend to favor vendors who assist them in making educated decisions. Investors who choose to buy and sell shares through a full-service stockbroker rather than on the Internet are effectively doing so on the basis of the knowledge transfer involved. In product sales, retail customers tend to value highly any genuine efforts to impart knowledge that enables them to make better purchasing decisions. Certainly, the highest levels of retail services are based on gaining deep customer knowledge and applying it to customized service.


## Shifting to Professional Services

The recognition of the value of the professional services model has been matched by action. Across a wide range of industries, product-based organizations have leapt to establish professional services and consulting divisions. The key driver has been businesses across the board recognizing that their core product business is rapidly becoming commoditized, and that their client relationships are eroding. It has become apparent that knowledge is a vital element of the value they add to clients. As such, it is valuable to formalize that by providing specific professional services offerings.

The most obvious example is how computer hardware companies have shifted their businesses to services. The stand-out example, IBM, has transformed itself from a company that primarily sold computer hardware to an organization that receives substantially less than half its revenue from hardware. This was already the case before its landmark acquisition of PwC Consulting, which bolstered its professional services staff by 30,000. HP's beginnings were in technical instrumentation, though over time computers became its core business. The firm has now sold off the division representing its original business line. In 1997, Hewlett-Packard set up HP Consulting, which in one fell swoop established a global consulting organization with more than 5,000 employees. When it acquired Compaq in 2002, it was buying a company for which almost a quarter of its revenue was derived from services. Network systems company Novell chose to buy the consulting firm Cambridge Technology Partners to create its consulting division.

However, the trend encompasses almost every industry, in which agricultural, heavy industrial, mining, and transport companies, among others, are establishing professional services divisions. United Parcel Service (UPS) has a burgeoning professional services division covering an array of logistics, project management, and engineering services. Continental Grain, one of the largest suppliers of grain worldwide, has established ContiTec, a consulting arm that provides focused internal consulting services through the company and services for select clients applying specialist knowledge on engineering and nutritional issues in their grain processing.

There is a range of key issues that must be dealt with in establishing professional services arms. The most important is the relationship of these new divisions to core product functions. Since the rationale for establishing professional services operations is often strategic, in terms of providing differentiation and enabling the development of highly interactive knowledge-based relationships, there should be a significant degree of integration of these services with core offerings. However, structural issues, including relationship management and remuneration, need to be addressed effectively.

## DRIVERS IN PROFESSIONAL SERVICES INDUSTRIES

Enron has a lot to answer for. The domain of professional services has been strongly buffeted over the last years, with strong forces that were in play in the late 1990s, such as deregulation and convergence, turned on their head by the corporate disasters of the first couple of years of the new century. Today, there are seven key drivers shaping professional services industries.

- Client sophistication
- Governance
- Connectivity
- Transparency
- Modularization
- Globalization
- Commoditization

Together these seven drivers provide a framework for understanding the forces on professional services firms today. Each driver also underlines the value and importance of shifting toward implementing effective knowledge-based relationships with key clients.

### Client Sophistication

One of the most inexorable trends is that of increasing client sophistication. In the past, professionals were hired to provide their lofty expertise, and were shown due deference. Over the years, clients have gained knowledge about service domains, have hired senior executives away from their service providers, and have refined how they work with external providers. One of their objectives has been increased self-sufficiency, or at the very least the ability to understand when and how it is appropriate to hire external professionals, and how to deal with them effectively. A new class of consultants has arisen to advise on how to issue requests for proposal, write service contracts, and manage service providers. In a number of service domains, including law and advertising, companies are often mandating that firms are engaged through their procurement departments, or through a strictly defined assessment process.

Client sophistication is usually correlated with size and with how much they spend on professional services. Although some professionals say they prefer less sophisticated clients, basically because they can exploit them, they are unlikely to have a promising career in the face of market trends. Those companies that have established rigid procurement make it difficult or impossible for service providers to work collaboratively with the clients. The professionals are being stuck in a box and inherently treated as commodities. The most sophisticated clients realize that this limits value creation, and are open to creating partnerships with their services providers, in those cases where it is justified. They understand that there has to be the opportunity for joint value creation and that it has to be worthwhile for the service provider, otherwise, they will not get the attention and resources they want.

Governance

Scandals galore over the last years have pushed governance to the top of the corporate agenda. The most important legislation to stem from Enron and the series of debacles that followed was the Sarbanes-Oxley Act, which among many other provisions established guidelines for how companies should deal with their auditors, in order to avoid conflicts of interest between verifying the accuracy of their clients' accounts and generating additional revenue from an array of other activities. However, the impact has gone far beyond that, with companies suddenly highly aware of the potential for conflicts of interest at their services providers. The real outcome has been a severe erosion of trust between companies and their professional services providers. Clawing that back will be a very slow process.

One specific provision of the Sarbanes-Oxley Act is that the lead audit partner at the audit firm must be rotated every five years for public company work. The intent is that personal relationships should not become too deep. One implication is that this makes it far more difficult for firms to know their clients extremely well. A real danger is that firms will not be able to create superior value for their clients because of lack of in-depth client knowledge. Although this legislation is specific to auditors, the attitudes have flowed across into other service domains.

Governance issues have turned on its head what was in the late 1990s one of the most powerful trends in professional services: convergence. The most pointed example is in how the major accounting firms established significant legal firms. In 2001, Andersen Legal (the legal services unit of Arthur Andersen) employed 2,880 lawyers, ranking it the second largest law firm in the world by number of lawyers.[3] All the other four global audit firms had significant legal operations. In the wake of Sarbanes-Oxley, these legal services operations have been sold off, shut down, or kept at arm's length. The heightened awareness of the potential for conflicts of interest has also placed dampeners on other convergent trends in the industry, such as between accounting and financial services.

## Connectivity

Professionals whose lives are now centered around e-mail find it stunning to recall that as recently as the early 1990s many of them had never sent an e-mail in their life. Few people had mobile phones, and documents were entrusted to the post office or couriers. Today, connectivity dominates the professional world, both in how work is done within firms and in how professionals communicate with clients.

One of the most evident impacts is in the pace of work. Expectations for how quickly professionals respond and turn work around have soared.

Although e-mail alone has had a massive impact on how professional work is done, there are now many layers to connectivity. Instant messaging is increasingly being used both within firms and with clients, web conferencing takes conference calls to the next level, and clients are able to access tailored information at will and to view work in progress. These are all commonplace today, yet the transformation from industries based primarily on physical documents has been swift — covering barely more than a decade — and dramatic.

As I explore in more detail in Chapter 7, connectivity is in many cases radically changing the nature of the professional/client relationship. When clients can both see every aspect of professional work as it happens and participate in whichever aspect they choose, the respective roles of client and professional have been redefined.


Transparency

In the 1970s, a large British company had a TV advertisement created for them by a leading advertising agency. Its invoice is reputed to have read: "Television Commercial: One Million Pounds." Today, clients regularly demand from their advertising agencies not only detailed itemization of their billing but also complete information on the agencies' costs and profit margins. To preempt the clients' demands, many agencies are proactively offering this information to their major clients.

Kemp Little, a U.K. law firm, provides its clients with an extranet that provides information on work-in-progress to its clients, enabling them to see unbilled time up to the previous day. This is a major shift from traditional law firm practices, in which clients only see time spent on their account until it is billed monthly. Increasingly, clients want to see not only billings but precisely how work is being performed and who is working on it. The experience of professional firms who provide greater transparency to their clients on processes and progress is that clients love it but do not necessarily choose to access it all the time. There is a great comfort factor in knowing they can see what is happening if they choose, and it is a significant differentiating factor in selecting their external providers. However, the issue is knowing it is there rather than using it.

In a connected world, transparency is a reality, and we have only seen the beginning. The future of business and society will be driven by increasing transparency. All businesspeople need to acknowledge this, and consider their strategic responses. In the present, transparency is a critical issue impacting professional/client relationships.


Modularization

U.K. law firm Lovells has a service it calls Mexican Wave, in which work from clients is allocated either to in-house lawyers or sent out to external firms that can perform routine work at lower cost. This example, which is described in more detail in Chapter 7, illustrates how it is increasingly easy to divide work into modules that can be performed in different locations or even different firms. This applies on two levels. First, professional services firms are increasingly able to outsource elements of their work. Second, clients find it far easier to select which components of a service they choose to be done externally and internally, or to be done by a particular service provider.

The ability for business to treat services as modular, able to be broken down into small components, is greatly supported by current emerging technologies. XML (eXtensible Markup Language) is a standard for attaching descriptions to pieces of information, so that any computer will know what any incoming information means, and how to treat it. Web services allow applications on different computers to interact and mesh seamlessly. Together, these are powerful enablers of modularization because they allow separate elements of business processes to be performed in different places and even different companies yet still be fully integrated.

The trend of unbundling of services into their components has been in place for a long time. However, this is now accelerating. This does not mean that clients necessarily choose to unbundle service provision. I will examine this issue in more detail later in the chapter. However, it is increasingly possible, and many clients are taking this up. Those firms that choose to sell monolithic services will find that their clients want to cherry-pick parts and get others performed by separate firms.

## Globalization

The shift to a more global, integrated economy is impacting every aspect of business, including professional services. The modularization of business means that those modules can readily be positioned not just outside the client or professional services firm but in a different country on the other side of the planet. Those elements that can be performed at lower cost in other countries will be relocated. A pointed illustration is the fact that many major investment banks, including JP Morgan, Morgan Stanley, and Citibank, are doing financial analysis and investment research in India.

The other key aspect to this trend is the fact that clients are increasingly global and integrated. The provision of services to multinational clients requires integration of practices, information flows, and client work. As I discuss in Chapter 9, professional firms need to be at least as coordinated across practice areas and locations as their clients are.

## Commoditization

The final outcome of many of the other key drivers, such as connectivity, transparency, modularization, and globalization, is the stark reality of commoditization. As in other industries, service and product offerings are being rapidly replicated by competitors and provided at a lower price. Elements of services that can be performed online are available as standalone, low-cost offerings. Companies are using requests for proposal and similar tools to compare service firms directly on price. Clients are increasingly prepared to source services globally.

Today, there is often considerably decreased loyalty on the part of clients, and strong internal drivers to decrease costs. The best offering at the lowest cost will be snapped up, and then ignored as soon as something better comes along. Yet despite the pressures of commoditization, there are many opportunities for professional services firms to transcend this drive, and create true partnerships with the client. The heart of the answer to commoditization is implementing knowledge-based relationships, and professional services firms are in the best possible situation to be able to create these. Later in this chapter and throughout this book I will examine how professionals can escape and move beyond the trap of commoditization.

## UNDERSTANDING PROFESSIONAL SERVICES FIRMS

Having recognized the existence of many important common elements and issues across all professional services industries, identifying and exploring these elements will help us develop a detailed understanding of the field. In addition, it will give us further insight into each professional services industry by revealing which elements differ from those in other industries. This approach enables us to determine what practices in one professional services firm are likely to succeed when applied or adapted to other related industries. Throughout our discussion, we will develop the theme of professional services firms as organizations based on specialist knowledge. We will look at the resources, inputs, functions, and the nature of relationships in professional services firms, and how they add value to their clients' functions. These elements are summarized in Figure 2–1.

### Resources of Professional Services Firms

The key resources of professional services firms are certainly not fixed assets such as plants and machinery. Trying to understand knowledge-

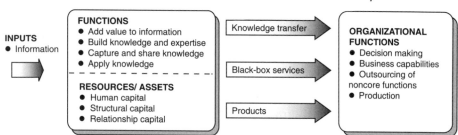

FIGURE 2–1  *A model of professional services firms.* Copyright © 2004 Advanced Human Technologies. Reprinted with permission.

intensive companies has driven the development of the new field of intellectual capital, which has provided us with frameworks for managing and beginning to measure the intangible assets of organizations. Of course, professional services firms as prototypical knowledge-based organizations provide an excellent illustration of the tenets of intellectual capital.

Frameworks for intellectual capital have been proposed by, among others, Sveiby,[4] Stewart,[5] Edvinsson and Malone,[6] Roos et al.,[7] and Brooking.[8] These frameworks all build on the original work of Sveiby, as such their basic structure and composition are very similar, with a few differences between authors over terminology and distinctions between the major categories of intellectual capital.

I will present my preferred framework for categorizing intangible assets, which is based on the work of all of the authors cited above, and uses definitions relevant to our purposes. The intangible assets of organizations can be separated into three categories.

- Human capital
- Structural capital
- Relationship capital

*Human capital* refers to the people who work for an organization, and their skills and abilities in creating value for the organization and its clients. *Structural capital* includes systems, processes, legally protected intellectual property such as patents, and organizational culture. *Relationship capital* includes relationships with clients, suppliers, alliance members, regulators, and other parties, as well as image and reputation.

Looking at this framework from the perspective of knowledge generation and transfer, human capital — essentially the people in an organization — is ultimately the key resource of professional services firms, and where the most valuable knowledge resides. Increasingly, organizations are attempting to capture that knowledge in documents, databases, and processes — that is, to make it part of their structural capital. Nevertheless, the ability to apply that knowledge to generate profitable business depends on the quality of the organization's relationship capital, notably its client relationships.

## Inputs of Professional Services Firms

The traditional inputs of industrial companies are basic commodities and low-level manufactured goods. What are the inputs of professional services firms? Information is the primary raw commodity used by knowledge organizations in performing their functions. These firms take information from external sources, and using their resources, including the knowledge held by their people, process that information in order to create value for their clients.

Financial markets are a clear example of a world completely driven by information and its interpretation by market participants. Financial market brokers and traders must have access to all major information sources, and their daily work is completely based around analyzing and making decisions based on that information. Walter Wriston, former chairman of Citibank, writes about how information flows through the nervous system of global financial markets to determine how money and prices move.[9] Similarly, lawyers can only perform their work on the basis of complete information about relevant legal cases, together with information and knowledge about their clients and the business environment.

Functions of Professional Services Firms

Professional services firms, when seen as knowledge-based organizations that add value to their clients through the execution of services, perform four key functions that draw on their resources and inputs.

- Adding value to information
- Developing knowledge and expertise
- Capturing and sharing knowledge
- Applying knowledge

Adding value to information is a key process in professional firms, which will be covered in detail in Chapter 3. It is a particularly critical function when knowledge transfer is an important issue, as much of the process of adding value to information lies in making it easy to internalize as knowledge, and readily usable in decision making.

Developing knowledge and expertise is an ongoing task for professional firms. The existing knowledge of their partners and staff is a base on which they must continually develop and build. The staff must both keep pace with knowledge development in their fields by reading journals, going to conferences, and keeping an open dialogue with their peers, and continually generate new knowledge by building on what they have learned, and applying the experience gained in working on client projects.

Capturing and sharing knowledge is at the heart of what is commonly called knowledge management. Particularly in larger firms, developing individual knowledge and expertise is less important than getting the most useful, valuable knowledge to be made available and used as widely as possible across the firm. To the extent that knowledge can be captured (i.e., made explicit), it can become part of the permanent structural capital of the organization rather than simply existing in one key individual's mind. As we saw in Chapter 1, sharing knowledge can happen directly or indirectly; both rich social interaction and the effective implementation of technology are essential.

Applying knowledge is the final step that makes the knowledge valuable. This application can be in product development, marketing, strategic decision making, performing services for clients, or any of the many activities that generate revenue and profitable business. Developing and sharing knowledge are only meaningful and useful if that knowledge leads to better business results through its application to the critical operations and functions of an organization.

## Adding Value to Client Functions

Adding value to clients is ultimately about enabling them to add greater value to their own customers. Black-box services enable clients to outsource specialist functions that can be performed more effectively or at lower cost than if handled in-house. This strategy adds value by achieving better outcomes at lower cost in noncore functions, and by allowing management to focus on their core capabilities and competencies. Knowledge-based relationships add value by resulting in better decision making, enhanced business capabilities, or both.

## THE DIVERSITY OF PROFESSIONAL SERVICES RELATIONSHIPS

The field of professional services is by no mean homogenous. Services delivery covers an entire spectrum of different styles of relationships. This is sometimes a function of the industry, though it frequently varies according to the relationship styles of the client and the service provider. Figure 2–2 shows some of the more important dimensions of professional services relationships.

- *Services scope:* Some professional firms, such as environmental auditors, provide very focused services, which dictates who they deal with at their clients and the nature of their relationship. Firms that offer a broad spectrum of services within or across industries have to deal with issues of multiple contact points and cross-selling across divisions.

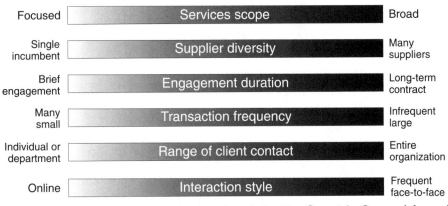

FIGURE 2–2   *The diversity of professional services relationships.* Copyright © 2004 Advanced Human Technologies. Reprinted with permission.

- *Supplier diversity:* Audit and often advertising, for example, are characterized by relationships with a single incumbent services provider, which results in issues with maintaining relationships and a focus on times when clients switch allegiances. This gives a very different relationship dynamic to a situation in which there is a panel of services firms, or simply a wide array of providers.
- *Engagement duration:* Some engagements, such as a focused press campaign or assistance with a pressing process problem, are quite short in duration. At the other end of the spectrum, clients have an ongoing, open-ended relationship with their suppliers, or potentially a long-term contract. The nature of the relationship reflects whether both sides are endeavoring to create value beyond the individual transaction or engagement.
- *Transaction frequency:* Financial market sales illustrate a situation with many transactions within an ongoing relationship. A bond salesperson may have multiple transactions with a single client in a single day. On the other hand, specialist mergers and acquisitions advisors may only have a transaction with a smaller client every few years.

- *Range of client contact:* Most professional services industries have a traditional locus for their client relationships. For law firms it is the general counsel, for advertising firms the chief marketing officer, and for audit firms the chief financial officer. In some cases the relationship remains focused on that key individual at the client and perhaps his or her direct reports. However, in these and other industries it is possible to build client relationships that span an immense diversity of positions and functions at the client.
- *Interaction style:* Increasingly, a number of professionals are finding that their client interactions are shifting to e-mail and document-based interaction, leading to a largely online relationship. Others still work in a primarily face-to-face mode, often through facilitating workshops or in coaching-style interactions.

It is useful to consider where your firm's activities are positioned along these key variables in professional services relationships, as well as where you would like them to be. If there is a discrepancy, this can be used as an input to strategic planning for the firm.

## Approaches to Services Procurement

One of the most powerful trends in professional services over the last decade has been the consolidation of relationships by clients, often referred to as "convergence." This is primarily a result of the key driver of client sophistication. Companies have realized that it does not help either themselves or their service providers to deal with too many suppliers. The narrow relationships caused by dealing with too many firms means that professionals are not able to get to know their clients well, companies do not get to know their advisors and their strengths and weaknesses, and spreading the business around too thinly means providers do not have a strong interest in the client. As a result, many organizations have formalized their services procurement, often creating highly selective panels of providers and allocating all of their work among this limited group.

Yet there remains wide diversity in how this consolidation is achieved and in how services procurement is implemented. It is now commonplace for panels of service providers to be selected through a bidding process, in which firms line up in a beauty parade, highlight their capabilities in bulky documents, and sharpen their pencils to propose highly discounted rates commensurate with the amount of work they stand to obtain through their privileged position on the panel. Although it is a trend for procurement departments within companies to be involved in purchasing not just raw materials and stationery but also specialized professional services, some firms have deliberately retained the latitude for executives to make judgments on which firms are best for them to use.

## One-stop versus Best-of-Breed

A perennial discussion is whether companies seek a single service provider for all of their requirements in a particular domain or prefer to access "best-of-breed" professionals, wherever they may be found. Certainly governance issues have shifted the emphasis significantly away from single-source providers, due to the potential for conflicts of interest. However, a handful of the global investment banks, some of the major strategy consulting firms, and the top advertising and media conglomerates are actively presenting themselves as "one-stop shops" for their clients.[10]

This positioning is designed to allow clients to focus all of their business with one service provider, based on the advantages of deep client knowledge and more effective communication. More importantly, significant advantages exist for global organizations in being able to work with a single supplier across their worldwide business units. The issue remains one of knowledge specialization. Corporate clients are demanding the greatest level of expertise, especially in new and emerging fields, and are increasingly comfortable selecting from a moving array of providers for the professional services they require. Almost all investment banks have given up trying to cover all global financial markets, and even the giants are presenting themselves as "multi-niche" providers.


## Professional Services Networks

One of the strongest trends in professional services is for networks of independent professionals to band together in loose networks to deliver services to major clients. The availability of collaborative tools that allow remote teams to work together has made this possible. However, one of the other key enablers has been that large corporate clients are increasingly willing to consider alternatives to the major suppliers. After Arthur Andersen failed and the remaining Big Four accounting firms laid off substantial numbers of their professionals, many small groups of professionals banded together to service former clients, offering the same services as the major firms at significantly lower fees. Many more structured "virtual firms" have arisen to provide clients with access to broad expertise without the overhead of major firms. New York-based Axiom Legal brings together a network of skilled lawyers to deliver high-level services to clients in highly inter-active relationships at competitive fees. Sense Worldwide, a London marketing strategy firm, draws on a global network of researchers and trend analysts. Marion Weinreb and Associates, a quality consulting firm for the pharmaceutical and medical industries, has two full-time employees based in California, and over 150 associates globally to deliver services to its clients.[11]

The gradual rise of professional services networks, especially as they grow more sophisticated, will prove to be a competitive factor for top-tier firms in some segments. Those that can provide access to top experts, effective project management, and integrated delivery capabilities will be able to carve out significant value.

## PROFESSIONAL SERVICES POSITIONING

For decades most professional services firms were based on the same strategy of hiring out professionals to do work for the client at an hourly rate, and taking the margin between their salary and the cost to the client. The powerful array of drivers of professional services relationships has created the need for new models and approaches. Unless firms can create real differentiation, they will struggle.

### Professional Services Models

The traditional model of the professional is the expert you call on for advice, and defer to in awe of their superior expertise. As you have already seen, this is an increasingly tough position to hold in the market, yet it is one possible positioning. In Chapter 1 I explored the difference between black-box and knowledge-based services. Another key distinction is whether professionals position themselves solely as content experts, or whether they focus at least in part on the process of creating and applying knowledge. Mapping these two dimensions against each other creates a two-by-two matrix of core professional services models, as shown in Figure 2–3.

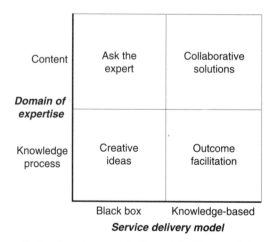

FIGURE 2–3   *Core professional services models.* Copyright © 2004 Advanced Human Technologies. Reprinted with permission.

Each of these four models has its place in the landscape of professional services, with its own value and challenges.

- *Ask the expert:* The black-box delivery of content expertise is the classic view of professional services, and still a significant proportion of professionals today think of themselves in this way. It is a viable position, but there is only space for a handful of firms in this domain. New York law firm Wachtell, Lipton, Rosen and Katz can justifiably claim this position. As a firm focused on mergers and acquisitions, it has deliberately taken the policy of not having long-term client relationships, as this could be a barrier to taking on other clients. However, this means that it cannot diversify beyond its core position. Many other firms that aspire to this model cannot realistically hope to achieve it.
- *Creative ideas:* Many of the major advertising and design firms, for example, claim unique insight into the process of generating valuable ideas, and sell their finished ideas to their clients. They are the creatives, and what they think of as their singularly uncreative clients should be grateful for their talent. This has proved an increasingly difficult market position as clients view this ability as a commodity, and look for results to be created in their organizations. This position still has a significant future, albeit a challenging one.
- *Outcome facilitation:* There exists an array of companies that present themselves to clients as facilitating outcomes. The expertise they bring to the client is of the processes that enable knowledge creation. Examples include innovation firms such as London-based ?What If! (see "?What If!" in material following), design firms such as IDEO in Palo Alto, and new-generation advertising agencies such as London's St Lukes and Mother. This is a growing domain, with increasing demand from clients, yet the reality is that it will always be

niche firms compared to the revenue streams from the other models.

- *Collaborative solutions:* The most rapidly growing professional services domain is the application of deep content expertise in knowledge-based service delivery. The outcome is collaborative solutions to problems that bring together the unique capabilities of the client and professional. Clients are increasingly demanding this model, and it is becoming a standard for the industry. This certainly does not mean that it will become the only professional services model, but each of the other models needs to be defined relative to this position.

On examining this array of professional services models, firms need to ask themselves a number of pointed questions.

- Where are we currently positioned in this array?
- If we use more than one model, how do these models relate to our market positioning?
- Do our current and emerging competitors have different positions?
- Do our clients perceive us the same way we perceive ourselves?
- If we choose to retain a model on the left-hand side of the figure, how can we sustain this position?
- How can we successfully shift our firm's positioning?

This last question is one of the most challenging. The issue of shifting to knowledge-based relationships is addressed throughout this book. However, shifting across different domains of expertise is also a critical issue. An example is advertising agencies seeking to compete with strategy consulting firms on high-level marketing and branding issues. They need to shift, both in capabilities and client perception, to deep content expertise on corporate strategy. In many cases the more challenging aspect is to change clients' perceptions of your expertise. However, this in turn means it is more difficult to attract and retain the professionals with appropriate experience.

Various challenges are involved in moving from content expertise to knowledge process expertise in terms of developing the capacity to facilitate idea development internally and with clients. This can be an extremely valuable complement to existing positioning, enabling the firm to have a broader scope of interaction with clients. However, this approach often does not fit the culture of traditional content expertise firms, and needs to be introduced in specific contexts to establish its value before being applied more broadly across client engagements.

### ?What If!

London-based ?What If! is an innovation company employing 100 staff, specializing in working with clients to help them enhance their innovation capabilities, often specifically to create new products and services. Clients in Europe, the United States, and the Asia Pacific include Coors, Southwest Airlines, Tesco, Cadbury Schweppes, Unilever, Microsoft, and the U.K. Cabinet Office. It claims to have added £2.5 billion of revenue growth to its clients over the last five years. Much of its client work is implemented in workshops, either for staff training or focused idea generation. Its training sessions in creativity and product and service innovation are often run across its clients as part of programs aimed at changing innovation culture. For these broader programs, it may begin with an innovation audit as a foundation for designing a company-wide initiative. It also runs an annual TopDog trip for diverse groups of its clients' chief executives and board members to show them the practices of some of the world's most innovative companies, in a format designed to stimulate their own creative thinking. ?What If!'s American TopDog tour visits companies such as Apple, Southwest Airlines, and Ritz Carlton, and a Scandinavian TopDog trip delves into organizations such as Lego, Ikea, and Bang & Olufsen.

One of ?What If!'s major clients had been working with the firm on and off for eight years, almost from the firm's inception. When one of its competitors came to ?What If! and asked it to run a major project, ?What If! went to its original client — which had not given them work recently — to see if it minded them taking the business. The response from the client was that they very much did not want ?WhatIf! to work for their competitor, and this triggered a sudden shift in the relationship. The client's recognition of the value they received from ?What If!'s work prompted a shared review of the client's needs, extended work in getting to know the client's operations better, and resulted in the development of a joint plan and commitment for action over the coming year. The range of services ?What If! delivered was not significantly different from its usual offerings. However, the up-front collaboration and commitment from both sides resulted in a highly coordinated approach that achieved superior results for the client, and a further bolstering of the relationship.

?What If! is unusual for a professional services firm in that it does business for itself as well as assist its clients. In the face of client criticisms that they were no longer innovators themselves, just talking about it, the company founded ?What If! Ventures, which provides seed capital and expertise to new, fast-growing consumer businesses. Ideas it has supported include an organic food business, an innovative fast-food chain, and a consumer events company. One of the benefits is continuing to learn from their own innovation and commercialization efforts so that they can apply those lessons for clients. In addition, it creates internal opportunities and provides greater work variety, contributing to ?What If! being named as one of the ten best companies to work for in the U.K.

## Dealing with Commoditization

Commoditization is a reality in professional services. As you saw earlier in this chapter, the modularization of business means that clients increasingly look at the various elements of the services they are offered, and want to ensure that each of those elements is provided in a way that maximizes the value created for the cost incurred. Professional services firms all talk about differentiation. It is critical to have a clear idea of how the firm is distinct in the eyes of the client. However, the reality is that high-end differentiated services will find it difficult to stand alone. If professionals shed every element of the services and activities provided to clients that can be readily duplicated by others, just a narrow sliver will remain. The danger at that point is that the client relationship is so thin that it breaks. Other firms that provide a more comprehensive array of knowledge-based services will have the personal relationships and client knowledge that will provide true differentiation and awareness of opportunities at the client. Even long-term strategic planning and mergers and acquisitions advice have process elements that do not need to be done by professionals on exorbitant salaries.

There are two key steps to addressing the pressing issues of commoditization. The first is identifying the elements of your business that currently are or will become commoditized. The second is deciding what strategies to take for these commoditized elements.

Identifying what is or can be commoditized from your business offerings is not always evident. Professionals like to feel that everything they do is differentiated. However, this is a dangerous stance. The clearest way to look at commoditization is whether your clients are prepared to pay more for any particular element of the services you provide. If they believe you are good, they are very likely to be prepared to pay more to spend time with you in a face-to-face meeting. However, unless there is something special about your invoicing and billing services they will expect these to contribute no more to the fees they are paying than they do to their telephone bill. If your clients know that your firm or other firms have created a similar document or report to the one they require, they will not be prepared to pay for it to be created from scratch again. In general, if something can be established as an automated process it will be commoditized. It is important to take a time horizon of at least three years for judging the scope for commoditization, as you will have to be prepared to act now if the landscape will change in that time frame. Firms need to look at three different levels in terms of what elements of their offerings are becoming commoditized.

- *Firm:* Which service offerings across the firm are becoming commoditized? An obvious example is routine property legal work. Many law firms have recognized that they are not able to demand premium pricing for this type of work, and are choosing to get out of this business.
- *Client:* For each of your large clients, examine the spectrum of services and service elements you provide, and determine what could be commoditized. In the next few years, what elements might they choose to buy from a more efficient provider?
- *Service line:* Within each service offering, what elements will remain distinct and justify premium pricing, and which elements may become commoditized?

Having identified those elements of your offerings that may be commoditized, for each of these you need to establish a clear strategy. In establishing your strategy for each element, there are three key considerations.

- *Positioning:* What is your firm's vision for its distinctive market positioning as commoditization and the other drivers described earlier in this chapter impact your business?
- *Independence:* Can the service element be run as a stand-alone offering, and can clients viably force you to unbundle it from the rest of your offering?
- *Relationship breadth:* What would the impact be on the scope and breadth of your relationship with key clients if you eliminated service elements from your offering?

There are four major options available to you for those service elements that are currently or in the process of becoming commoditized.

- *Eliminate:* If a service offering is independent of other service offerings, is not likely to be highly profitable in the future, and will not adversely impact positioning and client relationships by its absence, then the offering can be eliminated.

- *Automate:* In many cases, service elements are either integrated into the service offering or are strategically important in client relationships. In this case, it is important to automate these to achieve efficiencies. Nondifferentiated elements must be done at the lowest possible cost.
- *Outsource:* An alternative to automated processes internally is to outsource them, or potentially to provide them to clients through an alliance. Outsourcing requires skills in managing these relationships, in integrating external processes into internal systems, and in quality control.
- *Keep:* It is difficult to justify maintaining a commoditized offering within your portfolio if you do not implement measures to do this as cost efficiently as possible. In the long term this is not a sustainable position. However, it is possible over a shorter time frame if the element is fully integrated into your other services and is not a large proportion of cost to the client.

The most important issue is for firms to look these issues squarely in the face. Ignoring the massively powerful trend of commoditization — which seems to be the default strategy for many professional services firms — is a recipe for disaster. This will play out over quite a few years, but the strategic thinking and positioning needs to be done before the landscape changes. The most important issue is that of developing true knowledge-based relationships with key clients. However, this needs to be set in the context of having an integrated portfolio of service elements that are either truly differentiated from the perspective of the client or can be done highly efficiently.

One possible response is to separate delivery styles into different companies. Nizan Guanaes, Brazil's leading advertising personality, has created a group of three advertising agencies under the banner of the Ypy Group, each positioned in a different market segment. Africa, his top-tier brand, began with the intention of accepting only nine clients, which it has achieved, and charges premium pricing. DM9DDB, which he originally sold to DDB Worldwide and has now bought back into, addresses the midmarket. MPM, which Ypy recently bought from the Interpublic group, deals with the more price-sensitive end of the market.

## SUMMARY: PROFESSIONAL SERVICES AND KNOWLEDGE-BASED RELATIONSHIPS

Professional services are business services based on the application of highly specialized knowledge. This definition includes a wide variety of industries, including not just the traditional professional service practices such as consulting, investment banking, and law but a far more diverse range of organizations, including internal services. The common theme of knowledge specialization underlying professional services means that all industries within the field have much to learn from one another, and the fundamental importance of knowledge in the economy means that indeed almost all organizations can use their approaches as a model.

There are powerful drivers at play across the field of professional services, however, that are resulting in accelerating commoditization. These include increasing client sophistication, governance, connectivity, transparency, modularization, and globalization. Differentiation is increasingly difficult.

To understand professional services firms, we need to look at the primary resources of human capital, structural capital, and relationship capital. The primary input of professional service firms is information, and its functions include adding value to information and developing, sharing, and applying knowledge.

Examining the diversity of professional services provides a foundation for adapting lessons from adjacent industries. Professional services positioning should be founded on recognizing the importance of relationship style, and focusing on which elements of services provided are being commoditized.

To this point I have covered the fundamental issues of knowledge-based relationships, and the professional service firms for which these are most relevant. The next step is to understand how knowledge is used in adding value to clients. The following three chapters in Part 2 deal with adding value to information, client decision making, and client capabilities. The nuts and bolts of implementation are covered in Part 3.

## NOTES

1    David H. Maister, *Managing the Professional Service Firm*, New York: The Free Press, 1997, p. xvi.

2    Tom Peters, *Liberation Management: Necessary Disorganization for the Nanosecond Nineties*, New York: Fawcett Columbine, 1992, p. 11.

3    Geanne Rosenberg, "Big Four Auditors' Legal Services Hit by Sarbanes-Oxley," *New York Lawyer*, January 5, 2004.

4    Sveiby.

5    Stewart (1997).

6    Leif Edvinsson and Michael S. Malone, *Intellectual Capital: Realizing Your Company's True Value by Finding Its Hidden Roots*, New York: HarperBusiness, 1997.

7    Johan Roos, Göran Roos, Leif Edvinsson, and Nicola Dragnetti, *Intellectual Capital*, Basingstoke, U.K.: Macmillan Press, 1997.

8    Annie Brooking, *Intellectual Capital: Core Asset for the Third Millennium Enterprise*, London: International Thomson Business Press, 1996.

9    Walter B. Wriston, "Dumb Networks and Smart Capital," *The Cato Journal*, vol. 17, no. 3, Winter 1998.

10    Bresnahan looks at some of the pros and cons of one-stop shopping, as well as issues of knowledge transfer in IT consulting. See Jennifer Bresnahan, "The Latest in Suits," *CIO Enterprise*, October 15, 1998.

11    Ray Ozzie, "Ray Ozzie Looks Back, Looks Ahead," *ZDNet*, December 6, 2004, at *news.zdnet.com/2100-9589_22-5479624.html*.

# PART II

*Adding Value with Knowledge*

# 3

# Adding Value to Information
## From Information to Knowledge

$\mathbf{W}$e are awash in information. Anybody can sit down in front of a web browser and access billions of pages of information with the press of a button. Whether you are a professional or the client of a professional, you have access to vast reams of potentially useful and relevant information. The question is, how does information become valuable and valued by clients?

As you saw in Chapter 1, the essential distinction between information and knowledge is that information can be digitized, while knowledge is the capacity to act effectively. Information in itself has limited value. It becomes valuable when it becomes knowledge, the ability to do things better. Knowledge can be transferred either directly between people through socialization or indirectly by delivering information people can internalize as their personal knowledge. Both means of transferring knowledge are fundamental to professional services, and although direct interpersonal contact is critical for rich knowledge sharing and relationship development the dynamics of technology and markets mean that information is playing an increasingly dominant role in shaping the world of business. In this chapter, I examine the dynamics of adding value to information in serving professional services clients.

## INFORMATION AND DIGITIZATION

Probably the best way of understanding the nature of information is that it is something that is or can be digitized.[1] As we have all experienced, the digitization of information allows it to be stored indefinitely, duplicated at will, communicated almost instantly anywhere in the world, analyzed and compared with other information, and accessed easily from vast databases. These are fabulous benefits, which has resulted in almost all information now being held in digital form. Moving far beyond data and documents, music, sounds, photographs, and movies are already primarily stored in digital format.

Digital communication will never completely replace face-to-face meetings and interaction. It will certainly grow very rapidly in importance as bandwidth becomes cheaper and more available, and videoconferencing begins to expose more of the subtleties of personal interaction. However, the real issue is that much of the value in interaction is created in the tangential yet often more productive conversations that happen before and after formal meetings. As the term *socialization* implies, much useful knowledge transfer happens informally and by osmosis, which requires being in the same location, and not always in a formal agenda-driven context.

So while face-to-face interaction and knowledge transfer will never be fully supplanted in high-value contexts such as professional services delivery, the role of information in adding value to clients is critically important. There is no question that information underpins our economy. However, in recognizing that information's primary value is when it becomes knowledge for our clients we need to understand how to add the greatest value to information, how to transform raw data into high-value information, and how that information can create value for our clients.

## INFORMATION OVERLOAD!

Perhaps the most obvious feature of our information-intensive world is the overwhelming flood of information in which we are swimming (or drowning!). We are deluged with articles, quotes, and data that tell us how much information we are receiving and how fast the information flow is growing, with commentators wailing that humans were never meant to swim in these turbulent waters, and that this type of society is not sustainable.[2]

This information overload is driven not only by the availability of information but by the fact that almost all managers find they need more information about more topics than ever before. Professionals need to keep up to date and informed not only in their own fields of specialization but also on their clients' industries, as well as on broader changes in the business environment, including the rapidly developing impact of technology. In a study commissioned by Reuters, 85 percent of middle managers agreed that they need as much information as possible to keep abreast of their customers and competitors.[3]

The Attention Economy

Information overload is a critical factor in the productivity of all knowledge workers, and is in many ways at the heart of the knowledge economy. One of its most important consequences is the competition for people's attention. Some argue that there is now no shortage of primary resources, capital, or information, and that attention is the only true scarce resource today — and thus that which drives the economy.[4] In the "attention economy," those who can attract and keep people's attention are kings and queens.

Seeing attention as the key economic resource helps us to understand many of the changing dynamics in the business environment. It has driven the shift of emphasis from product marketing to customer relationships, which in turn has been an important factor behind global consolidation in financial services and other industries. The rise of "one-to-one marketing," which focuses on customizing products and services to individual customers, also reflects this trend.[5]

The same principles apply in sophisticated professional services, in which clients are often overwhelmed with high-value information from service providers and would-be providers. Information must be able to cut through the massive information overload clients experience to capture their attention. This critical ability underscores both the vital roles of relationships, which are often essential in getting even the first glance at your information, and the importance of designing information that captures and keeps attention.

## The Democratization of Information

The increasing availability and access to information that are driving spiraling information overload are also having a major impact on the economics of information. Once information is created, it can be duplicated at virtually no cost, resulting in constant downward pressure on the market value of information.[6] Most information is now commoditized, and in fact an enormous amount of information is being made available for free. The Internet allows anyone who so wishes to make information broadly available, accelerating the pace of commoditization.

The nature of the media industry is fundamentally changing in that customers now have access to much of the same raw information as it does. Customers are no longer forced to go to newspapers, magazines, and television for their news, but can often get it directly from the same sources as the media, or through other filters such as blogs or independent web sites. People will choose to go through media only if value is added to the original information. This is just as true in business. Clients usually have access to the same general information as their service providers, and will only pay for information to which high value has been added.

These trends have substantially changed how professional firms add value to clients with information. Access to information used to be a significant differentiator, but that is far less the case today. Clients can find much of the raw information they need for free on the Internet or for a small fee from databases. The emphasis is increasingly on adding value to information, providing context, and applying it in the client's situation. This has always been the case, of course, but now that clients have access to information that is the same or similar to that available to their service providers, professional services firms are being driven to add increased value to information.

## Internal and External Orientation

Effective information management systems must address the issues of information overload, striving for the delicate balance between delivering and giving access to the most vital information people require in performing their functions, without overloading them. However, to date these systems have been primarily oriented to internal use in organizations. The dynamics of adding value to information with an external orientation — that is, for clients — are substantially different. Most importantly, there is far less control over information dissemination, and in contrast to internal systems, which hold a quasi-monopoly of their users' attention, external suppliers must compete with a host of other information sources.

## THE VALUE OF INFORMATION

For professional services firms, the most relevant and useful way of thinking about the value of information is the practice of how to add value to it from a client perspective. I will address this question in some detail later in this chapter. But what *is* the value of information, and how can we measure it? It is difficult and in some ways almost meaningless to try to attribute an absolute "value" to information. However, to be most effective in adding value to information it is worth briefly examining the nature of the value of information.

## Value Depends on Context

The value of information and knowledge is entirely dependent on the context in which they are made available. A report on the best practice in implementing customer relationship management (CRM) could be worth millions of dollars in savings to a large company planning to embark on such a project, substantially less to a smaller company or one already well down the track on implementation, and nothing to an individual or company with no plans to implement CRM. For information to be valuable to an organization, the organization must be in a position to act on it, and the profitability of the resulting action will relate to the information's value.

In addition, the way any information adds value to an organization depends substantially on the context of all other information it receives and to which it has access. If a client has little knowledge of a specific field, the most valuable information will be an overview of the situation. More often clients already have access to fairly rich information on any given topic. Thus, general information is likely to be of lesser value, and what will be most valuable is specific information and recommendations for action that build on the client's existing knowledge.

Every year IBM Research produces what it calls its Global Technology Outlook (GTO), which is its vision for the future of information technology. This includes forecasts, technology trends, emerging applications, and implications for business. It is used internally for IBM's strategy development, but is also shared with selected clients and partners. This is always delivered as a presentation, supported by a comprehensive handout, customized to the industry, and sometimes to the individual organization and types of executives participating. In this case, information is provided within a highly specific context in a way that is designed to create most value for the client.

## High-, Low-, and Negative-Value Information

Although the value of information varies with context, it can also be seen across contexts in its capacity to create value. Information that will affect the valuation of a company in a multi-billion-dollar takeover can easily be worth hundreds of millions of dollars, while knowing how many ice cream cones the corner shop sold yesterday will never be worth a fortune to anyone. Some information has more value than other information.

What is less obvious is that information can have negative value, as Karl-Erik Sveiby points out.[7] The value of anything equals the benefits from using it, minus the costs of using it. In a world of information overload, the cost of "using" information in terms of the time and effort required to read it is often more than the benefit gained from that information. When people send you a glut of information that is not highly valuable to you, they are in fact subtracting value from you. Time and attention are the most valuable resources we have. To take a case in point, the value of your time and attention in reading this book is certainly many times greater than the price you paid for it.

The objective of professional services firms, or indeed any organizations that disseminate information, is to take low-value information and use it to create high-value information. As you saw in Chapter 2, the primary input of professional firms is information. However, this is usually low-value information, generally available in the market. One of the key functions of these firms is to use this input to create high-value information for their clients, as well as for use in their own operations.

## Knowledge and High-Value Information

Having seen that information can have high, low, or negative value within a given context, it is useful to revisit the distinction between information and knowledge. Many people state or imply that high-value information is knowledge, while low-value information is information. Using these definitions, it is impossible to say what distinguishes information and knowledge. At what point does information become valuable enough to call it knowledge? This issue emphasizes the importance of differentiating between information and knowledge by understanding that knowledge is inseparable from people. Having made that distinction, we can then better understand the domain of information by distinguishing between different levels of value.

Although we can talk about the value of information, the value of knowledge can only be regarded as a general concept. Knowledge as the capacity to act effectively cannot be subdivided into components — it is an integral whole. Yes, knowledge is valuable, having perhaps the greatest value there is, but because it resides within the individual only the sum of his or her knowledge could be effectively valued, and not any discrete part of the total. For information to have a very high value it must be easy to internalize as knowledge. As you will see, the ease of assimilating information is a key factor in determining its value.

## ADDING VALUE TO INFORMATION

The rapidly developing importance of information means that adding value to information represents a substantial, growing proportion of the process of creating value in the economy. The steps and processes in making information more valuable to clients are at the heart of value creation, and are core professional services activities. Implementing and continually improving these processes within an organization are vital to its success.

The business of providing data or low-value information will remain important, and certainly many clients are prepared to purchase information for input into their own value-adding processes. The nature of this business, however, is commoditized and low-margin, and I will focus here on the delivery of high-value information as a source of differentiation, significant client value, and premium pricing.

### The Role of People

The processes that add the most value to information are those performed by people and that cannot be computerized or automated. This is certainly true at the moment. Over time computers will be able to perform more and more of the processes that add value to informa-

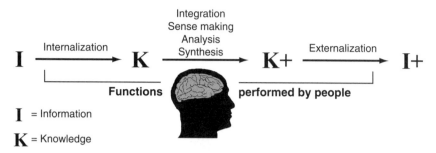

FIGURE 3–1    *How people add value to information.*

tion. However, people will still add the greatest value. There are two key reasons for this observation. Knowledge is about combining and synthesizing information based on meaning and context, which cannot be done without understanding. Computers are a long way from being capable of understanding. And anything that can be automated will become commoditized in fairly short order, meaning that differentiation will continue to depend on the abilities of intelligent people.

For people to add value to information, they must first internalize it as knowledge. This means integrating it into their existing knowledge, adding value to that knowledge — which often happens in the process of internalization, as well as through subsequent analysis and synthesis — and then externalizing it as value-added information. This process is illustrated in Figure 3–1.

How Information Is Used

Information can be used in a wide variety of contexts and situations. Decision making is the most obvious application of information. This issue is covered in detail in Chapter 4. Information may be intended simply to keep managers informed of what is relevant and important in their business environment, and to help build the knowledge that provides a broad backdrop to decision making and business activity. In most cases, managers do not acquire knowledge to address a specific situation, but draw on their existing knowledge to act effectively, and seek to develop their working knowledge on an ongoing basis.

Information is not always used by people, of course — it is now often used as raw input into computer systems and models that perform specific analysis or that look for patterns or generate rules for behavior, as with neural networks. Most of the raw information used by these systems is commoditized, and the major issues in information delivery in this situation are in data validation and formatting. I will not examine these issues in detail here, as this creates little value compared with providing information for use by people.

---

### Powell Goldstein

Law firm Powell Goldstein LLP is based in Atlanta and Washington, D.C., with over 300 attorneys covering a wide range of practice areas. The firm has built a new service line based on assisting its clients to protect themselves from serial litigation. Many national companies find they are targeted by litigation, sometimes in every state. In many cases, the plaintiffs actively share information, trying to find chinks in their targets' armor. Because there are no law firms that operate in every state of the United States, to defend themselves companies must hire different law firms for every state or region. Since each of these defense firms will need to go through a discovery process with their client to respond to the plaintiff's demands, this imposes a substantial burden on the defending company's resources and creates the potential for inconsistent information to be provided to plaintiffs as well as the company's own defense lawyers, weakening the defense cases.

For two large national clients, Powell Goldstein has created discovery guidelines and databases to assist in defense against coordinated litigation. It first samples the information being requested across the various jurisdictions, and creates a template it uses to interview relevant staff at its client, sometimes as many as 100 people. It then consolidates the knowledge it has gathered to establish a database of key documents and information that is made available to the defending lawyers nationwide. In addition, it creates a cross-referenced indexed book that contains factual answers about the defending company to the questions being raised by the plaintiffs, with state-specific details where applicable. The systems can then be updated on an ongoing basis so that the client is pre-emptively prepared for other litigation, and to ensure that historic information is maintained when companies lose key staff or information in the process of rapid growth.

In essence, Powell Goldstein is acting as an information gateway, performing research deep into its client's operations, putting that in a useable format, and making it available across the network of the client's law firms. Other law firms have tried to play the role of coordinating counsel for their clients in similar situations, setting defense strategy and instructing the individual state-based law firms in turn. Powell Goldstein's approach differs in that it does not seek to play a strategic role but simply to be an effective information broker for its clients' defense network, based on its deep client knowledge.

Powell Goldstein is also an innovator in its implementation of Six Sigma processes in its client work. Six Sigma is an information-intensive methodology for improving quality, originally developed by Motorola, that has been implemented across many major corporations. One of the foundations of Six Sigma is identifying critical success factors for achieving company objectives. In the case of one client that had an established Six Sigma program, the legal department was already accountable on preestablished measures such as early case disposal, costs, and litigation outcomes. Powell Goldstein worked with the client to align its processes and remuneration with the legal department's internal objectives, including reducing hours billed and introducing relevant success fees. As a result, the firm now handles all of that client's litigation work nationally. If clients have not established internal Six Sigma processes, Powell Goldstein's attorneys may interview their clients to help them establish appropriate success factors, and use these to improve the effectiveness of service delivery from the client's perspective and assist the client with implementation of its own business objectives.

## THE PROCESS OF ADDING VALUE TO INFORMATION

There are seven key processes in adding value to information. Here I will focus on adding value to information users outside the organization, although the same principles apply to adding value to information for use within an organization. These seven processes are:

- Filtering
- Validation
- Analysis
- Synthesis
- Presentation
- Ease of access and use
- Customization

You saw earlier that the value of information depends on the context in which it is used, and most of these processes can be performed effectively only if the context is specified. Customization can actually be considered part of each of the other processes. I have chosen to distinguish it as a separate process, however, as a critical aspect of adding value to information.

### Filtering

Filtering is a process of reducing the quantity of information by assessing its relevance and value. In most cases this can only be determined relative to the intended audience. The narrower the audience, and thus the greater the specificity of assessing relevance and value, the greater the value of the filtering process.

Technology can help with low-level filtering, for example, by selecting documents that contain specified key words. Agent software takes this a step further by learning user preferences over time on the basis of feedback. Still, computers may be good at processing information, but remain very poor at assessing its relevance and usefulness.

Collaborative filtering technology works by getting people to grade the relevance and value of all documents they read, and pools those assessments to provide recommendations to other people with related job and interest profiles. This means that all levels of executives can input their evaluations of the documents they read, leading to far more useful assessments of the documents' value than would be achieved by dedicated administrative staff.

Nicholas Negroponte writes of the importance of serendipity in information searches: stumbling across unexpected and unsought valuable discoveries.[8] Receiving information that is too highly filtered reduces the chances of coming across other useful information. Although focused information sources, such as legal technology newsletters, should be filtered within tight parameters, when providing a larger proportion of your clients' overall information requirements it is best to strive for a balance between a high degree of filtering and allowing for serendipitous discoveries.


Validation

The reliability and trustworthiness of information from the client's perspective is a key element of value. The first aspect of validating information is ensuring that the information provided is indeed correct, or instead assessing and rating its reliability. The second aspect is making your clients confident that your validation is itself reliable. If they have faith that information you supply is accurate and correct, it can save them substantial time and effort in checking and cross-referencing, and allows for instant action.

The reputation of newspapers, magazines, and wire services is largely dependent on the perception that the information they provide is accurate. Elaborate checking procedures are usually in place to ensure that incorrect information does not go out, often at the cost of timeliness. Companies are prepared to pay substantially more for information provided by Reuters or Bloomberg, for example, than for the same information on the Internet, in part because they can be confident the information is correct. The reputation of these firms for information quality has been built up over time.

Information validation is to a significant degree a manual process. Some of its elements can be automated, especially those providing an alert to potential spurious data. However, human judgment and supervision are required. Fortunately, much of the information validation process can be performed by fairly low-level, inexpensive staff. Organizations may choose to establish centralized information validation functions. Alternatively, teams can set up quality systems to cross-check each other's work, which is a common practice in major consulting firms.

## Analysis

Analysis includes a wide variety of approaches and techniques for manipulating, categorizing, and correlating information. In many cases, analysis is performed with computers. However, selecting the type of analysis to be performed usually remains a human task.

Categorization is a type of analysis, as it gives a context — and thus some meaning — to information. Identifying correlations in data adds substantial value, as it reveals trends that can lead directly to profitable action, or at least a deeper understanding of the business environment. This is a prime task for number-crunching machines, though people still play an important role. An example of this type of analysis is found in visual data mining software, which shows visual representations of the patterns underlying enormous bodies of data, and in turn enables people to pick out relevant correlations and trends.

Analysis includes the use of many quantitative tools and models. Proprietary analytical approaches, in particular, can turn data into information directly relevant to decision making. An example is found in credit rating agencies such as Moody's and Standard & Poor's. Their detailed access to many companies' accounts over an extended period has enabled them to assess the relative importance of different data in determining credit quality. This evaluation has produced proprietary models that assess credit risk for each industry, and can be used to analyze data in ways that add substantial value. It is important to note, however, that these quantitative analytics form only a part of the rating agencies' assessments, and human judgment is a major component of their rating processes.

## Synthesis

Synthesis of a wide array of disparate information in a meaningful way can create massive value. For the purposes of this discussion, I will treat synthesis as an ability that — for the present time, at least — can be performed only by people. Only people can leap between different levels of logic and categorization in order to draw meaning or sense from a world of information. Internalizing information requires it to be related to existing knowledge, so simply understanding new information or experience is already an act of synthesis.

The ability to recognize patterns in one's business environment and organization is one of the most fundamental and valuable skills in management, as the doyen of strategic planning, Henry Mintzberg, and others have pointed out.[9] Pattern recognition, which discovers the hidden relationships within information and puts them into a useful framework, is a very powerful form of synthesis. Recognizing patterns creates enormous value, and the ability to do it well can command extremely high fees. In a similar vein, all creation and innovation can be said to be based on synthesizing different perspectives, as suggested by Arthur Koestler.[10]

Synthesis is generally a senior-level function, since to be most valuable it must draw on very broad experience and knowledge. It is a role commonly performed by the most senior team members, who are generally only brought in to provide the "big picture" as to how all of the strands are to be woven together. While the ability to synthesize information and recognize patterns is founded on broad experience, there are also skills involved that can be developed and improved. Traditional courses on creativity address some of the required skills, but rarely cover more fundamental issues such as broadening perceptual filters and developing approaches to structuring patterns.


## Presentation

The fact that information's primary value is found in being internalized by people as knowledge means that presentation is one of the most important parts of adding value to information. If information had intrinsic value, its presentation would be irrelevant. As it is, the presentation of information must be designed very specifically with the intention of making it as easy as possible for the intended audience to internalize or assimilate as useful knowledge.

In the first instance, we want to minimize the "cost" of using information in terms of the time and effort required. In a world of information overload, only information that is extremely easy to use and internalize will capture limited attention. Furthermore, we want to help our audiences to get the most value from the information by integrating it deeply and easily into their knowledge frameworks.

There are many key elements involved in the effective presentation of information, including effective writing and structuring, and the use of visual representations. Readability has a major impact on value. If a document is written in an easy-to-follow style and format it will be far more valuable than if it is written in jargon such as legalese. Simple quantity of information can be a critical factor. An effective one-page summary is often far more valuable than a 100-page document, simply because of the relative time investment required.

Immense amounts have been written on these fundamental communication skills. However, very little specific attention has been paid to the communication of knowledge, and the customization of communication for different audiences. These are extremely important issues in the knowledge economy (a detailed background is provided in the Appendix, and some approaches are covered in Chapter 12).

## Ease of Access and Use

There is a critical distinction in information management between information push — in which information is "pushed" to users automatically — and information pull, in which users actively seek information ("pull" it) for themselves. Achieving an effective balance between information push and pull is at the heart of a good information management system. In a world of information overload, however, users increasingly prefer to access information themselves rather than being presented with pre-specified information. The most important issues are the ability to access relevant information with minimal time and effort, flexibility in accessing that information, and subsequently being able to manipulate it easily.

User access issues include providing facilities to search for information based on key words and other criteria, structuring information in hierarchies of detail, and providing alerts to notify users that new information is available. In addition, how information is presented or formatted can strongly impact its value. For example, providing data in spreadsheet format can be far more valuable than simply presenting a chart of the data, as clients may wish to manipulate the data themselves rather than just see the output. These are primarily technology issues. Much of the current focus of information and document management relates to how to improve ease of use and accessibility of information.

## Customization

Customization is intrinsic to almost every aspect of adding value to information, as well as to all knowledge transfer. Information's potential value is limited by the breadth of its intended audience. Information targeted to a broad cross section of business executives, such as that in national business magazines, can never command a high price. However, information produced for a very narrowly targeted audience can sometimes justify a very high price.

Customization can be considered a process in its own right. It begins by understanding the client's situation, and processes information specifically to add maximum value in that context. In effect, customization consists mainly of filtering, analysis, synthesis, and presentation, with each of these processes performed within a very specific context. Each of these can be performed without a specific audience in mind, but this approach will strongly limit the value created. Validation and ease of access can generally be implemented effectively without customizing for a specific client or user.

One important aspect of customization is translation, which involves framing information or messages in the language or format that will be best understood by the client. On a basic level, this can refer to the actual language in which the message is written. However, just as important are the language and style of communication favored by the culture of the target individual or group. The way in which engineers like information to be presented is very different from the preferences of human resource managers or bond traders, for example, and each group uses different language and specialized terminology in its communication. In Chapter 8 I will return to the theme of customization in the context of designing client contact in firm-wide relationships. Customization is fundamental to the implementation of knowledge-based relationships.

## From Information to Knowledge

The process of making information into personal knowledge is internalization, as you saw in Chapter 1. The essence of this process is in establishing new connections and associations to and within existing knowledge. This happens by perceiving associations and similarities to prior experiences, thoughts, and mental structures. The Appendix examines in detail the nature of knowledge, how experience and ideas are internalized as understanding, and how to communicate knowledge more effectively. Here I will introduce these topics, as they are fundamental to the issues of effective knowledge transfer.

## Generic and Customized Knowledge Communication

How can we design and present information so that our clients can easily internalize it as knowledge they find useful and valuable? This objective can be accomplished on two levels: first, in making it easy for people in general to understand your communication; and second, in designing the communication specifically for one person or a small group, based on their preferences and approaches to taking in information.

To maximize the value added to broad audiences, we need to understand how people take in and think about information. The field of cognitive psychology provides us with many useful lessons. What is of most interest is how people take in conceptual information and think about complex situations, rather than low-level functions such as how they perceive objects or comprehend spoken words.

## Cognitive Styles

In tailoring our presentation of information for specific individuals or small groups, we need to understand the *differences* in how individuals take in information, analyze it, and make decisions. We can learn useful distinctions by drawing on the study of *cognitive style*, which examines the range of preferences people express in their cognition and personality. There can be dramatic differences in how people go about making decisions, and if we do not understand that diversity and the particular cognitive styles of the people involved it is far more difficult to communicate in ways that create value.

Far too often, professionals unwittingly design client communication in line with their own cognitive style, which is fine when the styles mesh but will mean that real knowledge transfer is limited when clients have different preferences. In addition, in the case of communication to a large group there is certain to be sufficient diversity of cognitive styles to ensure that any presentation designed within one style will be poorly understood by a significant portion of the audience. It is a fundamental rule that effective knowledge transfer to large groups must be designed to cater to a range of cognitive styles. As such, an understanding of cognitive styles should be a core skill of all professionals who communicate with clients, and a significant component of training programs for them.

When interaction is focused on an individual or a small group, understanding their cognitive styles can allow the tailored design of communication for maximum impact and client value. Failing to consider these issues can result in miscomprehension or worse.

## Visual Representations

One of the most useful ways of improving the internalization of knowledge from information is the use of visual representations. The use of visuals is a very powerful tool in the effective presentation of information, as well as in actually enhancing people's understanding and knowledge. This theme is developed in more detail in Chapter 12, and supporting evidence for the benefits of visual approaches is presented in Appendix A.

## DEVELOPING INFORMATION AND KNOWLEDGE CAPABILITIES

Understanding the process of adding value to information is one thing. Improving organizational performance at these processes is another. The following framework for developing the information and knowledge capabilities of professional services firms will help in achieving this. It is applicable both internally in firm's operations and externally in adding value to clients. Adding value to information and knowledge are dynamic processes. Rather than thinking about "managing" knowledge, it makes far more sense to focus on developing information and knowledge capabilities. This emphasis on capabilities recognizes that these can always be developed and improved.

## Domains and Means

There are two key domains in developing information and knowledge capabilities: the individual and the organization. As you have seen, people are at the heart of the processes that add the most value to information. It is crucial to focus on developing the capabilities of individuals in dealing with information. Individuals, however, work within an organizational context, which brings people together in useful ways and provides direction and coherence to their efforts. The organizational level is fundamental in enhancing capabilities, particularly in developing the flow of knowledge.

Technology is an essential means of enhancing information and knowledge capabilities at both the individual and organizational levels, reflected by how much money is poured into information technologies. However, technology is far from sufficient in its own right. Developing skills and behaviors is also a vital means of achieving enhanced capabilities, but is often neglected relative to technology, in part due to the difficulty of implementing initiatives and measuring their success. However, the return on investment in developing skills and behaviors is usually greater than incremental investment in technology. Certainly, technology is worthless unless people have the skills and behaviors to use it effectively.

## Fields for Developing Capabilities

If we intersect these two domains — the individual and the organization — with the two means of development — technology, and skills and behaviors — a matrix for developing information and knowledge capabilities is created, as shown in Table 3–1. The four quadrants mapped by the matrix represent the key areas for developing information and knowledge capabilities. Since the matrix covers each of the most important fields in developing information and knowledge capabilities, it can be used to assess whether existing knowledge initiatives are broad enough in their scope to achieve success. Many so-called "knowledge management" initiatives address just one or two of these four fields, which greatly limits their potential effectiveness.

- *Individual technology:* How can technology assist individual knowledge workers in the process of adding value to

TABLE 3–1   *Developing organizational information and knowledge capabilities.*

|  | *Individual use of information* | *Organizational flow of information and knowledge* |
| --- | --- | --- |
| Technology | Search engines<br>E-mail filters<br>File organizers<br>Intelligent agents<br>Information visualization | E-mail and instant messaging<br>Collaborative spaces<br>Discussion forums<br>Knowledge yellow pages<br>Videoconferencing |
| Skills and behaviors | Filtering information overload<br>Information search<br>Analysis and synthesis<br>Effective decision making<br>Knowledge communication skills | Collaborative culture<br>Diverse internal networks<br>Team structures and processes<br>Sharing and reciprocity<br>Facilitation skills |

information? Examples include the effective filtering of "push" information, as in collaborative filtering, e-mail filters, and being able to use search engines to "pull" the information workers require. Intelligent agents acting on behalf of the user, in this case, searching for relevant information as well as learning the user's interests and inclinations, are likely to play an increasingly important role. Another valuable tool is information visualization software, which assists in making sense of and finding patterns in large amounts of data, and for communicating information usefully to others.

- *Organizational technology:* This quadrant covers the technological tools that assist in the organizational flow of information and technology. Many practitioners of "knowledge management" seem to think that addressing this field is all that is required. The tools start with e-mail, and include intranets, collaborative workspaces, discussion forums, videoconferencing, and knowledge yellow pages, which are databases to help identify who within the organization has expertise on specific topics. These initiatives are absolutely

essential in providing the means for large distributed
organizations to leverage their internal knowledge. However,
in and of themselves they function far more as enablers than
as a source of value creation.

- *Individual skills and behaviors:* This quadrant focuses on
the absolutely vital field of information and knowledge
skills. Professionals are the quintessential knowledge
workers. Their entire function is managing knowledge,
whether using it to achieve results or transferring it internally
or to clients. Very few knowledge workers, however, have had
any specific training and development for the skill sets on
which much of their role is based: dealing with and adding
value to information and knowledge. Some core skills in
which professionals are usually already proficient, but can
always develop with substantial improvements in productivity,
include setting information objectives, filtering information
overload, reading and note taking, analysis, synthesis, using
information and knowledge to make decisions, and in
particular the ability to communicate knowledge effectively to
others.

- *Organizational skills and behaviors:* Very little can happen in
developing an organization's information and knowledge
capabilities without the skills and behaviors that support
knowledge flow in the organization. Much of this process is
based on organizational culture, and ultimately the propensity
to share knowledge with others. The motivation for skill
development can stem partially from remuneration and
recognition structures that explicitly reward knowledge
sharing, but these must be supported by congruent signals
from management with leadership and example.[11] Specific
skills and activities for development include building teams
around information flow, establishing group processes for
sharing knowledge within and across teams, and facilitating
rich two-way communication of knowledge.

Developing Capabilities

Since professional services firms are based on specialized knowledge, developing their information and knowledge capabilities is fundamental to their competitiveness and sustainability. All firms are investing in the development of their internal capabilities in some ways, though few are effectively addressing all four quadrants of the matrix presented in Table 3–1. To do so requires not only implementing projects and efforts within the spheres of technology and human resources but also coordinating these to produce results both for the individual knowledge worker and the organization as a whole.

## Summary: Adding Value to Information

Information is anything that can be digitized, while knowledge is the capacity to act effectively, an attribute unique to people. Information's real value emerges when it is internalized by people as their own personal knowledge, and creates better action and results. The rapidly increasing pace of information overload is changing the nature of the value of information, making attention the most valuable resource, and giving wide and easy access to information. Information can have a high, low, or even negative value, depending on the context. A primary function of professional services firms is adding value to information from the perspective of their clients.

The key steps in the process of adding value to information include filtering, validation, analysis, synthesis, presentation, facilitating ease of access and use, and customization. Each of these steps can be performed at least partially with the help of technology. However, the greatest added value almost always involves people.

To add the most value to information, organizations must develop their information and knowledge capabilities. The two key domains that must be developed are the individual and organizational levels, while the two primary means for developing capabilities are technology, and skills and behaviors. These form a matrix covering the critical areas that need to be addressed in any comprehensive information and knowledge initiatives.

There is an increasing emphasis on information in business communication, and it is therefore critical to understand how information adds value. Adding value to information can be seen as the first stage of the process, but the real value is created in the application of information by the client. In the next two chapters I will examine adding value to client decision making and client capabilities. Both of these depend strongly on high-value information generated in the ways covered in this chapter, but also require rich personal interaction in order to be effective.

## NOTES

[1] This tallies with the definition of information given by Carl Shapiro and Hal Varian, *Information Rules: A Strategic Guide to the Network Economy*, Boston: Harvard Business School Press, 1998, p. 3.

[2] I disagree that information overload is necessarily a liability. See Ross Dawson, "Information Overload — Problem or Opportunity?," *Company Director*, October 1997, pp. 44–45.

[3] Reuters, *Dying for Information?*, London: Reuters, 1996.

[4] See Thomas H. Davenport and John C. Beck, *The Attention Economy*, Boston: Harvard Business School Press, 2001.

[5] See Don Peppers and Martha Rogers, *The One to One Future: Building Relationships One Customer at a Time*, New York: Currency Doubleday, 1993, and *Enterprise One to One: Tools for Competing in the Interactive Age*, New York: Currency Doubleday, 1997.

[6] Shapiro and Varian.

[7] Sveiby, pp. 108–111.

[8] Nicholas Negroponte, *Being Digital*, New York: Knopf, 1995.

[9] See, for example, Henry Mintzberg, *Mintzberg on Management: Inside Our Strange World of Organizations*, New York: Free Press, 1989, p. 38.

[10] Koestler coined the term *bisociation* to describe this. He proposed that creation always stems from operating on more than one plane of thinking. See Arthur Koestler, *The Act of Creation*, London: Hutchinson, 1964.

[11] See Ross Dawson, "Performance Management Strategies for Knowledge Organisations," *Reward Management Bulletin* 2, no. 3, February/March 1998, pp. 183–186.

# 4

# Adding Value to Client Decision Making
## Better Strategic, Line, and Portfolio Decisions

The final outcome from information and knowledge, that which provides value to organizations, is decisions. Indeed, economics Nobel Prize winner Herbert Simon contends that management *is* decision making.[1] The greatest value added to clients with knowledge is ultimately found in better business decisions: those resulting in better outcomes for companies in terms of profitability, shareholder value, or other chosen measures. Of course, action and implementation must follow decisions if they are to have value. Effective implementation, however, is itself a sequence of decisions and actions based on knowledge.

To help clients make better decisions for themselves, we must understand *how* they make decisions. This enables you to help them enhance their decision-making processes, and to tailor the way you communicate knowledge so that it can be usefully integrated into their decisions.

## TYPES OF DECISIONS

Organizational decisions can be divided into strategic, line, and portfolio decisions, as you saw in Chapter 1. It is useful to delve into these three categories a little further. They are relevant specifically within the context of professionals working with clients in knowledge-based relationships. Each type of client decision requires different approaches from the professional in order to add the greatest value.

## Strategic Decisions

Strategic decisions are those that determine the direction and positioning of the organization, usually within unlimited or very broad boundaries. Strategic decisions are normally made by top management, though there may be input from across the organization. They are based on the decision makers' understanding of the organization, its environment, and the relationship between them.

Strategy consulting firms explicitly target this area. The value of better strategic decision making is obvious, and premium pricing is available for those firms that can convince their clients of their ability to add real value in this area. Strategy consulting can be delivered with a wide variety of relationship styles, ranging from "ask the expert," defined in Chapter 2, to highly collaborative approaches, some of which are described later in this chapter.

## Line Decisions

Line decisions are those made within a defined scope, usually at line management or staff level. All knowledge workers make line decisions in performing their functions. Since line decisions are individually less important than strategic decisions, it is usually not cost effective to engage a professional services firm to assist with specific issues. To add value to line decisions, a service provider must develop the ability of knowledge workers to make better decisions within an organizational framework.

In this situation, the distinction between information and knowledge is clear. Giving managers information in the form of documents is next to useless. They are usually placed on a shelf and left there. What managers need is knowledge they can readily incorporate into the thinking behind their decisions. A good example of adding value to line decisions is found in risk reduction, which entails all decisions and actions being implemented in full consideration of critical potential risks.

Law firm Blake Dawson Waldron's "preventive lawyering" solutions, implemented through its online training (see "Blake Dawson Waldron Legal Technolgy Group"), provides a prime illustration. This shows the stark difference between delivering legal information — often in the form of hefty procedures manuals — and transferring knowledge. The interactive nature of e-learning, which involves presenting relevant information and stories and gets users to answer questions on content, means that real knowledge acquisition and understanding are far more likely to be applied by client staff in day-to-day decision making.

---

**Blake Dawson Waldron Legal Technology Group**

Blake Dawson Waldron (BDW), an Australian law firm with 190 partners and offices in four countries, has a well-established Legal Technology Group that is a distinct profit center for the firm. The group has won awards worldwide for its innovative products and practices. One of its earliest and best-established innovations is what the firm calls SALT, for self-administered legal training. Now entirely online, the product addresses clients' compliance issues by ensuring that staff and line managers across the organization understand their legal obligations and how these need to be considered in their actions and day-by-day decisions. Topics include trade practices, occupational health and safety, privacy, corporate governance, and insider trading. Training is delivered online, so staff can do it at their own pace. Tests throughout the learning process ensure that staff have acquired the required knowledge, and that individual and company-wide understanding of critical issues can be monitored. Although line managers may not be highly motivated to learn about these issues, effectively imparting this knowledge to them can have a major impact on avoiding potential legal liabilities, resulting in substantial value to clients.

*(Continued)*

Originally BDW provided its clients with individual customized training programs, delivered either on CD-ROM or integrated into its clients' intranets. Today, the use of online systems and the development of standardized e-learning platforms means that a common template can be used across its training programs, with integrated links to scenarios specific to the client. This provides efficiencies, lower costs, and means that users of the system are still presented with real-life situations directly relevant to their company and work environment seamlessly integrated into the program. Increasingly, large clients have their own learning management systems implemented internally, so BDW uses industry standards to deliver its content in a format its clients can use within their in-house systems. One of the reasons SALT has been successful is that it is founded on integrating legal expertise into training products in an accessible way. Lawyers are trained extensively in instructional design and work with specialist lawyers to convert their knowledge into training programs that are suitable for non-lawyers. Other products provided by BDW include what it calls Virtual Lawyer Systems, which use expert systems technology to automate functions that have previously been performed by in-house lawyers. These are described in more detail in Chapter 7.

The firm's Legal Technology Group also provides technology consulting services to the legal departments of its clients. This includes general issues such as improving efficiency, establishing intranets, and implementing practice management systems. It also works with its clients to set up automatic document generation systems and other approaches that enable the legal department's internal clients to obtain self-service for their simple legal requirements. This frees up in-house lawyers from mundane contract drafting to focus on higher value-add activities. BDW does not perceive these services as cannibalizing potential work for the firm, but rather as an opportunity to create additional value for the client and position itself extremely well for the complex, desirable work generated by the company.

## Portfolio Decisions

Portfolio decisions refer to the ongoing management of a portfolio of assets, liabilities, or risks. This concept most obviously applies to financial markets in fields such as funds management, corporate treasuries, and bank lending. However, it is also relevant to a host of corporate functions, including risk management, property management, and research and development. Many organizations are now being managed specifically as a portfolio of businesses and opportunities.

The essence of portfolio decisions is that they are made on a continual basis, reflecting changing conditions in the market or business environment, as well as evolving parameters for portfolio objectives. These decisions must be made on the basis of interpretation of all information as it becomes available. While computer models are increasingly used across the full range of portfolio management situations, they remain tools that can only be used with human guidance and judgment. High-level portfolio decisions are made by individuals or groups based on their experience, and knowledge of the current environment and context. As you will see, that knowledge is based on how these managers organize and structure information into frameworks and perspectives as it becomes available.

## MENTAL MODELS

All of our decisions are based completely on our *mental models* of the world or the situation within which we are working. A mental model is the representation we hold in our minds about the way we believe the world or some part of it works. People can only think and make decisions about their environment based on their understanding of it. That understanding is represented in their mental models.

From the time we are born, we start to build models and develop ideas about the way our world works, and how we can usefully interact with it. When we observe a consistent pattern in our environment we start to build an implicit model of how it behaves, and act on the basis of that model. Early in life we build models of simple mechanical and interpersonal interactions. Later we build conceptual models of how the world we live in works. People's mental models about simple mechanical interactions are usually very similar. However, in more complex areas such as business, society, and interpersonal relationships we find an amazing diversity of mental models.

The term *mental models* has been popularized in the business community by Peter Senge with his influential book *The Fifth Discipline*,[3] but the concept has been used by cognitive psychologists for decades, and applied extensively in many contexts. Among many others, Kenneth Craik wrote about mental models in 1943,[4] Henry Mintzberg referred to mental models in a management context in 1973,[5] and Chris Argyris has proposed the very similar idea of "theories-in-use."[6]

Since all decisions are made on the basis of the decision maker's mental models, professionals must understand their clients' mental models in order to be effective in adding value to their decisions. Throughout this chapter I will build on the concept of mental models and how to use a better understanding of them to add greater value to our clients. Because of the critical importance of mental models in all knowledge acquisition and transfer, I have provided detailed coverage of the topic in the Appendix.

## Rich and Impoverished Mental Models

The mental models people use to make decisions in their business and personal lives can be rich in taking into account many issues and allowing diverse perspectives, or they can be impoverished in being locked into a single simple way of looking at things. In a simple world, simple mental models can be very effective. In the highly complex and dynamic business environment we work in we need similarly rich and diverse mental models. A related perspective is how flexible or rigid a person's mental models are. Flexibility means the ability to change not only our views and opinions but also the very basis of those views.

Rigidity is the inability to change views and opinions, even when these prove to be less than useful.[7]

The law of requisite variety, drawn from the field of cybernetics, states that for a system to be successful it must display at least as much variety as its environment. In other words, you are completely subject to changes in your environment. You effectively have no choices, unless you have at least the same degree of flexibility and complexity as the system in which you operate.[8] What this means is that our mental models must be at least as rich, diverse, and flexible as our environment. In our increasingly complex world, rich and flexible mental models are essential for business survival.[9]

In the context of dealing with clients, we can add immense value if we can assist our clients in developing richer, more flexible mental models. This represents the highest level of adding value to client decision making, and one closely tied to developing intimate and profitable client relationships. On another level, if our clients have impoverished, rigid mental models it is extremely difficult for us to add value. If we can help to enrich their mental models, we are adding immense value and paving the way for ongoing further added value and business within the context of a powerful knowledge-based relationship.

## Risk Management and Risk Awareness

In practical terms, constructing and effectively utilizing richer mental models means taking a broader range of factors — and their interrelationships — into account in all decisions. One very important implication of this process is that people with impoverished mental models simply fail to recognize many potential sources of risk. Helping our clients build richer mental models is central to effective risk as well as opportunity management.

Risk management can never be fully computerized, because it is about perceiving risk, which is unbounded in nature. One of the greatest risks in business is that of *model risk* — that the implicit and explicit models we build and use do not cover the full spectrum of what is possible or even plausible. Analytical risk valuation techniques such as "value at risk" are extremely valuable. However, the heart of effective risk management is about ensuring that senior managers have the richest possible mental models of what could impact their business, and the ability to respond effectively when the unexpected happens. Scenario planning, described later in this chapter, is a valuable tool in qualitative and quantitative risk management, and particularly in helping executives perceive the broadest possible scope of risk.[10]

## Mental Models and Decision Making

We use our experience to build mental models of the world, so that we can then use them to understand and predict what will happen in the future. We think through and assess possible courses of action by applying them to our mental models of the situation, and seeing what results are likely based on our understanding. In this way, all decision making is based on our mental models.

Figure 4–1 illustrates how mental models guide our decision making. Our mental models form the framework within which all of

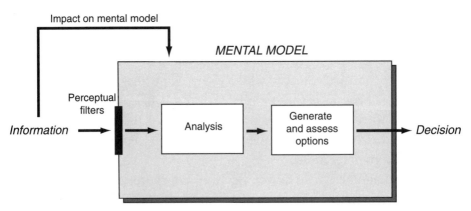

FIGURE 4–1    *Mental models in decision making.*

our thinking and decision making take place. They are in fact all we have available to us. New information and experience can be interpreted within our mental models in two ways: in being filtered by what our mental models allow us to perceive or in actually changing the mental models. People's mental models dictate their perceptual filters, which determine what they actually sense in their environment, and how it is interpreted. The degree to which people use new information to adapt and enhance their mental models as opposed to interpreting it on the basis of their existing models is a measure of the flexibility or rigidity of their mental models.[11]

Traditional decision-making theory is based on establishing criteria and assessing options for action relative to those criteria. Real-life decision making by people is rarely as straightforward. However, the two phases of analyzing and thinking about the situation, and generating and assessing options for action, are central aspects of the decision-making process. Both of these processes are subject to the constraints of the mental models of the decision maker. From these a decision will be made, which should reflect what is most likely to result in the desired outcome of the decision maker given his or her mental models.

## DECISION MAKING IN ORGANIZATIONS

In adding value to decision making in our clients, we need to understand the realities of how decisions are actually made in organizations, in a way that can usefully guide our interaction with them. Much decision-making theory is difficult to apply in practice, although there are some frameworks and perspectives that can help us be more effective in working with the processes of organizational decision making.

### Decision-Making Theory

Decision making has been a focus of management theory for many decades. The operational term has mostly been "theory" —

developing idealized models of how decisions should be made rather than examining the reality of how decisions are actually made in organizations. Much of the early research — and still a considerable proportion of current practice — revolves around "rational" decision making, and is prescriptive in describing how decisions should be made to optimize outcomes given input criteria. The main downfall of this school of decision making is simply that the criteria in all but the most trivial situations are too complex to yield to ready quantification or use in rule-based models.

Herbert Simon, together with colleagues James March, Richard Cyert, and others, helped to focus the debate on the more practical issues of how decisions are actually made in real business situations. They introduced the concept of "bounded rationality," which suggests that people are not rational in their decisions but work within the limits of their attention, comprehension, and the availability of information. One key consequence is that managers "satisfice," that is, make satisfactory rather than optimal decisions.[12]

## Decision-Making Content and Process

It is useful to distinguish between the *content* and *process* of decision making. The content of decisions consists of the information that goes into them, the recommendations considered, the content of the mental models of decision makers, and the actual final decisions themselves. The process of decisions consists of the steps and manner in which they are actually made. This process includes how information is gathered, the players involved and their relative roles, and the communication to, within, and from the decision-making team.

Most professional service providers focus on the content of decision making, and mainly on the information input to that content, not the client's current structure and way of thinking, which is at least as important in producing decisions and action. Just to be able to provide content relevant to decisions in a valuable way, the process aspects of decisions must be considered. In addition, adding value to the process of decisions itself has greater impact on the client. Wherever possible, professional service providers should endeavor to add value to both the content and process of decisions.

## Adding Value to Decision Making

As you have seen, all decisions are made within the context of the mental models of decision makers. New information and experience are filtered by mental models for use in decisions, and can also impact the models themselves. The filtered information is then analyzed and considered, and then options are generated, developed, and selected in order to produce decisions. In this chapter I will examine how value can be added to decision making within the context of existing mental models. Following that I will look at how we can add value to the mental models themselves.

The three major stages of decision making in our model include taking in information, analysis, and generating and assessing alternatives. Since most input to decision making takes the form of providing options and recommendations, we will look at these issues before we examine the stage of analysis. This results in three phases of adding value to decision making.

- Providing key information
- Providing options and recommendations
- Analysis and thinking

### Providing Key Information

One of the most obvious ways of adding value to decision making is in providing information that is highly relevant to the decision at hand. This was addressed in Chapter 3. As you saw, the value of information rests in its application in making better business decisions, which is achieved by customizing information for the specific decisions the client must make. Customization includes providing all information necessary to make the decision at hand, filtering out everything else, and presenting the information in a format that is easy to understand and relevant for the specific decision.

As information becomes increasingly commoditized, high-value information must be geared toward being directly relevant to client decision making. Companies that are able to command premium prices for business information are those deliberately focusing on providing input to executive decisions, such as the Economist Intelligence Unit, credit rating agencies such as Moody's, and industry-specific market research companies.

## Options and Recommendations

All decisions — both in formal processes and in quick informal situations — depend in some way on generating options or alternatives, which are then evaluated to choose a path of action. Generating decision options, assessing these, and presenting recommendations for action is a key role performed by professional service firms in many industries. Much of the advisory work in the legal and consulting industries, for example, consists of these functions.

We have seen that generating and assessing options takes place within the scope of the client's mental models. As such, any options or recommendations must make sense within the context of their mental models. If not, they will be rejected out of hand. This emphasizes the importance of understanding the client's mental models, even when clear recommendations are being made.

In some situations clients may be actively looking for ideas that fit their world view. An example is the case of portfolio managers, who have distinct mental models of the financial markets or whatever portfolios they are running, and will reward any salesperson who can provide them well-thought-out actionable ideas that take advantage of their views and opinions. The portfolio managers implicitly understand that they have their own mental models of the markets, and want professionals who can understand these models and provide recommendations consistent with them.

Black-box service providers will tend to present recommendations as the outcome of the engagement. In knowledge-based relationships, clients are helped to generate and assess options for themselves, and can be provided with additional alternatives and insights to ensure that the broadest range of issues are considered.

The investment consulting industry provides services primarily to the trustees and executives of superannuation and pension funds. The trustees have the responsibility of making considered decisions in structuring portfolios and selecting asset managers. The investment consultant's role is to assist trustees in those decisions. In some cases, pension funds effectively outsource the decisions to the consultants, simply rubber-stamping their recommendations. In other situations, consultants provide useful input to the trustees' decisions. The highly dynamic nature of regulation and developments in the investment world mean that education is always an important part of the consulting function.

Mercer Investment Consulting, a member of the Marsh & McLennan group of companies, is one of the largest investment consulting firms worldwide. Mercer maintains a broad range of relationships with its clients, from individual projects through to ongoing retainers, and fully implemented consulting through to broad input to decision making. Information and recommendations are provided through regular reports, supplemented with presentations to trustees. Often the way these are presented will be developed in consultation with the trustees' chairperson, and individual meetings with board members may be scheduled where significant education on critical issues is required, or where a range of opinion is represented. In situations in which clients more actively make their own decisions, Mercer will present three or four reasonable positions, with full cost/benefit analysis of each. To emphasize that none of these is suggested as a preferred option, they may be presented in alphabetical order in the report.

## Analysis: The Thinking Behind Recommendations

The presentation of recommendations to clients is often performed as a black-box function. It is opaque to the client how these recommendations were generated. In this case, any decision generated is not so much one made by the client as one made by the consultant and endorsed by the client. There are situations in which the client only wants this type of recommendation. However, clients increasingly want to make their own decisions, and to use the thinking behind the generation of options and the final recommendations in future decisions.

One important reason black-box recommendations generally yield less value than providing the content and process behind them is that they "collapse" the richness of the thinking that went into the recommendations down to a single outcome. An excellent example of this phenomenon is economic research in whatever field it is applied. Economists go through a detailed process of examining all issues and uncertainties in looking ahead. When they collapse or condense all of that thinking into a single set of figures representing their economic forecast and the justification for that most-likely outcome, the richness of the thinking that went into developing the forecast largely disappears for the client. While many clients simply want some numbers to slot into their budgets without much discussion (a dangerous but common approach), economists are inherently limiting the potential value of their work to clients by leaving out the breadth of the analysis behind their views.

On a related front, investment bank Morgan Stanley, in its financial market research, rather than giving "house" opinions on what will happen in global economic and financial markets occasionally publishes lively debates between its senior analysts, sometimes expressing very different views. These published debates allow clients to take on the richness and diversity of thinking behind the issues for integration into their own thinking, rather than being given a single perspective. Similarly, Goldman Sachs has published a range of possible global economic scenarios and the thinking behind each, and has encouraged clients to allocate their own weightings to these scenarios and to explore their implications.

## ADDING VALUE TO MENTAL MODELS

Decision making can only be done within the context of the mental models of those making the decisions. As a result, usually the area in which the most value can be added to client decision making is in impacting the mental models themselves. This can be done in three ways.

- Making mental models explicit
- Integrating mental models
- Enriching mental models

### Making Mental Models Explicit

An important part of adding value to clients' mental models is helping to make them explicit or visible. Mental models are almost invariably beyond the awareness of the individual or group, and depending on the situation they can either be useful or a barrier to success. In either case, making the mental models explicit and clear will be valuable in assisting clients to make better decisions. Helping a client's senior managers understand the way they are currently thinking about their business, and their underlying assumptions, is itself extremely valuable and paves the way to help them take on new perspectives.

Kees van der Heijden, Professor of General and Strategic Management at Strathclyde University, U.K., and former head of Royal Dutch/Shell's Group Business Environment Division, uses the concept of the "business idea," which he describes as "the organization's mental model of the forces behind its current and future success."[13] He emphasizes the importance of articulating managers' business ideas in building shared understanding in the management team, and focusing the dialogue that must take place to develop the organization's distinctive competencies.

More and more consulting firms are offering services designed to make the mental models of their clients explicit, often as part of a broader process of facilitating strategic decision making. The methodologies usually involve developing a visual representation of the group's mental model, using principles based on systems dynamics. *Cognitive mapping*, which is used to build maps for individuals or organizations of the way they understand their business situations, developed as a prominent field in the 1990s, supported by considerable academic research and use by management consultants. The basis of these approaches is explained in the Appendix.

Clearly, deep trust of service providers by clients is required for engagement in working with them at the level of their mental models.[14] Equally, the degree of intimacy inherent in the process will help to develop far deeper relationships and trust.

## Integrating Mental Models

Integrating the mental models of individuals on decision-making teams at client organizations, especially around broad themes such as the business or investment environment, is one of the most valuable services possible. The idea is certainly not to make people's mental models the same. Differences and divergence in individual ways of thinking within a group are invaluable. Integrating mental models is about developing a common framework that allows team members to share the ways in which their mental models are different. The process also provides a basis for constructive communication, and builds a richer mental model that incorporates a wide variety of perspectives, as represented in Figure 4–2. The importance of integrated or shared mental models in organizations has been emphasized by a number of practitioners, notably those associated with the learning organization movement, such as Peter Senge and Ray Stata.[15]

Making a team or organization's mental models explicit is an important means of integrating the mental models of individuals within the

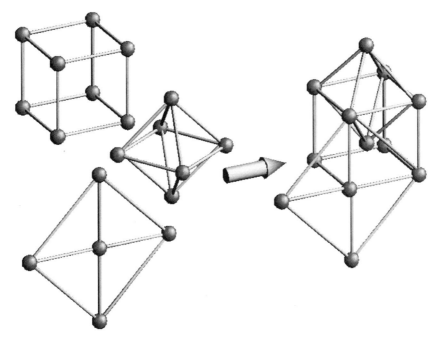

FIGURE 4–2    *Integrating individual mental models produces richer group mental models.*

group. It allows people to understand how they are thinking and how that differs from others, and it provides a foundation for meaningful dialogue. More generally, skillful facilitation is about finding a common ground for productive discussion, which often draws on similar approaches. These are vital foundation skills for professionals seeking to add value to their clients' decision making.

## Enriching Mental Models

You have already seen the importance and value of richer mental models. Any service provider that can effectively enrich the mental models of its clients, and link that enrichment to better decisions, will create immense value. All interactions have the potential to help clients gain richer and more useful perspectives, and this should be a core intention behind all conversations and meetings. If, however, clients explicitly give "permission" to help enrich their ways of thinking, the potential impact can be far greater, and clients are far more aware of its value.

One approach is simply challenging clients by presenting alternative views that require them to think beyond their current mental models. Doing this poorly can easily result in clients rejecting those views and becoming alienated. Ideally, the alternative views will take into account the clients' cognitive styles, existing mental models, and how these can best be developed. A key aspect of enriching mental models is bringing assumptions to light. People's assumptions are their blind spots. Often people do not perceive certain issues because they are taken for granted, so bringing these issues into their field of perception is extremely valuable.

Outsights, a London-based consultancy, was approached by a client that wanted help in implementing "real options" (a quantitative approach to assessing strategic choices). The consultants responded by noting that this is only useful if you examine and understand the assumptions made in developing the models. Outsights ended up helping the client examine and uncover its business assumptions, resulting in the client deciding that it did not need to use the real options methodology.

There are any number of more formal techniques and methods for enriching mental models. Some of the most effective methodologies include scenario planning and war gaming. One approach explicitly focused on enriching mental models is what Global Business Network (GBN) calls "learning journeys" (see box on "Global Business Network").

## Facilitating Decision Making

In general, it is more valuable to help clients make decisions for themselves than to go through the analysis process externally and provide them recommendations. Facilitating clients in their own decisions is a good example of knowledge elicitation. The assumption is that the client has most of the knowledge required to make the best decision, but can be assisted in drawing that out and working with it so as to result in the desired outcomes. Indeed, it is difficult for a professional service firm to suggest that it knows the client's organization better than the client does. However, it can certainly provide expertise in decision making and the business environment that results in better decisions for the client. In most cases, facilitating decision making not only contributes value to the decision at hand but also enriches the client's mental models and ability to make better decisions in future situations.

Here I will present two structured approaches to facilitating client decision making that have gained currency over the last years: scenario planning and war gaming. While other approaches are often used, those presented here are representative, and probably have the longest pedigrees of success.

## Scenario Planning

Scenario planning is a well-established approach to strategic decision making. It first became widely known in the business community when Shell had developed a scenario for a sharp rise in oil prices before the onset of the 1974 oil crisis, and as a result was better positioned than its competitors to respond effectively. Since then, scenario planning has become broadly used across a variety of industries, with a resurgence of interest in the wake of the manifold shocks of the last years, as businesspeople have been forcibly reminded that the future is unpredictable.

Scenario planning is a process of developing a number of scenarios or stories for the future that are plausible to decision makers, complementary in that together they cover the broadest possible scope of uncertainty in the organization's environment, and relevant to the key decisions the organization faces. The methodology usually involves getting broad participation in uncovering the underlying trends and critical uncertainties in the organization's environment, building these into engaging narratives that form the scenarios, and using these to generate, explore, and refine a cohesive and robust strategy in the face of uncertainty.

The history of scenario planning has seen it applied mainly to making major decisions and developing organizational strategies. However, it is increasingly also used as a tool for developing the ongoing interactions and processes within the organization that result in effective decision making. Even today, all major investment decisions at Shell must be assessed against a set of scenarios. Scenario planning is increasingly being implemented in-house as an intrinsic part of the strategic planning process in many of the largest corporations worldwide. Most commonly, external organizations are involved, because of their value in introducing fresh perspectives as part of projecting beyond what scenario planners call "the official future," which is essentially the organization's mental model of its future.

Pierre Wack, considered the guiding light behind the development of scenario planning and the writer of two seminal *Harvard Business Review* articles on the topic,[16] introduced the concept of "remarkable people" to the practice of scenario planning.[17] Since building scenarios useful for strategic decision making requires examining and challenging existing mental models, the role of these people is quite simply to present very different ways of thinking in order to shake up decision makers.[18] This is a primary role of Global Business Network's individual members, who are often used in GBN's scenario planning engagements with its clients.

War Gaming

War gaming has gained currency as a powerful approach for adding value to strategic decision making. As the name suggests, its genesis was in the simulations that have been used extensively by the military for centuries. In the context of organizational management, it provides an intense simulation of real-world business environments and decision making.

One professional service firm that uses war gaming extensively is strategy consultant Booz Allen Hamilton, though others, including

McKinsey & Company and PricewaterhouseCoopers, are adopting similar services. Typically, Booz Allen involves 60 to 80 senior managers from its client organization over about three days.[19] The managers divide into teams that play their own company, a selection of their major competitors, their customers, and potentially other players such as regulators. Each team is given critical background information, with the team playing the customers given detailed customer research to guide its response to the developing range of offerings available through the game.

The game proceeds through a sequence of moves by each team, which can be measured in months or years. Each move is based on the outcomes of the previous move, resulting in a dynamic and evolving competitive marketplace. External discontinuities in the market such as deregulation can be designed into the game, or strategic innovations introduced by the teams.

Similarly to scenario planning, war gaming challenges the implicit assumptions of managers about the dynamics of their industry and how it will evolve, and helps them to think through how they will respond to previously unforeseen circumstances. The highly experiential nature of the game and the approach of forming teams for different players in the industry results in powerful learning opportunities for participants, and the dynamic nature of war gaming can bring new issues to light. However, it generally does not cover the scope of uncertainties that is the essence of scenario planning.

---

### Global Business Network

Global Business Network (GBN), based in Emeryville, California, was established in 1987 by five colleagues, most of whom had been involved in scenario planning in Royal Dutch/Shell during the previous 15 years. A member of the Monitor Group since 2000, GBN's 40-person staff serves as the hub of the network, connecting corporate and individual members that represent an eclectic range of expertise in the arts, literature, sciences, social sciences, government, and business.

*(Continued)*

GBN offers three primary services: a membership organization for foresight professionals, scenario and strategy consulting, and scenario training. At its core is the Worldview membership service, which is primarily geared toward global corporations, but includes governments and nonprofits as well. For an annual fee, members have access to a variety of GBN resources, including regular publications of GBN research and insights; the monthly GBN Book Club; access to a proprietary web site and online forums; attendance at GBN's meetings and conferences, which examine key issues affecting organizations now and in the future; and preferential access to GBN's training and consulting services, which are available to any interested clients (not just members).

While GBN provides extensive content knowledge on the issues facing different industries and on the future of business and society, its consulting focus is perhaps more oriented toward process, such as how to conduct an effective scenario planning project and then use that learning to generate an ongoing strategic conversation. GBN does not attempt to hold on to that process knowledge, but actively teaches its clients how to do it for themselves. Furthermore, it has welcomed to its training courses representatives of many organizations that could be considered competitors, such as the major professional service firms. The entire philosophy of GBN, and the basis on which it was designed, is about enabling interactions and learning from others in emergent and collaborative ways, often across traditional boundaries, reports Nancy Murphy, head of communications at GBN. The network structure and nature of the interaction between GBN members is designed to bring together different knowledge, experience, and perspectives to create new understanding, with GBN playing the role of catalyst and facilitator as well as participant in the resulting discussions.

An illustration of the approaches used by GBN to elicit useful knowledge and broaden mental models is what it calls "learning journeys." These experiential tours take executives to visit innovators and organizations at the leading edge of change in areas relevant to their industries and decisions at hand, though often in tangential and unexpected ways. GBN sometimes designs scenario planning exercises to include learning journeys, and has designed week-long learning journeys to achieve specific learning outcomes with groups of executives.

## SUMMARY: ADDING VALUE TO CLIENT DECISION MAKING

Arguably, management *is* decision making. As such, adding value to our clients' ability to make better business decisions can create immense value. For the purposes of adding value to clients, we can distinguish between strategic, line, and portfolio decisions. Each of these requires different approaches in order to add value effectively.

People make decisions on the basis of their mental models, or ways of thinking about the world they live in. By understanding group and individual decision-making processes, we can add value to those decisions, and the mental models clients use in their decisions. The greatest, longest-term value is created by enriching clients' mental models, which allows clients to incorporate a broader perception of issues into their thinking and decision making.

A range of specific methodologies is available to facilitate clients in making better decisions. One example is scenario planning, in which clients develop a number of plausible scenarios for the future of their business environment as a tool for making better strategic decisions. War gaming immerses clients in a simulation of their business played against their competitors, to give them a better understanding of the potential issues they face.

While business is about decision making, this only happens within the context of the organization. Organizations are defined by the competencies and capabilities that enable them to create value for their customers or clients, and will survive only if these remain superior and distinctive. Knowledge is at the heart of those capabilities, and a fundamental role of professional service firms is adding value to the capabilities of clients. This is the subject of Chapter 5.

## NOTES

[1]  As pointed out by Chun Wei Choo, *The Knowing Organization: How Organizations Use Information to Construct Meaning, Create Knowledge, and Make Decisions*, New York: Oxford University Press, 1998. See, for example, Herbert A. Simon, *Administrative*

*Behavior: A Study of Decision-Making Processes in Administrative Organizations*, 4th ed., New York: The Free Press, 1997, p. 305.

2   SALT is a registered trademark of Blake Dawson Waldron.

3   Peter M. Senge, *The Fifth Discipline: The Art and Practice of the Learning Organization*, New York: Currency/Doubleday, 1994.

4   Kenneth Craik, *The Nature of Explanation*, Cambridge, U.K.: Cambridge University Press, 1943.

5   Henry Mintzberg, *The Nature of Managerial Work*, New York: Harper & Row, 1973.

6   Chris Argyris, "Single-Loop and Double-Loop Models in Research on Decision Making," *Administrative Science Quarterly* 21, September 1976, pp. 363–375.

7   Markides notes that "very strong mental models can hinder active thinking and the adoption of new ideas . . . we tend to hear what already supports our existing beliefs and ways of operating, while any new information that does not support what we believe we discard as wrong and not applicable." See Constantinos Markides, "Strategic Innovation," *Sloan Management Review*, Spring 1997, pp. 9–23.

8   Originally proposed in W. Ross Ashby, *An Introduction to Cybernetics*, London: Chapman & Hall, 1956. The law of requisite variety originated from the field of cybernetics, but has been very influential, recurring across a wide range of disciplines, including anthropology and social ecology (see, for example, Gregory Bateson, *Steps to an Ecology of Mind*, London: Paladin, 1973); management (Nonaka and Takeuchi nominate it as one of the five enabling conditions of organizational knowledge creation); and neurolinguistic programming (NLP), in which it is one of the basic presuppositions of the field.

9   Paradigms can be considered to be the highest level of shared mental model, which are the most difficult to shift. See Thomas S. Kuhn, *The Structure of Scientific Revolutions*, Chicago: University of Chicago Press, 1970, and Thomas Clarke and Stewart Clegg, *Changing Paradigms: The Transformation of Management Knowledge for the 21st Century*, London: HarperBusiness, 1998.

10  See, for example, Ron S. Dembo and Andrew Freeman, *Seeing Tomorrow: Rewriting the Rules of Risk*, New York: John Wiley & Sons, 1998, pp. 38–45. For a coverage of applying scenario planning to financial risk management, see Ross Dawson, "Did You Forecast Asia? Scenario Planning in Portfolio and Risk Management," *The Australian Corporate Treasurer*, August 1998.

11  Isenberg suggests that good managers continually test and revise their mental map of the problems and issues facing them. See Daniel J. Isenberg, "How Senior Managers Think," *Harvard Business Review*, November/December 1984.

12  For an excellent review of this approach, see James March, *A Primer on Decision Making: How Decisions Happen*, New York: Harvard Business School Press, 1994.

13 Kees van der Heijden, *Scenarios: The Art of Strategic Conversation*, London: John Wiley & Sons, 1996, p. 59.

14 In the context of articulating the "business idea," van der Heiden notes that the "choice of the facilitator is important, and will normally be limited to team members or well-trusted outsiders" (van der Heiden, op. cit.).

15 Stata explicitly writes about shared mental models. See Ray Stata, "Organizational Learning — The Key to Management Innovation," *Sloan Management Review*, Spring 1989, pp. 63–74. Senge refers to the related concept of "shared vision."

16 Pierre Wack, "Scenarios: Uncharted Waters Ahead," *Harvard Business Review* 63, no. 5, September/October 1985, pp. 73–90, and "Scenarios: Shooting the Rapids," *Harvard Business Review* 63, no. 6, November/December 1985, pp. 131–142.

17 Peter Schwartz, *The Art of the Long View: Planning the Future in an Uncertain World*, New York: Doubleday Currency, 1991, p. 10.

18 Janis, in examining the highly relevant issues of "groupthink," suggests that outside experts should be invited in to challenge the views of core team members. Irving L. Janis, *Groupthink: Psychological Studies of Policy Decisions and Fiascoes*, Boston: Houghton-Mifflin, 1982, pp. 266–267.

19 The description of the Booz-Allen & Hamilton war gaming process is drawn from John E. Treat, George E. Thibault, and Amy Asin, "Dynamic Competitive Simulation: Wargaming as a Strategic Tool," *Strategy & Business*, 2nd Quarter, 1996.

# 5

# Adding Value to Client Capabilities
## Enhancing Processes and Skills

Every company's ability to compete and survive is based on developing and maintaining distinctive capabilities that are relevant to its business environment. Organizations must draw on both internal and external resources in order to develop and evolve the capabilities on which their future depends. Harvard Business School's Dorothy Leonard notes that most or all companies must import knowledge from beyond their boundaries in order to build core capabilities.[1] The sources for that knowledge include customers, suppliers, partners, educational institutions, and other organizations.

Any organization assisting others to enhance their capabilities, whether categorized as a professional services firm, product vendor, research organization, alliance partner, government body, or anything else, is creating immense and often irreplaceable value. This role of external capability development is at the heart of our increasingly interconnected economy.

## DEVELOPING CAPABILITIES

Organizational capabilities are the abilities underlying performance in specific spheres of business. These could include activities such as attracting and retaining staff, manufacturing with consistent quality and at low cost, or marketing to high-income consumers. The related domain of competencies, as defined by Hamel and Prahalad, refers to fields of often technological knowledge and expertise that can be combined and applied to the provision of a broad range of products or services. Examples include miniaturization, precision optics, and building alliances.[2]

Capabilities and competencies form the source of competitive advantage for an organization. As such, it is critical that they be continually reinforced by investment and management attention, and adapted in line with changes and anticipated developments in the business environment. Companies need continually to develop their knowledge and internal expertise, and to enhance their processes and skills. External service providers can play a critical role in assisting companies in these endeavors.

## Processes and Skills

The two essential components of business capabilities are processes and skills. Processes in organizations are knowledge that is encapsulated in methodologies, or in systematic sequences of actions. These processes can be formal or explicit in that they are clear, documented, and replicable. However, more often they are informal or implicit, in that they are embedded in "the way things are done," and their efficacy is not understood in detail.[3] Business systems of all types including accounting systems, workflows, and reporting systems, can all be considered processes.

Skills, in the same manner as knowledge, are unique to people. Skills are a vital component of knowledge. They usually refer to tacit knowledge, they must be used in the context of an individual's overall knowledge and experience, and they are a significant component of the action in the "capacity to act effectively."

From an intellectual capital perspective, introduced in Chapter 2, processes and systems are part of structural capital, and skills are part of human capital. By definition, structural capital remains, whether the people are there or not. Certainly formal processes, which are documented or embedded in technology, are part of structural capital. Many informal processes, which are built into the way teams work, will survive people leaving and being replaced by others who learn the processes on the job. In this case, they are also part of structural capital. If, however, the processes are so informal that they do not survive the departure of key staff then they are effectively part of human capital.

Capabilities are in practice a fusion of both processes and skills. A process alone is not valuable without the skills to perform the process effectively, while skills in themselves are of limited use unless they are applied within an effective process. As such, the processes and skills on which capabilities are built are an inseparable system; that is, each depends on the other to have value. In developing our clients' capabilities, we must focus not only on processes and skills individually but also deal with them as an interdependent system.

## Capabilities and Meta-capabilities

Capabilities create high performance in a specific sphere of business. Capabilities in areas such as attracting and retaining high-quality staff, total quality manufacturing, or efficient back-office processing are primary sources of competitive advantage. Organizations place a very high value on firms that can assist them in developing and enhancing those capabilities.

Perhaps the most valuable capabilities of all are those that contribute to developing and enhancing other business capabilities. These can be called *meta-capabilities*, as they act on other capabilities.[4] The relationship of meta-capabilities to capabilities is illustrated in Figure 5–1. Some of the capabilities that can be considered meta-capabilities or to support meta-capabilities include the following.

- Rapidly learning new processes and skills
- Open communication throughout the organization
- Sharing and leveraging knowledge internally

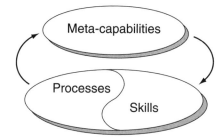

FIGURE 5–1    *Meta-capabilities enable the development of other integrated capabilities.*

- Taking in knowledge from outside the organization
- Flexibility and adaptability of organizational structure

Clearly, enhancing clients' capabilities at this level is more valuable than working with capabilities that apply only to a limited range of functions. Developing client meta-capabilities is potentially immensely valuable, but more difficult to achieve than with other capabilities. In the first instance, the client must recognize the value of these initiatives, which is not easy when there is a short-term result orientation. In addition, it can be a major challenge to identify or quantify the results of programs that act at this level.

### Organizational Learning

Organizational learning has been one of the most influential management trends of the last decade. John Browne, CEO of BP, says that "to generate extraordinary value for shareholders, a company has to learn better than its competitors and apply that knowledge throughout its businesses faster and more widely than they do."[5]

The concept of organizational learning in fact encompasses the ongoing development of all meta-capabilities within an organization. Organizational learning is the process by which organizations and the individuals within them continually develop their ability to further

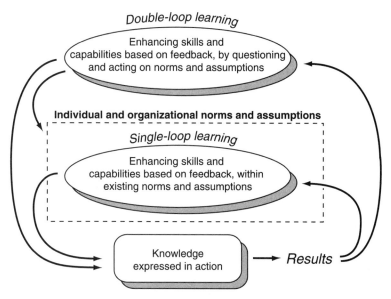

FIGURE 5–2    *Single-loop and double-loop learning.*

develop their own capabilities. This has to be implemented in processes and skills, particularly those that involve observing results achieved by current processes and actively experimenting with new approaches. In practice, organizational learning is particularly difficult to influence from outside the organization.

Chris Argyris of Harvard University has proposed a distinction between what he calls single-loop and double-loop learning.[6] Single-loop learning refers to learning processes and skills within the context of established norms of the organization, looking mainly externally, while double-loop learning requires individuals to question their own and the organization's assumptions and norms by looking inside, as represented in Figure 5–2. This is very similar to the distinction between working within the scope of an individual's or group's existing mental models and actually changing or enriching those mental models, as described in Chapter 4. As such, the lessons learned in adding value to decision making can also be applied in assisting organizations to develop organizational learning.

The fact remains that it is very difficult to add value to clients at the level of developing organizational learning without already having a very close relationship. To be effective, organizational learning initiatives must be ongoing and embedded in the organization's leadership, culture, and projects, with results assessed primarily at a group level. As such, the existence of a top-level commitment within the client organization will be a key success factor.

## Approaches to Enhancing Client Capabilities

Enhancing organizational capabilities depends on the development of both processes and skills in a coordinated fashion. The primary focus of the service provider may be on either processes or skills. However, both fields will always have to be considered if the goal is to achieve an impact at the level of clients' business capabilities.

Throughout this chapter I will examine both process-oriented and skills-oriented approaches to developing client capabilities, as well as approaches that integrate both aspects in a more holistic manner. The objectives behind initiatives should always be framed at the highest possible level. This can transform, for example, a training initiative into a program that develops organization-wide business capabilities and generates substantially greater value.

Professionals need to understand how to develop specific business capabilities as well as meta-capabilities. Since meta-capabilities are in fact a type of capability, in general the same principles apply. However, as you have seen, the focus should be on the level of attitudes and mental models in addition to the basic processes and skills involved in continual learning and improvement. One of the most important aspects of developing meta-capabilities is that they are generative, in the sense of acting as a foundation for further capability development beyond the time frame and scope of the professional service firm's engagement.

## Process Implementation and Enhancement

One of the most straightforward means of developing client capabilities is in implementing effective business processes. This is a core element of many professional services offerings. In selling or implementing processes, there are two possible situations: the client does not have a formal process in place to achieve the desired results or is willing to discard its existing process, or it wishes to develop and enhance the processes it is currently using.

In some situations, implementing a new process can be relatively straightforward in simply giving the client a series of actions to follow. However, in many cases processes need to be adapted to the client's culture, or to the organizational context in which the new process will be embedded. To enhance existing processes, a deeply interactive approach is required, starting from studying those processes, designing enhancements, and helping to implement those changes in the existing process.

### Process Documentation

Processes are often provided to clients in the form of written documentation, which details all steps in the process or its implementation. There are clearly substantial limitations to the effectiveness with which process knowledge can be transferred through documents. Simpler processes, such as software registration procedures or immigration compliance for new staff, are clearly far more amenable to transfer through documentation than complex and diverse processes, such as replicating best practice or implementing enterprise-wide software.

There are, however, advantages to both providers and clients in that once documentation has been produced it can be sold and resold without requiring any additional professional time, and is relatively inexpensive for clients. Process documentation as a standalone means of knowledge transfer can be very useful for smaller clients who cannot afford or justify the dedicated time of expensive professionals.

Naturally, process documentation is most valuable when combined with other means of knowledge transfer, so provides a complement to more experiential approaches, as well as an easy and accessible reference source when required. When used in isolation it is of limited value and impact in knowledge transfer.

## Software

Software offers many advantages over documentation for process implementation, in part because the business process can be embedded in the way the software works and is used. As such, it is increasingly used as a means of encapsulating and transferring processes. This is perhaps most obvious in workflow-based software, which in its usage actually dictates a specific sequence of actions by people with nominated functions in the organization, and coordinates communication flow between them.

The implementation of process software must be accompanied with training and specialist advice in order to add maximum value to clients. Ultimately, implementing software in itself is unlikely to provide a competitive advantage. One reason for this is that software generally embeds knowledge implicitly, and thus that knowledge is far less available to the client to work with, adapt, and use. In addition, purchasing a commercially available software package can never provide differentiation from competitors. It is only in combining it with the development of skills or enhancement of processes that the potential exists for major value creation. This is illustrated by the massive consulting projects involved in the implementation of enterprise resource planning (ERP) software such as SAP or PeopleSoft. The value resides more in the customization, adaptation of processes, and training than in the software itself.

## Process Reengineering

Business process reengineering, affectionately known to many as BPR, reached its zenith about 1995, when it was estimated that corporations spent $51 billion on these initiatives.[7] The basic principle of BPR involves looking at organizations from a process and workflow basis, and reengineering those processes to achieve greater efficiencies. The acronym of BPR is no longer popular, in part because many of the initial round of BPR initiatives had substantial inadvertent negative impacts. However, the approaches are still practiced extensively in evolved forms.

BPR is itself a process, and can be performed either as a black-box service or as a knowledge transfer project that enables the client to perform BPR for itself. When BPR was extremely popular in the early to mid 1990s, Ernst & Young chose to offer it only as a package that included a single implementation of BPR within the client organization, combined with training and licensing the client to implement the process for itself whenever it was subsequently required. Ernst & Young implicitly recognized that the client would in any case learn the process to a substantial degree in the implementation, and so chose to make that learning embedded in the offering and pricing structure. Since BPR is about enhancing existing processes, teaching clients to implement BPR can certainly be considered to be developing a meta-capability.

---

### RiskMetrics Group

RiskMetrics Group (RMG) provides software-based services, data, and training for financial institutions and corporations to enable them to better manage financial risk. RMG was originally the risk products group of JPMorgan, and was spun off in 1998, with Reuters and the employees of the new company joining the bank as shareholders. In mid 2004, a group of private equity partners bought out the remaining equity of what had become JPMorgan Chase, leaving the firm entirely independent.

RMG's original product — RiskMetrics — was released in 1994, when sophisticated financial risk management was in its infancy. The Risk-

*(Continued)*

Metrics methodology was and still is provided free of charge to the entire industry, with technical documents specifying the methodology available from its web site. The data sets required by the methodologies could also be downloaded daily. The release helped establish it as an industry standard, promoted greater transparency in the market, and helped reduce overall risk in the financial system. In line with the philosophy behind openly releasing the methodologies, all calculations performed in the software are fully documented and accessible to clients.

The company now provides a suite of for-fee software-based risk management services, as the centerpiece of a range of services to help its clients manage their financial risk effectively. RMG has shifted to offer its software services almost exclusively on an application service provider (ASP) basis, in which RMG hosts the application and clients access it over the Internet. Clients have recently become far more comfortable with having sensitive portfolio information held outside the firm, though will sometimes conduct security audits to support their confidence.

In addition to the provision of risk management software services, clients look to RMG to find out global industry best practices in risk management. RMG has always provided both classroom training and e-learning on risk management to its clients. However, it is placing less emphasis on these formats, usually just running a one-day classroom program for relevant executives when the system is initially installed. Now it focuses more on providing one-on-one training and coaching to client executives. Many of its researchers and senior risk advisors spend a substantial portion of their time at client sites, providing clients with coaching to implement the risk processes effectively. There is no traditional help desk, with calls going directly to specialists who can respond to their clients' issues. The intention of the multifaceted rich interaction with clients is to ensure that not only is the software service available but that it is fully implemented into clients' processes, along with the necessary skills to create high-level risk management capabilities.

## Client Education

Developing the skills of client staff is critical to enhancing the organization's capabilities, both in its own right and as a complement to the implementation of processes. Skill development is often separated from other aspects of organizational development and knowledge transfer when engaging professional services firms. Many organizations treat skill development as purely a training issue, and they bring in training companies to address specific development needs, often without placing these needs in an overall strategic context.

Skill development needs to be treated as a far broader issue by service providers and their clients, in terms of addressing skills as a source of organizational capabilities and sustainable competitiveness and in terms of applying the full range of approaches that result in effective development. Classroom training and workshops are just two ways of developing skills and knowledge. Practical knowledge is most effectively gained through experience, however, which emphasizes the importance of experiential learning in client interaction.

The Australian operations of global banking group ABN AMRO have for several years run a simulated trading game for junior executives at its fixed-interest funds management clients. Over three days, for about 16 people, it provides product education and guest speakers, embedded into a multi-stage game. The executives are allocated into teams of three or four people, with one ABN AMRO staff member on each team. All teams are given fictitious portfolios to manage over the three-day program, competing with each other to make the most money through trading. Members play the roles of both bank traders and clients, so that they can understand how their counterparts at the bank perform their work. All game participants are given versions of the bank's in-house pricing sheets, which they can use on their laptops to see how pricing is structured from the bank side, and apply this within the game. They are able to take these pricing sheets with them at the end of the game.

During the game, teams are informed of news announcements and changes in market conditions, which they have to respond to in their portfolio strategies. Versions of ABN AMRO's range of research reports that provide commentary on the game's economic and market environment are supplied to teams as input to their decision making.

ABN AMRO finds that the trading game is a valuable relationship tool, and plans to roll out the game for its London clients in the near future. The game provides a context for demonstrating the value of the bank's tools and services, creates value by developing the skills of clients' staff, and builds relationships with future decision makers. One energy utility that provides energy trading products and that has worked with ABN AMRO has chosen to implement the game for its own corporate clients.

## Client Education in the Professional Services Offering

Client education, implemented through classroom training and e-learning, is a significant standalone sector of professional services. This can be considered a very pure form of knowledge transfer, as the outcome is explicitly skills, knowledge, and the capacity to act effectively. However, client education has a critical role to play within almost any professional services relationship. It is important in many ways, as it adds substantial value, builds closer relationships, and develops more sophisticated clients who can gain greater value from high-level professional services.

In fact, client education is one of the most powerful ways of engaging a client in knowledge-based relationships, by demonstrating the ability to create additional value for the client. In one case, a global investment bank was in discussions with a state-owned organization in Eastern Europe that was considering going through a privatization and initial public offering of shares. The investment bank offered to spend several weeks with the organization's senior executives, training them on what was entailed in the privatization process, the key success factors, and the step-by-step activities to achieving a successful result.

In the process, the bank demonstrated its expertise, gained deep knowledge about the organization, and built solid personal relationships with senior management. It was no surprise when it won the mandate to privatize the company.

The advertising industry has traditionally offered training courses as part of its suite of services. These are sometimes packaged as part of the overall relationship, or are made available separately for an additional price. The basic intention of the training courses is to develop the client's ability to use advertising effectively. They usually include topics such as the advertisement development process and media placement. The intention is that the client and advertising agency are able to work together more smoothly, and better results are achieved. The agencies have a strong interest in seeing their clients achieve value for the cost of their advertising.

Advertising agency DDB London has been running a "Creative Role-Reversal Course" since 1970. It is designed to place its clients in the role of an advertising agency so that they can better understand the process of how advertising is developed, though the course is now open to any young marketer or brand manager who deals with advertising agencies. Over an intensive five days, participants break into syndicates that play the roles of agencies pitching for business. The subject is usually a real-world situation in the agency, and the syndicate presentations at the end of the week are judged by a panel, including a senior representative of the relevant client and the top management of DDB. Each syndicate is assigned a tutor who acts as a mentor and sounding board for the group as they work. While there are instructional talks and exercises throughout the course, the primary emphasis is on developing advertising ideas in a realistic situation.

CIBC World Markets, the investment banking arm of Canadian Imperial Bank of Commerce, has established the School of Financial Products, which provides structured training programs in the use of financial derivatives for its clients and prospects. The spectacular losses in derivatives of Orange County, Procter & Gamble, and other organizations led to a tendency among corporations to shy away from using complex financial instruments, despite their value in portfolio and risk management. CIBC World Markets chose to establish formal training programs for its clients, examining not only the practicalities of dealing with financial derivatives, including risk management, but broader strategic issues such as establishing policies and procedures for managing sophisticated financial products. The School of Financial Products runs more than 30 formal programs in its New York offices, as well as in other locations in North America and worldwide. These are provided free of charge to any organization introduced by CIBC World Market's front-line sales staff and relationship managers.

## EXPERIENTIAL LEARNING

For the majority of people, the most effective way to learn a process or skill is by doing it. Textbook or classroom learning is usually not sufficient in itself to enable a person or team to develop skills effectively, or to learn how to implement or run a business process. Knowledge acquisition is almost always substantially more effective if it is based on practical experience. Over the last couple of decades the training industry has taken into account the clear evidence that experiential learning yields the best results, and training is now usually strongly oriented toward activities, simulation of real work environments, and learning by doing. Action learning — which embodies the same principles — has emerged as a key framework for internal development initiatives.

While the principle of experiential learning often guides the design of training programs, it should also be implicit in the design of all client interaction intended to facilitate knowledge transfer. This principle directs how many professional service firms implement knowledge transfer — by taking clients through a real-life process in such a way that they can then implement the process unassisted. This was the case with Ernst & Young's provision of business process reengineering services. Ernst & Young trained the client to perform BPR by actually carrying out the process in one of its business units or operations, and worked with key client staff at all stages. Thus, the client experienced how to resolve major challenges throughout the process.

The reality is that anytime an organization engages an outside consultant to perform a process for it the hiring organization learns many essential components of how to perform that process. This is true whether or not the consultant explicitly attempts to transfer that knowledge, and even whether or not the client deliberately tries to learn as much as possible from the interaction. Since the client will in any case learn substantively how to perform the process for itself, it is often worth formalizing the knowledge transfer, doing it effectively, and specifically charging the client for it or gaining recognition for the value added. Attempting to hang on to this knowledge is not as profitable in the long run as explicitly selling it.

## Joint Client/Service Provider Teams

If experiential learning is about doing, the design of client projects should be based on getting clients to work through the processes for themselves. The black-box style of professional services is closely related to the premise of all work on a project being performed by the service provider, while knowledge-based projects are often founded on teams comprised of staff from both the service provider and the client. Implementing project teams that substantially involve client staff not only results in strong experiential learning but also provides the ongoing rich interaction between professionals and client staff that results in socialized knowledge exchange, and closer personal and organizational relationships.

Choosing whether and how to build joint client/service provider project teams is a fundamental element of project design. Whether it is appropriate in a given instance depends on the nature of the project and the client culture, as well as the usual approach and stance of the professional services firm. Certainly joint project teams are increasingly the norm in many professional service industries. Having chosen a high level of involvement in conjunction with the client, the issue becomes how to design interaction throughout the project to optimize useful knowledge transfer.

Consulting firm ksbr Brand Management, based in Hertfordshire, U.K., uses intensive consumer research as the basis of brand planning for its clients. Rather than doing the research, developing a theoretical framework to understand it, and then presenting that to the client, ksbr encourages its clients to become involved from the very beginning of the process. Moving beyond the practice of simply having clients attend several focus groups and interviews central to the research, the firm offers to assist clients in running the focus groups themselves. For each project it works on, ksbr helps establish a range of focused teams within its client organization, with responsibilities including managing the project, generating ideas, and approving the internal recommendations. The firm participates in the client teams to assist them in creating a rich variety of output from their ideas and work, including physical objects and videos that can be presented to senior management, in the process often challenging and debating with teams on the value of their findings. Its approaches are based on the belief that to achieve change in the large service businesses that represent many of its clients the internal project team itself must be influential. Team formation and internal communication from the project are all designed to achieve a lasting impact.

## Project Induction Training

One of the most critical milestones in running joint projects is the launch, which establishes common ground between the client and professional service firm. This is often addressed in formal project induction training. This training is not intended to provide the ultimate desired outcome in its own right, but rather to pave the way for effective interaction and learning by the client in the process of the consulting engagement.

At global consulting firm McKinsey & Company, for all projects that involve a joint McKinsey/client team the client team members attend a one- to three-day induction session to establish ground rules and the basic approaches, thinking, and methodologies to be used in the project. This forms a reference point for the thinking processes the joint teams use throughout the project. As such, it enhances the experiential learning of applying these processes and approaches throughout the project, and maximizes the clients' ability to use them for themselves in subsequent situations.

Similarly, Strategic Decision Group, a decision quality consulting firm based in Menlo Park, California, takes its new clients through a two-week training course that is essentially the same as that used for the induction of its own new consultants. This training course is intensive and highly interactive, with participants leading workshops and coming up with recommendations in the course of running simulated consulting projects.

---

### Celemi

Celemi, based in Malmö, Sweden, with offices across Europe and in the United States and China, provides learning solutions to its clients. These include simulations run interactively around actual models of companies, lasting between one-half day to several days. One of its simulations, named "Apples and Oranges," takes employees at all levels in an organization through an understanding of the company's key financial indicators, and how their individual actions contribute to these indicators. Another tool, "Tango," simulates several years in the life of a knowledge-based organization, with teams playing rival firms who must compete for clients, talented staff, and challenging projects.[8]

Complementing these packaged simulations, a substantial portion of Celemi's business is the customized development of learning tools for specific client situations. One example is its work with Sainsbury's, the United Kingdom's largest food retailer, which had identified a need to

*(Continued)*

enhance its customer service. Celemi developed a series of learning tools that simulated real-life situations in the stores, which employees used in discussion groups to establish their own approaches to improving service. Taiwanese PC retailer Acer wanted its employees to "live the brand," as a way to help improve positive awareness in the community. To support this, Celemi created a three-part learning solution including an e-learning component, custom-designed posters with interactive activities, and fostering dialogue in the company on these issues.

Celemi's clients have gone on to use its products to develop the learning and capabilities of their own clients. Pfizer Pharmaceutical Sweden was seeking to add value to the medical community through education programs, but was finding that traditional-style lectures were not resulting in any changes in behavior. It established the DAISY program, which is intended to enable practitioners to diagnose illnesses faster and more accurately, and to recognize the benefits of new drugs and treatment programs so that they will feel comfortable prescribing them.

The program usually involves an initial two-day session that takes participants through a specific illness in the context of the human system, its causes and effects, and the pros and cons of available treatments. Celemi develops for Pfizer interactive learning tools for each targeted illness, including visual diagrams and case studies. Participants usually meet again several weeks after the workshop to review and discuss what they have learned in a practical context. The DAISY program has reached 70 percent of Pfizer's target group of primary care physicians in Sweden.

## CLIENT COACHING AND MENTORING

*Coaching* and *mentoring* are rapidly gaining currency across a very broad range of organizations as valuable tools in internal skill development and knowledge transfer. Coaching is an approach to skill and knowledge development that encourages and guides people in their own knowledge acquisition, especially by providing focused, constructive feedback. Mentoring is usually implemented as a one-to-one relationship maintained over an extended time period, in which an experienced person assists a more junior colleague in his or her career and personal development. This process can cover a very broad range of work and other issues. The popularity of these approaches is based on their success in achieving personal development, which is largely a result of the richness of interaction allowed by the relatively unstructured approach.

Coaching and mentoring are most obviously applicable within a single organization, in part due to confidentiality issues. In addition, these relationships are most useful when they are open-ended rather than defined within the time and resource constraints of a contract or external relationship. Still, there are many opportunities across a broad range of industries for companies to engage in a coaching- or mentoring-based style of interaction with their clients in order to maximize knowledge transfer and added value.

The flexibility and "bandwidth" of effective coaching or mentoring relationships mean that they can be exceptionally effective at knowledge transfer. In addition, the closeness implicit in these relationships again demonstrates the deep ties between knowledge transfer and client relationships.

*Coaching* is usually a better term in client relationships, as clients may not be comfortable with the implications of seniority or greater experience suggested by *mentoring*. Interactive marketing agency Arc Worldwide, described in Chapter 8, refers to "co-mentoring" with its clients, to imply that each has knowledge to transfer to the other, while emphasizing that this transfer is achieved through an ongoing highly interactive relationship. Whatever words are used, formalizing client contact so that the broadest experience of the professional can be applied in a fairly unstructured way to the issues facing the client results in substantial benefits to both parties.

## Implementing Client Mentoring

Mentoring is commonly referred to and used in the field of software development. When organizations have their own software development teams, their productivity and effectiveness can be greatly enhanced by having regular access to people who have had substantial experience with similar challenges in development and project management.

Many high-level software and programming training companies offer a package whereby trainees in advanced programming languages such as C++ initially undergo a multi-day training program. This training program is followed by a period of several months in which trainees have access to a mentor to guide them in the on-the-job application of the principles they have learned. For example, LearnQuest, a technology training firm based in Pennsylvania, frequently includes mentoring components in the education programs it designs for its clients. Classroom training is followed by mentors working onsite to assist programmers in implementing the tools they have learned in the context of the specific project at hand.

Similar approaches can readily be adapted to other industries and situations. As discussed, mentoring may not always be the best description for marketing the services, but the underlying principles and philosophies are among the most effective in achieving knowledge transfer and adding substantial value in skill development.

## Providing Unstructured Advice

Providing unstructured advice is an excellent means of adding value and developing and broadening client relationships. In essence, this is a specialist coaching relationship, which allows professional expertise to be available when required. Being in a position to provide ad-hoc advice depends on a high degree of trust and is usually built from an existing relationship. This type of relationship, which can arise spontaneously or be suggested by the professional, is an excellent vehicle for knowledge-based relationships, helps to develop close personal relationships, positions the professional as an advisor and sounding board, and very importantly starts to broaden the perceived expertise of the professional.

Many senior lawyers, accountants, consultants, bankers, and other professionals sit on company boards, reflecting the scope of their relevant business experience. Establishing mentoring-style relationships enables professionals to broaden their relationships beyond their nominal field of specialization to encompass far more of their general business experience and expertise.

It is important to recognize that many "soft" and interpersonal skills are required in effective coaching and mentoring, which are not part of the core expertise or repertoire of many professionals. These include strong questioning and listening skills, giving feedback effectively, demonstrating respect, and letting people explore their own learning opportunities. Whenever possible, professionals who are entering a coaching-style relationship with a client should be given at least introductory training and development in some of these foundation skills.

## SUMMARY: ADDING VALUE TO CLIENT CAPABILITIES

A company's competitiveness is based on its capabilities. These stem from a fusion of effective business processes and skills. The greatest value, however, is in developing "meta-capabilities," which enable clients to continually improve their own capabilities. There are a variety of approaches to implementing and enhancing business processes, including implementing process documentation, software-based methodologies, and business process reengineering. Client skill development is intrinsic to developing effective capabilities, and should be built into all professional service relationships.

The processes and skills that form capabilities are best developed through experiential learning, which means implementing project teams involving both the client and service provider. Coaching and mentoring represent excellent models for the types of ongoing and highly interactive relationships that result in real development of capabilities and in greater client intimacy.

Over the past three chapters I have examined in detail how knowledge is used to add value to clients. Adding value to information is a primary function of professional service firms, and increasingly important to clients as the scope of digitization develops. Clients' ability to make better decisions at all levels of their organizations is central to their success, and is one of the most valuable outcomes of effective knowledge transfer. Enhancing the processes and skills that constitute clients' business capabilities can result in powerful and lasting value creation. In Part 3 I will cover the practical issues of implementation: what professional service firms must do to use knowledge to add greater value to clients, as well as stronger and more profitable client relationships.

## NOTES

[1]   Dorothy Leonard, *Wellsprings of Knowledge: Building and Sustaining the Sources of Innovation*, Boston: Harvard Business School Press, 1995, p. 135.

[2]   Prahalad and Hamel.

[3]   Badarraco distinguishes between "migratory knowledge" (which can move readily and quickly between organizations and across national boundaries) and "embedded knowledge," which resides in relationships between individuals and groups, and affects the way information flows and decisions are made. Embedded knowledge, although essential to the success of the firm, cannot be easily understood and captured and thus can only move slowly between organizations. See Joseph L. Badarraco, *The Knowledge Link: How Firms Compete through Strategic Alliances*, Boston: Harvard Business School Press, 1991.

[4]   The term *meta-capability* has been used by Jeanne M. Liedtka and John W. Rosenblum, "Shaping Conversations: Making Strategy, Managing Change," *California Management Review* 39, no. 1, Fall 1996, pp. 141–157.

[5]   Prokesh.

[6]   Argyris.

[7]   Thomas H. Davenport, "The Fad That Forgot People," *Fast Company*, no. 1, November 1995, p. 70.

[8]   See Thomas A. Stewart, "The Dance Steps Get Trickier All the Time," *Fortune*, May 26, 1997.

# PART III

## Implementation

# 6

# Enhancing Client Relationship Capabilities
## Implementing Key Client Programs

The real value in knowledge-based relationships is in making them happen. However attractive the concepts, they are worth nothing until they are implemented in the organization, and can bring benefits to both clients and the firm. If they are brought into practice, this allows far more value creation than in traditional black-box relationships.

This third part of the book is devoted to implementation; that is, how to bring knowledge-based relationships into reality in your organization. Much of the action that needs to be taken is in the field, bringing practices to bear in working with specific high-value clients. However, there also needs to be an overarching framework within which this is done. This chapter introduces this skeletal frame, which is fleshed out in the subsequent five chapters.

Since the 1980s, many firms have implemented programs to improve how they work with their most important clients. However, the first phase of this movement was largely driven by industrial and consumer products firms, usually labeling the focus of their initiatives "key accounts." Diversified technology vendors were innovators in their account management approaches, though their orientation was very strongly toward closing sales rather than deepening relationships. Large financial services firms were next to follow, at least in establishing early and often simple versions of these programs.

It was only in the late 1990s that many professional services firms began in earnest to work to apply their efforts more effectively to client relationships. Part of the fault lay in organizational structures. Partners or senior professionals were allocated client relationship responsibilities without the mind-set or skill base to develop the relationship actively, rather than simply performing work for the client. In addition, firms in many professional services industries were still too fragmented across country operations, service lines, and partners to be able to develop effective, coherent practices and processes. Marketing functions within firms until recently have all too often been focused on producing brochures and managing entertainment. The 2003 annual conference of one association of professional services marketing executives was titled "Beyond Golf Balls and T-Shirts." One would certainly hope that most of them had gone way beyond that stage by then.

However, by now, most professional services firms around the world are at least beginning to get their act together. Firm leaders are recognizing that the major competitive field of play in their industries is the ability to develop deeper, stronger client relationships. If they are not effective at this, they are in the process of becoming commodities.

Many firms are focusing on increasing their sales capabilities. This can be a worthwhile endeavor. However, this must be done within the context of developing relationship capabilities. Sales efforts should be subsumed under relationship initiatives. The most important emphasis is developing deeper, more profitable relationships. Sales activities need to be positioned to create and concretize specific revenue opportunities within those relationships.

## ENHANCING CLIENT RELATIONSHIP CAPABILITIES

Every firm has a certain set of capabilities in developing high-value client relationships. All successful firms will have at least reasonable capabilities in this domain, even if this has not been an overt focus in their management activities. The issue, whatever the current state of those capabilities, is how to continually enhance them. As you saw in Chapter 1, doing quality work is not enough. At every level from the top end of the market down, differentiation will increasingly stem from how well firms manage their client relationships. What was good enough a few years ago is not good enough today, and what is good today will simply not be adequate a few years from now. As illustrated in Figure 6-1, there are five key domains firms must address in order to enhance their client relationship capabilities on an ongoing basis.

- Strategies
- Structures
- Processes
- Skills
- Culture

Professionals must understand that these five domains are inseparable. Any initiatives must take into account each domain and how it interacts with the others. For example, for many firms the first step will be to introduce foundational structures for selecting and dealing with key clients. However, for this to be effective the design must stem from a clear understanding of the firm's strategic directions, and front-line professionals must have the relevant skills in building broad client relationships. Certainly it would be challenging at best to obtain significant business results from these initiatives without a firm culture and behaviors that support the initiatives. As such, firms must identify where they should focus their initial efforts in enhancing their overall client relationship capabilities, while always keeping in mind the broader context.

Here I will introduce the five key elements of enhancing client relationship capabilities. Each of these is discussed in more detail in the next five chapters, with a consolidation of these themes in regard to creating an action plan presented in Chapter 12.

## Culture

Attitude of client partnership, collaboration, and respect
Collaboration and effective communication with relationship team members
Transparency with the client and inside the firm
Using firm-wide client relationship processes and systems

## Skills

Setting and implementing relationship objectives and strategy
Leading and participating effectively in relationship teams
Customizing relationship and communication styles to clients
Managing client expectations

## Processes

Selection of client relationship team members
Relationship team communication and collaboration
Developing and monitoring client relationship strategies
Ongoing client feedback and its application

## Structures

Key client selection and segmentation
Selection and allocation of client relationship leaders
Cross-selling remuneration and recognition systems
Account management and customer relationship management systems

## Strategy

Role of client relationship style in firm differentiation
Targeted client profiles, client industries, service lines, and service delivery
Role of online service delivery within firm strategy
Long-term strategic directions and positioning

FIGURE 6–1   *The five domains of enhancing client relationship capabilities.* Copyright © 2004 Advanced Human Technologies. Reprinted with permission.

## Strategies

Many professional service firms fail to specify adequately how their business development initiatives relate to their strategic directions. Simply in order to be able to allocate relationship development efforts appropriately across existing and prospective clients, firms must have a clearly articulated vision of which industries, service lines, and types of service delivery they wish to develop. This requires examining how their business environment is shifting. One of the most useful approaches is to apply scenario planning to "the future of the client," examining how in 5 to 10 years your clients and client industries may have evolved, especially in how they want and expect service delivery. This will inform current strategies and emphasis of business development activities. Whatever approach is used, it is critical to build a vision of how your clients and the marketplace are changing, and how you want your firm to be positioned in this future world.

## Structures

Many firms have tended to focus on the relatively easy issues of underlying relationship structures, including selecting and segmenting key clients and establishing account management planning and customer relationship management (CRM) software. Other key issues include implementing effective remuneration and recognition systems for cross-selling, and clear approaches to allocating client relationship leaders to key clients. Some of these can be overlaid on existing firm structure, but in other cases they require reappraisal of the formal structures. A common example is how many firms have substantially reorganized around industry lines in order to more effectively bring together disparate practice areas in creating client value.

## Processes

Clearly defined processes should to be in place to support professionals in relationship development activities. These include processes for client relationship team formation, developing and monitoring client relationship strategies, and gathering useful client feedback. One of the most important issues is having clear processes in place for effective relationship team communication and collaboration, discussed in more detail in Chapter 9. Some of the processes can be formalized as standard practice. However, many of the processes are essentially tools made available for relationship leaders to apply in running smooth and effective client relationship teams.

## Skills

A core challenge for professional service firms is that their senior executives have all come from a deep functional specialization, and have rarely had specific skill development in client relationship management. The issue is taking technical professionals and making them into true leaders that can inspire aligned action across the firm to address client challenges. High-level communication skills are required to manage client expectations effectively in complex relationships, and to customize service delivery and client communication according to the client's relationship style. Leading client relationship teams in particular requires key skills in setting and implementing relationship objectives and strategies, and fostering collaboration across diverse teams. Leadership development is discussed in Chapter 12.

## Culture

Even if all of the other four key elements are in place, success is unlikely unless the firm has a culture that supports the development of deep client relationships. Professionals need to be driven not only to enhance client service and client knowledge but also to collaborate with colleagues across different service lines and locations. Every firm must focus on continually enhancing their culture in supporting client relationship capabilities, through consistent and aligned communication, relevant remuneration structures, and effective leadership.

## IMPLEMENTING KEY CLIENT PROGRAMS

The general intent of a key client program is to identify the most important current and potential clients of the organization, and to create focus around building those relationships. However, the specific intent is often still mired in a sales-oriented mentality: "How do we sell more to our clients?" I am far from suggesting that this is not an appropriate objective. Absolutely, you want to generate higher, more consistent flows of profitable business from current and existing clients. However, the most effective route to this is not in focusing on how to sell more services to them. It is in striving to build deep, trusting, knowledge-based relationships with your clients that allow you to create greater value for them. If you can do that, it will then be extremely easy to sell specific projects and services. The mentality behind the design of a key client program is critical. I have seen major firms implement programs in which the rhetoric is about relationships, but the reality is that they are predicated on feeding the sales pipeline. If the focus is on meeting quotas, the relationship will suffer, and revenue will eventually dry up. If the focus is on the relationship, sales will prosper.

The program needs to establish structures, processes, and activities implemented across the organization. It also needs to provide approaches and tools that will assist the relationship teams that work on the most important clients for the firm. Below is an overview of firm-wide initiatives and work on key client relationships. This provides a foundation that will be expanded on over the following five chapters, notably in Chapter 9 on relationship teams and in Chapter 12 on creating action plans.

### Launching the Program

Launching a key client program is not something to do halfheartedly. A failed initiative will set you back rather than advance you, and it is therefore critical to do it well. Support from senior executives is crucial. If that is not in place, it is possible to implement "stealth" programs that gradually create results and buy-in across the firm. However, this is a path for the brave only. The most important issue is establishing a staged program, which does not bite off too much initially, and allows successes in limited domains to build over time. Particularly when shifting how professionals and business development executives work, incremental change is preferable.

Establishing an identity for the program is important as a reference point, so that it can be branded internally. This could be as simple as "key client program," or a more adventurous title. From the outset key stakeholders need to be provided with initial education on the concept, intentions, and benefits in order to gain buy-in, and to bring into the open and address concerns. There are two key aspects to developing and launching a key client program.

- Establish a firm-wide program
- Enhance selected key client relationships

The firm-wide program is most importantly about establishing the structures and processes that guide and support client initiatives, including how firm resources are allocated to clients. This provides a framework within which initiatives can be established to develop relationships with selected clients. In the following two sections I describe some of the broader issues involved in establishing a firm-wide program and in enhancing selected client relationships. The client relationship efforts are the primary responsibility of the client relationships teams. This is covered in detail in Chapter 9.

### Zurich Financial Services

Zurich Financial Services is an insurance-based provider of financial services, operating in 50 countries, with 62,000 employees. In 2003 its operating profit reached $2.3 billion. The provision of complex insurance and risk management services is challenging because major multinational clients direct their insurance business through brokers, creating a three-way relationship among insurer, client, and broker. In addition, insurance in any specific business domain, which can range across shipping, property, technology, and many other areas, must be assessed, priced, and offered by a specialist underwriter. However, there are many benefits to more focused client relationships to both clients and the insurer, including developing a greater understanding of client issues, providing integrated offerings, and sometimes clients being able to learn more about their own global operations and issues.

In mid 2000, having experimented with providing clients with multiple service lines on a single contract, Zurich chose to establish a division called Zurich Strategic Relationship Management (SRM), responsible for representing all of Zurich's business units to its major global clients. The unit has hired and trained relationship managers, selected key clients, established structures and processes, and established a central role in the global organization. SRM received a strong boost when James Schiro joined Zurich as CEO from PricewaterhouseCoopers (PwC), where he had been CEO and the architect of PwC's relationship management model. Terje Lovik, CEO of Zurich SRM, says that it is impossible to implement a strategic management unit without top management support.

Zurich SRM has grown to 18 strategic relationship managers covering 150 key clients. The unit has built a rigorous process for introducing clients to the program and developing deeper relationships over time. It has established three categories of clients: Suspect, Target, and Hot. These reflect the potential value of the client to Zurich. It also has defined three levels of client relationships: Start, Good, and Deep. Each of the categories of clients and client relationships has strict criteria. For example, with a Hot client with a Deep relationship, Zurich would expect to get a final opportunity to make the best offer for any deal the client was considering.

Much of the relationship managers' activities are centered on developing greater client knowledge, and on bringing together key resources from across the company. They often come from a high-level enterprise risk management background, and can thus more easily broaden their relationship beyond their clients' risk managers to senior management such

*(Continued)*

as the CFO. One of the tools they use is introducing a two-way confidentiality agreement early in the relationship, in order to encourage more open discussions. A strong emphasis is placed on customizing products and service delivery to best suit the client, for example by creating tailored claim-handling mechanisms or risk-sharing structures.[1] This has to be based on deep client knowledge.

Strategic plans are established for all strategic clients, and these are visible only to key client stakeholders. The plans include key client information, short-term and strategic goals, and relationship activities. These are used to create briefing sheets for senior executives when they are going to meet clients, either formally or in a social context. Every key client has an executive sponsor from Zurich's top management team, helping to ensure resources are available when required, and building visibility for SRM through the company.

## Developing Strategic Clarity

Most professional firms have a reasonable idea of their current market positioning. However, if you start to explore a little deeper there is often a lack of clarity, particularly on how the firm's positioning will evolve over the next few years. A clear picture both of the clients that fit your current desired profile and the specific types of clients and client work that will assist the firm to create its future vision is an essential foundation of any key client program.

Two of the most fundamental questions are the firm's target clients and its targeted types of services. Target industries can be examined both from the perspective of likely growth and shifts in the demand for the services offered by the firm. The relative desirability of smaller and larger clients is an important issue, as is determining the most appropriate criteria in assessing this. For example, a human resources consulting firm will be more interested in a prospective client's number of employees and employee turnover than in its revenues. The service offerings the firm expects to be most attractive in the next few years can be examined using the steps for responding to commoditization described in Chapter 2.

The professional services models framework (see Chapter 2) provides one approach to thinking through firm positioning in terms of service delivery style. As for other issues, these should be considered in terms of both current desired profile and how the firm would like this to evolve over the coming years. In creating a future vision for the organization, it is important not only to envisage how the firm and its client relationships will shift over the next few years but to imagine a timeline for how this is expected to progress. A key question is specifically what new types of services and offerings will be in the firm's portfolio in, for example, three years. Lack of any intended changes should be a loud warning bell of business risk.

A key aspect of strategy clarity is a high degree of alignment among the firm's executives. This is best achieved through getting broad involvement in developing the firm's strategy. The discussions and interactions in examining key challenges and dimensions for the firm's present and future are essential to moving to a common understanding. A written outline of the firm's strategic positioning, including targeted clients, industries, service lines, and service delivery, will provide a reference point for clarifying to what degree a particular client or client engagement fits the firm's core directions.

One of the most noteworthy outcomes of this process is identifying the characteristics of the clients that will help the firm move toward its strategic vision. Targeted industries in which the firm does not currently have a significant presence means that clients in that industry are highly desirable. Penetrating these sectors requires the development of industry experience and a reference client. Where the firm wants to develop new service lines, it will want to seek specific opportunities to showcase these, or sometimes to help develop the necessary capabilities and experience.

## Key Client Selection

The next step is for firms to apply to specific clients the insights gained in refining their strategic vision. It is critical for firms to allocate their efforts and resources where they will have the most impact and also further the firm's core directions. In Chapter 1 you saw that the relationship style of your client is a major factor in the effort you put into developing the relationship. If they will never provide you with an opportunity to build strong relationships and create superior value for them, you will not want to invest excessive resources into the account.

There are a range of other reasons you will choose to focus firm resources on developing a particular client, ranging from profitability to prestige. It is essential to bring these together into a clear framework, so that firms can readily decide which are their key clients that merit preferential attention. This framework should be able to be implemented at two levels. It should provide a clear guide for the firm to allocate resources to its relationship development initiatives. It should also be a useful tool for individual relationship leaders in assessing the potential of their existing and prospective clients, and in allocating their own time and energy. There are three key factors in assessing client value and potential.

- Direct value
- Indirect value
- Relationship investment

The client's potential value is the sum of the direct value and indirect value, divided by the relationship investment. Each of these needs to be assessed in order to get a clear idea of the priority of the client in allocating resources.

## Direct Value

A client's direct value needs to be assessed both in current terms as well as in future potential. Wherever possible this should be measured by profitability rather than revenue. There are still relatively few firms that have reliable profitability measures for their clients. Whether the model used for client profitability is simple revenue and cost assessment or more complex approaches such as Economic Value Added,[2] the difficulty lies in allocating costs to activities. There is no "correct" way to do this, and the process is fraught with the perils of internal politics. Yet even a preliminary exercise can start to uncover the relative profitability of clients, which can provide a basis for effective decision making. If you do not have any profitability measures, you are flying blind. This is particularly relevant when major clients attract significant discounts, sometimes to the point of them becoming unprofitable to the firm without this being apparent to firm management.

It is important in relationship strategy to know your client's total spending on the range of services you offer, and thus your current share of this pie. The first issue is simply in defining the scope of where you are competing, that is the total pie for which you are competing. Sometimes this is clear, but redefining this scope, particularly as the organization changes its positioning over time, will affect how you assess the potential value of the client.

Often you will not know your client's total spending on the services you provide. One approach is to make an educated guess. The other is to ask your client. This brings us back to the nub of building knowledge-based relationships. If you are currently not comfortable asking your clients their total spending on your services, clearly you must build further trust, and clearly demonstrate to the client why it is valuable for them to be more open with you.

### Indirect Value

Indirect value is any way in which working with a client provides value that is not in direct billings. The first way is flow-on revenue, in which you gain revenue from other clients as a direct result of working for an organization. This could be through direct referrals or when organizations are closely tied. For example, one bank that was working for a credit union association began providing services to members of that association as a direct result of the work performed.

The other aspects of indirect value are all aspects of "strategic fit." There are four key ways in which clients can support strategic objectives.

- Reputation enhancement
- Enter new client industry
- Enter new product or service market
- Develop intellectual property or enhance capabilities

Firms need to have developed a high degree of strategic clarity in order to know which potential clients meet these objectives. Once the profile of what forms a fit with the firm's strategy has been developed, clients or prospects can immediately and easily be assessed as to how well they fit the firm's strategy.

## Relationship Investment

The third key aspect of assessing client potential is relationship investment. This includes how good a match there is between the firms, the effort required to achieve results, and how stable the revenues or relationship are likely to be. Depending on the industry, the key criteria are likely to include the following.

- Ability to provide superior value to the client
- Competitive intensity
- Cultural fit and ease of working together
- Sales or relationship investment required
- Existing industry experience
- Stability of client, relationship, and revenue

It is not uncommon to put in massive effort in developing a strong relationship, and then seeing your key contact at the client replaced by an alumnus of your arch rivals, or even more decisively the client going out of business. These types of events cannot be predicted, but an assessment of their likelihood should inform your decisions as to how much effort to put into developing the relationship.

In assessing client priorities, it is critical to assess the likely investment required to build a solid, mutually valuable relationship. If you only assess the potential value of clients, you may neglect what is required to realize that value, meaning firm resources are misallocated. Taking a wider approach allows this to be an effective tool for managing the firm's clients and prospects as a true portfolio, allocating resources where they are the most likely to be fruitful.

The type of framework for assessing client potential just presented can be applied both in selecting the firm's key clients and as a tool for individual relationship managers to allocate their efforts effectively. It is all too easy to get caught up in specific opportunities and lose sight of where energy is most likely to achieve worthwhile results. A simple framework covering the key criteria of direct value, indirect value, and relationship investment can be encapsulated in either paper or online form as a tool for relationship managers. Some firms implement systems such as these by ranking each of the selected criteria on a scale of 1 to 10, attributing an importance weighting to each of these from a total of 100 points, and multiplying these to come up with a single number to assess the client's potential. This can be useful. However, just as often it can obscure key criteria in the all-important decisions of allocating firm resources.

It is possible to build more complex models for assessing potential client value, for example using net present value (NPV) measures to discount the value of future revenue streams and incorporate uncertainty factors. However, the inputs to these models are highly judgmental, and in most cases this more quantitative approach yields little or no improvement to providing a loose framework for judgment by front-line professionals.

In a staged key client program, the firm is likely to choose not to establish a complete set of key clients in the first stage, but rather identify the most promising candidates in a first round. One approach is to allow relationship leaders to propose one or more of their clients to enter the key client program. These can be assessed within a broader framework to ensure that the initial key client list is representative of the firm's current and desired client mix.

In building a more comprehensive program, the firm needs to ensure that it is addressing both existing and potential clients. A common way of allocating target clients in a key client program is to place them into the categories of current high-value clients, existing clients with significant untapped potential, and companies that are not currently clients but that match the firm's strategic profile for targets. Allocating responsibilities for relationships with the top companies on each of these lists ensures that both near-term and long-term opportunities are being addressed.

## Segmentation and Migration

Not all clients are equal. The single most important way of segmenting clients is through the key client selection process presented above. However, there are many other dimensions that can be applied to segment clients usefully. For high-value clients, the most important outcome of this segmentation is creating customized service delivery. Some of the more obvious segmentation issues involved in achieving this include client size, service spending, industry sector, organizational style, relationship style, and buying behaviors.

In knowledge-based relationships, the most important issue is client value relative to service delivery styles. Figure 6–2 charts the types of relationships that stem from the client value and client's desire to interact. This relates strongly to the client leadership framework presented in Figure 1–2 in Chapter 1. However, it applies these dimensions to how to change interaction and service delivery with key clients. If a client has low current and potential value, but wishes to interact extensively in the course of service delivery, this will be a loss-making relationship. Depending on firm strategy, it can be appropriate to deal with low-value clients. However, in this situation it is essential to focus on resource efficiency in service delivery. In this case, the firm will want to migrate its clients to more efficient ways of dealing with the client, often using online tools and process-oriented offerings. Here the balance of power resides with the service provider, who can offer incentives to clients or simply restrict their choices. For example, some banks with online foreign exchange services offer

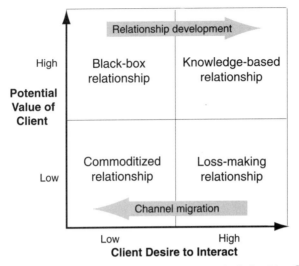

Figure 6–2  *Segmentation and migration in knowledge-based relationships.* Copyright © 2004 Advanced Human Technologies. Reprinted with permission.

preferential pricing to their corporate clients that use the service rather than deal on the phone with their foreign exchange dealers.

At the other end of the spectrum are high-value clients that are happy to be in a black-box relationship that requires little interaction with their service providers. The firm's efforts should then be focused on migrating its clients to a richer and more interactive relationship style. In this case, the power rests with the client, so the firm must educate the client as to the range of service delivery styles, and the benefits of more interactive approaches. In one case, a bank chose to show a major corporate client its internal measures of the client's profitability to the bank. The client was surprised to find that its extensive relationship was only marginally profitable to the bank. Since it valued the relationship, it promised to direct more profitable types of business to the bank.

The migration process needs to be implemented at both firm and relationship manager levels. Companies must establish a clear plan for how to migrate their clients. This needs to be more detailed than the very simple framework presented above. For each meaningful client segment, it should examine the current array of communication and service delivery models used, and establish a desired balance of client communication channels. For instance, a law firm looking at a segment of medium-size property investors may decide it wishes to deal with its regular property transactions primarily through an online interface it has developed, but ensure that all senior executive contact is directly with its relationship partners. It then needs to introduce a strategy to introduce any new channels to the client, and shift interactions to their desired balance. If the intended balance of client interaction is not clear, it will happen by accident or according to the client's preferences rather than yours.

The reality is that the migration process is implemented by the relationship managers responsible for the clients. They need to have the necessary conversations with the clients on how they would like to deal with the client, and why. This requires subtlety, and can be supported by effective training. The most important principle is that the migration process takes time. It can be a disastrous mistake to decide on how you want to migrate your clients and trying to make it happen immediately. If the migration period is expected to happen over an extended period, a phased approach to leading clients into new relationship styles is far more likely to be effective.

The ultimate form of downward migration is sacking the client. Again, this needs to be done with subtlety. Engendering ill will means you will likely never be able to deal with this client again, and certainly has the potential for a negative impact on your reputation in the client's industry. If you do want to stop dealing with the client, it is preferable to do this in a phased manner so that it is not a surprise to the client. Informing them along the path of shifts in your firm's strategy, criteria for dealing with clients, and effective timing help them to understand this is a business decision. It is even possible to offer an "outplacement" style of service that helps them to find and transition to an alternative supplier. Regional accounting practice Vanacore, DeBennictus, DiGiovanni, Weddell chose to fire a group of clients, suggesting they switch to an alternative accounting firm and assisting the transition.[3]

## Remuneration and Recognition

One chief executive of a leading investment bank told me that his single highest priority was finding effective ways to allocate rewards for major client work across operating divisions and key staff. Dealing with remuneration across complex multidivisional multilocational clients is highly problematic, but is an essential element to supporting client relationship capabilities.

The starting point has to be the ethos and existing reward structures for the firm. Lock-step partnerships, which in principle allocate shares in firm profits only on the basis of seniority, have no scope for rewards for generating revenue. The theory is that the systems engender a more collaborative attitude than those driven by individual performance, and for a number of the remaining firms that use this type of structure this indeed appears to be the case. The situation is easier when dedicated salespeople or relationship managers are in place. However, for most professional services firms practicing professionals are responsible for client relationships and business development.

Almost all firms have implemented some form of performance measurement system for their senior professionals, including direct financial measures such as personal or team billings, indirect financial measures such as firm business development and cross-selling, and nonfinancial measures including staff development and teamwork. For example, Ernst & Young U.K. shares profits among its partners by allocating units relating to personal objectives, including client service, revenue growth, and operational excellence.[4] Other firms explicitly use a balanced scorecard covering key areas. Before its acquisition by Pfizer, Pharmacia & Upjohn used in its key client team remuneration a balanced scorecard covering nine measures in four groups: financial, operational efficiency, innovation/creativity, and customer/team satisfaction.[5] Across these systems, the issue is identifying the behaviors or outcomes (preferably measurable) the firm wants to encourage and reward. For example, at several leading investment banks individuals are assessed by people they have worked with on a client team or project during the year. Each individual is asked to nominate who they would like to assess them. However, everyone has the opportunity to assess any other team member if desired. The outputs from this process provide a significant input into year-end bonus allocations.

There is an array of quantitative techniques used to reward cross-selling, each technique with its own problems. No single system will provide effective incentives for the desired behaviors at the level of the firm.[6] Probably more important are the nonfinancial rewards and recognition. Usually the most powerful reward in a professional services firm is promotion. If this is explicitly tied to collaborative behaviors, or even more powerfully if promotion is denied to executives that do not build client relationships beyond their own practice area, this can be a strong enabler of effective relationship development. Recognition by peers — implemented in the right way — provides very powerful support to desired behaviors.

## DEVELOPING CLIENT STRATEGIES

Enhancing client relationship capabilities at the level of the firm constitutes the big picture. However, the reality is that where the rubber meets the road is in working with individual major clients of the firm. Ultimately, the responsibility for working on and developing key clients resides with the relationship leaders and their teams. Chapter 9 covers in detail the selection and responsibilities of client relationship leaders and team members. Here I examine the process of developing and implementing client strategies.

Developing powerful, profitable, knowledge-based client relationships does not happen by accident. The intent needs to be there from the start, and consistent aligned action taken to get there. The critical enabler is effective strategic thinking and action. In Chapter 1 you saw how relationships must have continued forward momentum. Too often professionals focus on their current projects or the next sale rather than work on the level of the long-term client relationship. Though many firms get their salespeople or relationship managers to write "account plans," this is usually a rather linear process focused on feeding the sales pipeline internal accounting machine. Professionals need to have a clear vision on where the relationship can go, how the client can begin to see its supplier as a true partner, and how the firm can effectively lock in its client through consistently superior value creation. Using that to generate strategies that flow through into focused action is the only way this level of value creation can be achieved.

## The Client Strategy Process

Client strategy should be set by the relationship team under the guidance of the relationship leader. If a completed strategy is handed to relationship team members, they are unlikely to feel a high degree of commitment to the implementation. In addition, the strategy must be based on the deepest possible knowledge of the client, which will come from everyone who has had any contact or dealings with the client. A full identification of potential opportunities for value creation is difficult for any single individual.

The basic client strategy process is illustrated in Figure 6–3. In the initial stage of *client assessment* the relationship leader applies the assessment framework used at the level of the firm in order to examine the likely client potential and to prioritize relationship efforts. The second, third, and fourth stages are *strategy analysis*, *setting objectives*, and *establishing a roadmap*, described below. The next stage is *strategy alignment*, which involves sharing strategies with the client. This is discussed in Chapter 9, as this is implemented by the relationship team. The final stage is one of *execution and revision*, in which the action plan is implemented and client feedback used as critical input to refining the strategy. The process of gaining and applying client feedback is also covered in Chapter 9.

| Client Assessment | ■ Client Potential<br>■ Client Prioritization<br>■ Preliminary Objectives |
| --- | --- |
| Strategy Analysis | ■ Client Analysis<br>■ Competitive Analysis<br>■ Leverage Points |
| Set Objectives | ■ Financial<br>■ Relationship<br>■ Strategic |
| Establish Roadmap | ■ Team Definition<br>■ Relationship Activities<br>■ Action Plan & Timeline |
| Strategy Alignment | ■ Discuss with Client<br>■ Set Joint Objectives<br>■ Communicate Internally |
| Execution & Revision | ■ Implementation<br>■ Client Feedback<br>■ Strategy Review |

FIGURE 6–3   *The relationship strategy process.* Copyright © 2004 Advanced Human Technologies. Reprinted with permission.

## Setting Client Objectives

Too often client relationship objectives are stated in purely financial terms. Financial objectives are clearly fundamental to commercial relationships. However, if the focus is purely on the numbers the mentality and activities of client engagement are always focused on generating sales, with no attention to the issues that will impact the progress (or otherwise) of the relationship. Clients readily understand what the true focus is of their suppliers, and more often than not they seek service providers that are more interested in building relationships than driving short-term revenue.

It is critical to implement what I call 360-degree objectives, which provide clear direction to client relationship development activities. There are three key categories of objectives that should be set for major clients.

- *Financial:* Aside from the obvious financial objectives of current and future revenue (or preferably profitability), often a more important objective is increased "share of wallet" (i.e., share of client spending on the services you provide). In addition, you can set objectives for direct flow-on business, as described above.
- *Relationship:* Relationship objectives measure progress in the relationship. These can include meeting specific new client executives; developing relationships with senior executives such as the CEO; establishing contact with new divisions, offices, country operations; selling specific new products or services to the client; gaining preferred supplier status or presence on a panel; and meeting or exceeding satisfaction levels on surveys. As for any other objectives, these need to be specific, measurable, and set to a time frame. These relationship objectives form the core milestones mapped out in the action plan, discussed below.
- *Strategic:* As described above, clients can be desirable not just for their revenue potential but in terms of how working with them can contribute to firm objectives and positioning. For any individual client, these strategic objectives could include gaining entry and profile in a new industry sector or service market, developing specific marketable intellectual property or new capabilities, or enhanced reputation or positive media attention.

The objectives that have been set across these three domains set the directions out of which the client strategy will emerge. They can then be used to monitor progress on the relationship, with the relationship objectives particularly valuable in indicating the strength of relationship momentum.

Citibank's Global Relationship Banking program has implemented a balanced scorecard for its operations that measures client momentum in terms of increased penetration of its client's wallet, or share of spending on banking services. However, relationship reviews across its key clients also provide critical inputs.

## Designing Knowledge-Based Leverage Points

One of the most critical aspects of a sound relationship strategy is applying the concepts of knowledge-based relationships to identifying key leverage points. If you review the virtuous circle of knowledge-based client relationships, you can note the four key elements of the circle. When you are trying to enhance progress around the virtuous circle, the key issue is not each of the elements in itself but how all of the elements are linked and flow one to the next, as illustrated in Figure 6–4.

In examining the circle, we start from client knowledge, the element at the bottom, and move backward around the circle, as each element depends on the one preceding it. This uncovers five key issues on

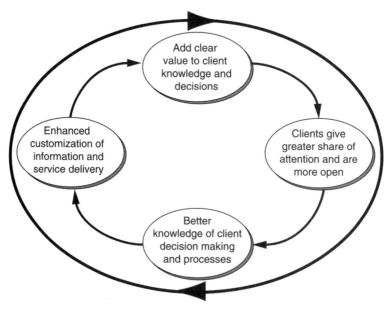

FIGURE 6–4   *Identifying leverage points in the virtuous circle.* Copyright © 2004 Advanced Human Technologies. Reprinted with permission.

which to focus in developing knowledge-based client strategies. Each of these throws up a series of key questions that need to be answered in order to enhance the circle. The most important issue is using these questions to generate specific action items that can be included in the client action plan.

- *Client knowledge:* In what areas do we know we need to improve our client knowledge? What action steps will enhance our knowledge in these areas? How can we uncover other issues at the client we do not know to ask about?
- *Client openness:* What can we do to get the client to be more open and disclose more? What will clearly demonstrate to the client the value of being more open? How do we gain greater client access, attention, and interaction?
- *Adding value with knowledge:* How do we add clear value to client knowledge, decision making, and capabilities?
- *Customization:* How do we apply deep client knowledge to customizing information and service delivery in ways that are meaningful to the client? How do we adapt our engagement style and interaction to the client?
- *Client recognition of value:* How do we demonstrate to the client we are using deep knowledge of their business to their benefit? How do we get the client to acknowledge the value of service customization and knowledge transfer? How do we shift to new pricing models that reflect the additional value created for the client?

This last key point of client recognition of value is about closing the circle, bringing each of the elements of the virtuous circle together to accelerate the ongoing deepening and development of the client relationship. To enhance its client relationships, advertising agency DDB Worldwide has implemented a relationship agreement that establishes clearly what each side expects from the other. With one of its major clients, DDB set up an agreement on how the relationship was to be conducted as a complement to the formal work contract.

When the idea was raised in discussions, client executives leaped at the idea, seeing it as a way to establish clarity on expectations. They specified that they expected DDB's work to challenge them, expressed understanding that creative work requires failures, and indicated that they wanted strategic thinking from the agency. On DDB's side, expectations of the client included sharing its business plans, and streamlining the advertisement approval process. Keith Reinhard, then Chairman and CEO of DDB, and the chief executive of the client, signed the relationship agreement, providing a foundation for a great relationship. This is an example of a practical tool that can leverage knowledge-based relationships by bringing key issues into the open. I challenge you to suggest this to your clients.

## Establishing Client Action Plans

The relationship action plan is the product of the strategy process, and a living template for all relationship activities. The plan is based around the relationship team and their roles and responsibilities. I examine how this is done in more detail in Chapter 9. Defining responsibilities in this way immediately creates clarity on how the action plan will proceed. Each of the three types of objectives — financial, relationship, and strategic — will be addressed in the action plan.

The development of the action plan needs to be done by the relationship team that will implement the plan. There are many approaches that can be taken to do this effectively. However, the most basic is simply generating a list of potential activities that will further the achievement of the stated objectives, and prioritizing these relative to available resources. The roadmap itself should incorporate all of the objectives, especially the relationship objectives, timed to produce a sequence of identifiable milestones that will indicate whether or not the relationship plan is on track. It is possible, for example, for short-term financial targets not to be met but for there to be clear progress in the relationship. In contrast, all financial objectives may be met, but without any expansion or deepening of the relationship, indicating vulnerability in the relationship.

In Chapter 1 you saw that no relationship is static. If it is not moving forward it is moving backward. A client relationship action plan has to embody this truth by ensuring that there is clear progress in the relationship, as measured by specific and tangible relationship milestones. Chapter 9 examines in more detail how the relationship team uses the action plan as a template for monitoring its activities and success.

## SUMMARY: ENHANCING CLIENT RELATIONSHIP CAPABILITIES

Professional services firms need continually to enhance their capabilities at developing client relationships. There are five key domains they must focus on: strategies, structures, processes, skills, and culture. While each firm will have a different area that affords it the greatest return on effort, the five domains must be considered as an interrelated whole.

It is increasingly common for professional services firms to implement key client programs, which select their top-tier clients and provide focused relationship development efforts. A key success factor is starting by developing greater strategic clarity on the firm's directions. For the nominated top-tier clients, strategies need to be developed and implemented that help lead them into deeper, mutually beneficial relationships.

This framework for enhancing client relationship capabilities provides a suitable kickoff on the topic of implementation, the subject of Part three of the book. The following chapters delve into more specific issues in implementing knowledge-based relationships, beginning with an examination of relationship channels in Chapter 7.

## NOTES

1   Terje Lovik, "Meeting the Challenges of SAM in a Service Environment," *Focus: Europe*, vol. 3, no. 2, 2nd Quarter, 2003, pp. 12–15.

2   Economic Value Added is a registered trademark of Stern Stewart.

3   Paul Dunn and Ron Baker, *The Firm of the Future: A Guide for Accountants, Lawyers, and Other Professional Services*, Hoboken, New Jersey: John Wiley & Sons, 2003, p. 23.

4   Ernst & Young U.K., Annual Review 2003, at *www.ey.com/global/content.nsf/UK/UK_Annual_Review_2003_-_Firm_managed*.

5   Noel Capon, *Key Account Management and Planning: The Comprehensive Handbook for Managing Your Company's Most Important Strategic Asset*, New York: The Free Press, 2001, p. 125.

6   See Charles J. Santangelo and William G. Johnston, "Tale of Compensation: Even in the Best of Times, Partner Compensation Isn't Easy," *Legal Management*, vol. 19, no. 1, January/February 2000.

# 7

# Relationship Channels
## Implementing Communication Portfolios

Knowledge-based relationships must be founded on rich two-way communication. For all truly high-value clients, face-to-face meetings will play a significant role. Since knowledge is an attribute of people, knowledge flows are greatest when people are together in the same room. At the same time, the dizzying rise and widespread availability of communication technologies are changing the entire landscape of client relationships. The broad adoption of e-mail in business beginning in the early 1990s has already transformed how professionals communicate with and deliver services to their clients. Now information flows to and from clients are routinely enabled through web-based interfaces, and significant elements of the service offering are performed online. Organizations need to examine and understand how to manage their client communication channels as an integrated portfolio, and strategically introduce online communication into that portfolio as new possibilities emerge.

## Managing Communication Channels

Some communication channels are far better suited to certain projects and situations than others. However, in client relationships the issue is not choosing the best single channel or channels, but managing the overall portfolio of channels to achieve the greatest impact. The issues of managing client contact from the perspective of relationship development is further covered in Chapter 8. In this chapter I will focus on how to use the communication channels available to maximize knowledge transfer and enhance relationship development, though the issues are closely linked.

## Information Richness and Media Richness

The concepts of *information richness* and *media richness* in organizational communication were first introduced by Daft and Lengel.[1] They defined information richness as the "ability of information to change understanding within a time interval." They also observed that communication media vary in their capacity to process rich information. This idea of "changed understanding" mirrors that of knowledge, and particularly embeds the ideas of how value is created for the counterparty.

The researchers reported that the richest medium is face-to-face meetings, because it provides multiple cues via body language, facial expression, and tone of voice, and provides immediate feedback so that interpretation can be checked. In addition, as the complexity of management challenges increases, richer information and media must be used in order to reduce uncertainty and clarify ambiguity.[2] This early research has spawned entire schools of study on information and media richness in organizations, which recently have begun to focus more and more on computer-mediated communication and its richness in achieving "changed understanding."[3]

## Enablers of Knowledge Transfer

Given the broad array of communication channels available to us, we need criteria to guide us in assessing their effectiveness in enabling effective knowledge flows. These criteria will allow us to design a strategy for communicating with our clients in a way that maximizes knowledge transfer. The following are the five key enablers of knowledge transfer in communication.

- Interactivity
- Bandwidth
- Structure
- Reusability
- Customizability

Each of these will be more or less important in any given situation. Examining each of these in more detail allows us to identify which communication channels will be most relevant in a particular client context.

## Interactivity

We have rapidly grown to expect interactivity in our communication across a wide variety of channels. We can best understand interactivity as the degree to which the flow of information between people or organizations is two-way as opposed to one-way. Printed documents and analog television, for example, have no interactivity. While you can choose what you read or watch, no information is communicated back to the organization that initiated the communication.

The greatest value creation for both clients and service providers stems from rich two-way knowledge flow. For example, information about client usage patterns of web sites can be captured and used to enhance the design of knowledge transfer processes. This is a form of interactivity, but in this case only limited information about a narrow range of behaviors flows from the client, which is far less powerful than if rich knowledge is flowing in both directions. Some media — most obviously face-to-face meetings — enable this rich two-way interactivity, while others limit the richness of flow in one or both directions.

The best and most basic model of interactivity is simply dialogue. Throughout the ages knowledge has always been developed through discussion and interaction with others, which is still true today. Technology increasingly allows us to interact in new ways. However, the closer the interaction is to an actual discussion, which enables people to question, probe, and elaborate their understanding, the greater its effectiveness.

The dynamics of interactivity depend on the number of people involved. Interaction between two people is already very high, although the potential benefits of interactivity increase with the number of people involved. There can, of course, be decreasing returns in adding more people, depending on the quality of facilitation within the group.

A different type of interactivity results when a person interacts with a machine, but the information is not necessarily captured. For example, interactive video games respond to users, but their input does not usually flow back to the manufacturer. Online e-learning can be very effective for knowledge transfer because it forces users to answer questions and to provide input that guides the information presented. Even if the users' responses are not captured, this type of interaction with the computer results in far more effective internalization of knowledge than by simply reading a document.

## Bandwidth

The concept of bandwidth is one of the most fundamental issues in knowledge flow. Broadly, it is the amount of information that can be communicated over a given period. Bandwidth is an essential element to media richness, certainly in terms of its ability to achieve changed understanding, that is, knowledge transfer. The more communication channels used within a client relationship, the broader the total bandwidth.

The effective bandwidth of a text document, for example, is quite narrow in terms of possible information transfer in a given period. The value of multimedia can be viewed as tapping greater bandwidth, by using sound, moving pictures, and other media to achieve richer communication. The sound and image resolution of even high-quality video, however, is still significantly limited compared with face-to-face meetings, in which the real flow of information is many orders of magnitude greater.

Global Internet bandwidth is increasing consistently at about 70 percent every year. While most businesses and affluent individuals in developed countries have access to high-speed Internet connections, the bandwidth available to them will also increase consistently, changing the dynamics of what types of communication channels are usable. For example, it is currently unusual for private bankers and wealth managers to use videoconferencing with their clients at home, yet this is likely to become commonplace, not as a substitute for personal meetings but as a way of achieving greater bandwidth than possible in voice calls.

Structure

The concept of structure in communication channels groups two related ideas. The first is how easily the relationships within and between ideas and information can be communicated. Greater structure means less ambiguity, and more clarity in implementation or further communication. Information customized for a specific client can be structured in a way to make it clear and usable in formulating action plans. The second idea is the ability to structure information so as to be aligned with the structure of your clients' mental models, which allows it to be most easily internalized as knowledge. This concept is developed in the Appendix.

While communication channels have varying capacities to convey structure, the importance of structure will also change depending on the type of knowledge to be communicated. For example, if knowledge is procedural in nature, such as how to implement software or report on a breach of safety regulations, the communication needs to be highly structured. In the case of developing strategic responsiveness to unforeseen developments, an unstructured approach is likely to be more effective. Global Business Network very deliberately designs conferences for its members so that valuable unstructured conversations take place, which enables new and unexpected perspectives and insights to come to light. Generally, knowledge communication (teaching existing knowledge) requires structured communication, while knowledge elicitation (drawing out the capacity to act effectively) favors unstructured approaches.

Reusability

The ability to reuse communication for other people or in other situations depends first on its permanence, which can be seen as the ability to capture the communication in a useful form, almost always digitally. This allows the communication — and the knowledge embedded in it — to be referred to again by the same or other people in the client organization, which can substantially increase its value.

Some media, however, while allowing content to be captured do not lend themselves to easy reuse. For example, even though a document can quickly and easily be accessed and utilized by many people, a video of a presentation is time-consuming to watch and difficult to reference by content, making it unlikely to be used again unless it is extremely relevant to the issues at hand. Technology is beginning to make this easier. Voice recognition software is enabling automated conversation transcription, and more ready access and reference to specific parts of conversations, as well as "conversation mining," in which patterns in conversations can be identified. The same technology can be used to provide automated indexing of videos, though this is still usually done manually.

The degree to which communication has been customized for a specific person, group, or situation will influence how valuable it is in other situations. We have seen how customization adds substantial value within a specific context, but by the same token this can make it less valuable in other situations. Recording a conversation that clarifies a client executive's concerns about a project is likely to be of limited value to anyone else. However, a presentation about the impact of e-commerce on the client's industry could well be valuable to many other people in the organization.

## Customizability

One of the most powerful possibilities of technology is the ability to automate the customization of information and service delivery to clients. A key aspect of the concept of customizability is that this can be automated, rather than having to be done each time by a person. For example, a face-to-face meeting is infinitely customizable, as each one will be unique, but it is not scalable because meeting participants have to be there for each one. However, information delivered through other communication channels can be readily customized to the recipient, if appropriately designed. A simple e-mail or word-processing document can be customized by manually going in and changing terms and phrases to make it relevant to an individual. Where the true power comes in is being able to automate that process. Mail-merge programs have for a long time allowed names and addresses to be inserted into a document to create a customized output. Now word-processing templates allow documents to be created for an individual or a specific circumstance, for example throughout the document selecting from a variety of different paragraphs depending on the context.

The degree of customizability of a particular communication channel will depend more on the way it is implemented rather than the channel itself. A word-processing document could either be not customizable or highly customizable. In a similar vein, e-learning modules can be designed to be customizable to the situation, for example by having the capability of readily inserting case studies relevant to the client rather than having to redevelop the entire module.

## MANAGING DYNAMIC COMMUNICATION PORTFOLIOS

As technology progresses, we still have all existing communication channels available to us. However, over time new channels, for example, instant messaging, become available, and the nature of some of the existing channels evolves over time through technological advances. Getting e-mail does not stop us being able to meet face to face and speak by phone. Yet over time, as more clients start to use broadband Internet access, it enables us to use e-mail in new ways, for example by sending attachments of high-resolution images of products or plant locations. In addition, as executives get continually more e-mails in the inbox, they change their patterns in how they use and respond to e-mail. This means that we must treat how we communicate with clients as a dynamic process. What worked for a particular client and context last year may not be appropriate this year.

Since we now have such a broad array of communication channels available to us, we need to consider them as a portfolio to manage. In any given circumstance, a particular array of communication channels will be most likely to achieve the best results. One of the most important factors will be the communication and learning styles of the key executives you are communicating with at the client. In the Appendix I explore some of the issues of preferences for different forms of communication. However, just as in any other portfolio management process the issue is not finding a single optimal configuration but over time adjusting the array of communication channels used to suit changing circumstances, and the shifting parameters of those channels.

A good example is instant messaging (IM). Not that long ago this was primarily used by teenage girls to share gossip. It is now becoming pervasive in U.S. organizations, and rapidly growing in usage in European and Asian companies. I did a web cast on professional services/client relationships for Microsoft in early 2004. In a poll of the web-cast audience of over 400 executives from a wide variety of professional services firms, 90 percent used IM internally, and 36 percent used it with clients. The sample may not have been representative, but it illustrates that what would have been for many professionals a completely new communication medium was rapidly becoming a staple of client communication. This requires not just familiarity with the tool but also an appreciation of how a particular set of communication channels facilitates both value creation for the client and the development of a deeper relationship.

Table 7–1 show the characteristics of a selection of communication channels in terms of facilitating effective knowledge transfer. The table includes the reasonable potential of each communication channel. However, this may require effective implementation. Note that the "customizability" attribute refers to scalable customization, allowing communication to be customized for many recipients. Clearly the ranking of the communication channels will change as technology develops. For example, IM originally included only short text messages. Increasingly, IM has a video component, and allows attachments to be sent, broadening the bandwidth available through this channel.

In selecting and managing a portfolio of communication channels, one of the prime considerations is maintaining sufficient personal interaction in a format that enables true two-way knowledge transfer. Meetings, facilitated workshops, and coaching represent some of the richest manifestations of human interaction. On the other hand, efficiencies are critical for both professional and client. If you can use channels that are structured, reusable, and potentially customizable to the client, maximum value can be created with the resources available in supporting the development of the virtuous circle of knowledge-based relationships. As bandwidth becomes more available, this enables more possibilities and leverage of communication. Meeting-capture tools such as Quindi enable meetings to be captured in multiple formats, referenced, and made available to people in different time zones. Next-generation web-conferencing tools such as Teleportec simulate the presence of someone in a room, enabling eye contact and a three-dimensional appearance.

## TECHNOLOGY IN CLIENT RELATIONSHIPS

The graphical web browser was invented in 1993. It has become a staple of our work lives extraordinarily quickly, but people's familiarity and comfort with the browser and the array of online tools

TABLE 7-1 *Knowledge transfer capabilities of various communication channels.* Copyright © 2004 Advanced Human Technologies. Reproduced with permission.

| Channel | Interactivity | Bandwidth | Structure | Reusability | Customizability |
|---|---|---|---|---|---|
| Printed documents | Nil | Low | High | High | Low |
| Digital documents | Medium | High | High | High | High |
| E-mail | Medium | Low to medium | High | High | Medium |
| Instant messaging | High | Low to medium | Low | Low | Low |
| Telephone | High | Medium | Low | Low | Low |
| Meetings | Very high | Very high | Low to medium | Low | Low |
| Web conferencing | High | High | High | High | Medium |
| Presentations and seminars | Medium | High | High | Low to medium | Low |
| Facilitated workshops | Very high | Very high | Medium | Low | Low |
| Training | Medium | High | High | Medium | Medium |
| E-learning | Medium | Low to Medium | High | High | High |
| Coaching | Very high | Very high | Low | Very low | Low |

surrounding it is relatively recent. It is only in the last couple of years that many smaller organizations have migrated from dial-up Internet access to broadband.

During the peak of the dot-com boom, professional services firms jumped on board, imagining that they too could participate in the massive boom and reap the rewards. Online services offerings proliferated. However, the client response was not always what was anticipated. Since the NASDAQ reached its peak in March of 2000, professional services firms have continued to try new approaches to delivering information and services to their clients, and gradually discovered what works and does not work. There is now a reasonable level of maturity in understanding what clients perceive as valuable, and in creating useful offerings. One of the key issues is how these new service offerings are integrated into the overall suite of offerings to the client, and the strategic implications of this.

One of the core drivers of online client communication and service delivery is transparency. As you saw in Chapter 2, transparency is a powerful force across all client/supplier relationships. The fact that it is now readily practicable to see into your service provider's work and activities has helped spark demand for transparency from clients. The next stage of this is client participation in business processes.

The connectivity enabled by the Internet is the foundational enabler of online communication between professional services firms and their clients. However, an entire suite of emerging technologies beyond that are now changing the very nature of client communication to a more collaborative approach.

Portal technologies are powerful enablers of collaboration, both inside and outside the organization. Microsoft's SharePoint server technology has a large market share, but similar functionality is available from a slew of other vendors. The most important aspect of portal technologies is that they enable complete control over who can access documents and other resources. Companies can select to whatever degree of detail they desire how much clients, partners, or even internal staff can see and participate in the work process.

There are two key domains in which companies can apply technology in their client relationships. One is in delivering services to clients via digital connectivity. The other goes a step further in getting the client to collaborate in the value creation process. Let's examine these two areas in more detail.

---

### Ernst & Young Online

Global professional services firm Ernst & Young's online initiatives deserve particular attention. In the mid to late 1990s the firm was a clear leader in online professional services, and as it has evolved its offerings in response to its clients and the market it has maintained a leading presence through its diverse range of services. In 1996, Ernst & Young established an online service it named Ernie. At its heart was the ability to ask questions on any business issue by e-mail. Ernie channeled these to the appropriate expert within Ernst & Young, guaranteeing a concise response within 48 hours. The proprietary content from the questions and answers was stripped off to build a database of previously asked questions, which not only gave quick and easy access to valuable information but also allowed clients to track the interests of their peers.

When Ernst & Young sold its consulting arm to Cap Gemini in February 2000, Ernie went with the sale, and was soon absorbed into Cap Gemini's operations. The development of Ernst & Young's online initiatives now reside in its Ernst & Young Online team, though each country operation of the firm focuses on providing a range of services relevant to its market. Most importantly, these services are all provided as tools for client engagement teams to use, so the internal dissemination of the tools and the recognition of their value by professionals across the firm is critical.

Ernst & Young Online currently includes the provision of customized content, tailored to the individual's company, industry, and interests and provided both in online format and through e-mail alerts. This includes relevant news, such as regulatory updates, as well as analysis, guidance, and checklists generated by the firm's experts. An online tax advisor similar to Ernie's e-mail question service is still available. This is now integrated as part of the service offered to major clients. Questions go directly to the client engagement team. However, there is a pre-established network of specialists to forward questions to if they go beyond the expertise of the core team. In these cases the question response is forwarded directly to the client from the specialist, with the engagement team kept informed of all communication.

A diverse suite of web-based tools under the banner of EYware provides both standalone services and offerings that complement major client engagements. The products include governance and compliance monitors, interactive tools that assist decision making in a variety of contexts, a platform for implementing 360-degree feedback within client organizations, and a tool that helps U.K. firms establish priorities for converting their financial reporting to International Financial Reporting Standards (IFRS). This latter tool is an example of a service that complements major client engagements, by providing a foundation for useful structured discussions between a client and Ernst & Young's professionals. Another online tool, named Enterprise Intelligence System, is being used within Ernst & Young Australia to provide its professionals with the capability of easily generating highly visual analysis and insights into clients' financial structures relative to their peers, again providing a basis for valuable knowledge-based conversations and relationships.

Over and above these structured online services, Ernst & Young is focusing substantially on providing collaborative spaces for clients and the engagement teams to work closely together. The collaborative spaces are built on IBM Lotus Quickplace, which can be very quickly and easily set up in a default configuration, but also allows a high degree of customization where required. The firm has implemented over 700 spaces for its clients. Although U.S. clients account for the single largest number of these spaces, overall significantly more activity has happened with Ernst & Young's European clients, notably in the United Kingdom, France, the Netherlands, and Sweden. The collaborative spaces allow a wide range of new ways of engaging with clients, starting from exchanging documents in accordance with clients' internal business rules through to sophisticated global business processes.

*(Continued)*

For one global advertising conglomerate with 400 subsidiaries in 40 countries, Ernst & Young created a customized space that embodies the global workflow required in the audit process. On the left-hand side of the screen client executives can access general information such as the audit methodology, process calendars, and other supporting information. The right-hand side shows the workflow deliverable process. This includes all information required in the audit process, who on the client and Ernst & Young side is responsible for providing it, who reviews and approves documents at each stage, and the current status of the process. All executives at the client who participate in the process, from subsidiaries through to the parent, are given customized access so that only what they need to see is visible. The new system does not change anyone's role, it simply models the process previously in place. However, it gives the client complete transparency on the workflow, being able to see what is being done both internally across its global operations and in its audit firm, and allows what previously took 10 days to be completed in two days.

While client uptake of online systems has been slower than was anticipated in the late 1990s, increasingly, more sophisticated clients ask for and expect these services. Lack of knowledge, perceptions of security risks, and cultural issues at clients have slowed the uptake of online services, but the pace is accelerating. Ernst & Young views its online services suite as a key differentiator, and a strategic complement to face-to-face contact as the role of the Internet in professional services delivery rapidly evolves in the marketplace. Ernie was originally aimed at mid-tier firms that were smaller than Ernst & Young's primary target markets. However, the current suite is firmly directed at its core market of top-tier firms.

## ONLINE SERVICE DELIVERY

It was not that long ago that the only means clients had of tapping the expertise of their professional advisors were face-to-face meetings, telephone calls, and documents sent by mail or fax. Within the space of just a few years a plethora of new communications channels have become available. This has opened up many new ways clients can gain value from their experienced professionals. The reality is that often a significant part of the value delivered to clients is through information, as you saw in Chapter 3. In this case, the information component of the service can be delivered through online media rather than more traditional approaches such as printed documents. This provides far greater benefits to clients, as clients can search the information, have it customized to their situation, put it into models for further analysis, integrate it into their systems, repurpose it within internal initiatives, and generally have complete flexibility on its application.

In addition, professionals' expertise can be accessed through online services in a variety of ways. One approach is using richer media for interacting with clients. For example, investment bank UBS uses Avistar Video Messenger system, which enables traders and investment bankers to use an instant-messaging style of interface to click on the names of their clients who have been set up with the system, instantly creating a video connection. Up to four people can be included in the video call, enabling discussion of trading ideas among multiple executives on both bank and client side. In another vein, online services can be created that provide valuable input for clients without having to incur the expense of the time of a seasoned professional. Ernst & Young's corporate governance online advisor (see "Ernst & Young Online") provides an example of this.

High-value Information

High-value information is at the core of many professional services offerings, as you saw in Chapter 3. Almost all of that information delivery is now on the Internet. There are two key dimensions to providing that information to clients in an online form. The first is providing clients with easy access to relevant information. The second is providing information customized to the client's situation, needs, and information preferences.

It is increasingly common for firms to provide clients with access to the same or similar information available to in-house professionals. For example, Microsoft provides its entire KnowledgeBase of support issues and resolutions online. HP has established a sophisticated internal methodology to ensure that the knowledge base available to its clients for its NonStop servers is current and readily accessible. The emphasis in their support processes is on balancing creating current information that clients can access to assist them and maintaining strict quality controls. Any support engineer who is working with a client to resolve a problem and believes that the current knowledge base should be updated can post the content they have generated to the system so that it is immediately available to be viewed by other clients. A council of senior engineers reviews a representative sample of the content posted by each engineer, and clients also post feedback, to ensure that the content is of prime quality.

Effective search capabilities are critical in providing clients with access to high-value information. This can be done through a keyword or other search engine. An alternative that can be highly relevant when clients are not sure of what they are looking for is a decision tree process, which guides the user through a series of questions. Linklaters, a London-based law firm that is one of the largest in the world, uses this approach in its BlueFlag financial compliance product. Users, who may be wanting to identify potential legal issues in launching a new financial product, are guided through a series of questions on what types of products, the jurisdiction, and so on, which leads them to a summarized view of the information relevant to their situation, with more details available as required.

Clifford Chance, the world's largest law firm, has been a pioneer in online service delivery since it launched its initial NextLaw service in May 1998. It now offers a wide array of online services to clients, ranging from customized information to advising major clients on implementing legal content management systems inside their organizations. It has increasingly shifted its service structure to make its online services relevant to particular functional areas in its clients. One of its target communities is mergers and acquisitions (M&As). Since most firms only make acquisitions irregularly, it is important for firms to continue to maintain contact and develop relationships on an ongoing basis, and the firm uses a variety of services to achieve this, such as e-mail alert tools focused on changes in specific industries.

One of Clifford Chance's current suite of offerings for its M&A clients is a Cross Border Acquisition Guide. Clients are initially presented with a wizard in which they select the range of jurisdictions and issues relevant to their situation, which generates an interactive report that gives them a high-level view of what they need to consider. They can then drill down into more detail on any of the issues, and can copy and paste any of the content into their own internal reports and applications as required. The service also includes a regular e-mail update on legislative changes.

Providing aggregated or comparative information can be very useful for managers, and is greatly enabled in an online environment. Global professional services firm PricewaterhouseCoopers provides an online Global Best Practices knowledge base that allows clients to see best practices in a wide variety of domains, including business processes down to the component level.[4] As companies participate in the knowledge base, comparative information across industries and geographies becomes available, assisting managers in understanding how their company is positioned relative to peers on specific business processes and issues. The online service functions as a standalone service in addition to leading clients into traditional consulting engagements.

## Online Services

Increasingly, online services are competing with the services of professionals. What used to require a person sometimes can now be provided by an interactive digital service. A great example is how "document assembly" technologies can be used to automate the creation of customized documents. This is becoming increasingly prominent in legal services. Many law firms are using this technology internally to streamline their work. If the creation of a legal document can be automated, why pay an expensive professional to do it? However, some firms are starting to offer this technology directly to their clients. London-based legal giant Allen & Overy, as part of its comprehensive Newchange suite of online services, provides its clients with the ability to apply document assembly technologies for themselves, being asked a series of questions that enables the specific clauses relevant to the situation to be inserted automatically.

As you saw in Chapter 2, many processes and activities previously performed by professionals can now be automated. The first stage is to implement these processes in-house. A number of leading firms, such as Allen & Overy, are starting to offer these to clients. In a more simple fashion, do-it-yourself will kits in both paper and online form are readily available.

Going to the more sophisticated level of expert systems, law firm Blake Dawson Waldron's Legal Technology Group, described in Chapter 4, offers a Virtual Lawyer Advertising solution. This is an expert system that embodies the experience of lawyers with substantial experience in assessing whether advertising copy is legally compliant. Users of the system submit their proposed advertising copy, and are then guided through a series of questions about the copy and the context in which it will be used, following its line of questioning dependent on the answers given. The system gives feedback to the user, who then has the option of modifying the proposed copy. The copy is then forwarded to a nominated reviewer for approval, together with an analysis noting any causes for concern. The Virtual Lawyer Advertising system has been implemented in for example a major national retailer, which creates a very large number of advertisements. Having the system inside the company takes a substantial burden off the in-house legal counsel, and obviates the need for hiring expensive external legal staff on mundane matters.

Ernst & Young's EYware suite of products (see "Ernst & Young Online") includes a number of online services that complement live service delivery. An example is its range of Corporate Governance tools, which assist its clients in monitoring internal activities to ensure compliance with a wide variety of regulations. Individuals in the organization are asked a series of questions to determine the current compliance situation, and are provided with action recommendations as a result. Again, this service provides value to clients who have been placed under a significant regulatory burden, without incurring the expense of high-level professionals.

Often online services are part of a broader range of service delivery mechanisms to create value for clients. Clifford Chance provides an e-learning service called Comply designed for businesspeople rather than lawyers, which was developed to assist clients in meeting compliance requirements, notably in antitrust and competition law. This can be bought as a standalone product, but is usually offered to clients as part of an integrated suite of services, including manuals and "dawn raid" simulations to mitigate risk.

## Implementing Collaborative Technologies

One of the most powerful shifts in the way professional services are and will be provided is the use of collaborative technologies. These, quite simply, are technologies that enable people to work together. Table 7–2 shows some of the core collaborative technologies that are available, applied to communication, information sharing, or workflow. Each of these domains can be applied for collaboration at the same time, sometimes called "synchronous" or "real-time" collaboration, or at different times, sometimes called "asynchronous" collaboration. All of these technologies are now commonly in use within organizations. The beauty of these tools is that they are usually almost equally easy to implement across organizational boundaries as within a company, thus transforming your ability to work closely with clients.

As the availability of bandwidth improves, collaborative tools are allowing richer interaction. It is now standard for salespeople in many industries to make presentations to their prospects using

TABLE 7-2    *Types of collaborative technologies.* Copyright © 2004 Advanced
Human Technologies. Reproduced with permission.

| Mode | Real time | Asynchronous |
|---|---|---|
| Communication | • Telephone<br>• Video conferencing<br>• Instant messaging | • E-mail<br>• Voicemail<br>• Courier |
| Information sharing | • Online presentations<br>• Desktop sharing<br>• Whiteboarding | • Document repositories<br>• Discussion forums<br>• Online workspaces |
| Workflow | • Real-time document modification<br>• Calendar/schedules<br>• On-demand e-learning | • Sequential workflow<br>• Collaborative design<br>• Project management |

web-conferencing technologies, and desktop video is gradually gaining
traction.

Instant messaging is one of the most rapidly growing communication tools. The most important aspect of IM is its "presence" functionality, which enables people to see when their colleagues inside or
outside their organization are in front of their computers or mobile
devices. Instead of sending an e-mail or calling on the telephone
without knowing whether the person is there, you can make contact
in the knowledge that they are currently available. The next phase of
software will embed this presence function into all aspects of work.
For example, when looking at a document that has been modified you
will be able to see whether the person who made those modifications
is currently available, and can inquire on the thinking behind these.

Generally, the availability of collaborative technologies changes
both the way professional services firms work internally and their relationships with their clients. Work can be allocated more effectively
across firms, and performed collaboratively in bringing together the
optimal combination of knowledge specialists in the firm. Work done
for clients will rapidly shift to be more collaborative.

Client Collaboration

The transition in clients' perception of their professional service providers often begins with increasing transparency. As clients grow more sophisticated and see the possibilities of greater information flow, they ask for visibility of how services are delivered to them. Once the workflow within the professional firm starts becoming transparent to the client, it is just a small step further to participate in that workflow.

In the wake of the passing of the Sarbanes-Oxley act that introduced regulation on services provided by auditors, global aluminum firm Alcan established strict approval policies for services delivered by its audit firm PricewaterhouseCoopers (PwC). PwC helped Alcan implement a virtual workroom that brought together over 200 PwC staff in 30 countries with key Alcan executives. This was initially used to ensure that any proposals for work by PwC throughout Alcan's global operations were visible and vetted by the relevant executives on both sides. However, the establishment of the workroom then provided a platform for greater collaboration and interaction on a broader range of work issues. The space is used to hold key documents, provide greater visibility of all client and PwC activities, and facilitate a range of work processes.

Ketchum PR, a public relations agency in the Omnicom group with over 1,100 people in more than 50 wholly-owned and affiliated offices around the world, implemented a knowledge-sharing portal it called myKGN for "my Ketchum Global Network." In the first phase this was used internally to share knowledge and provide a common workspace for professionals working on global client accounts. A modified version of the service was then made available to clients. In the first instance it allowed clients to see what was happening on work Ketchum was executing for them, but it also enabled staff in different offices of the client to communicate and coordinate around what were often global projects. Finally it began to be used for both Ketchum PR professionals and executives at their clients to collaborate on projects, getting input where required from clients and making work an increasingly shared process.

As professional work becomes more collaborative, more tools are launched to enable visibility and client participation. The idea of the "deal room" is an online space in which all information relevant to a deal or transaction is visible to all participants. General Electric Commercial Finance has created the GE Dealroom, which is a platform for GE executives and clients to liaise and communicate about all aspects of financing transactions that GE is executing for its clients. Most major law firms provide deal rooms in some form to their clients for large transactions. There are several parties involved in any major financial transaction, including at least a client, an investment bank, and a law firm, and often other participants such as a merger partner, independent valuer, or others.

Trying to coordinate time-sensitive and document-intensive activities using physical documents would be a major constraint. Using e-mail may seem to be an improvement, but there are many problems, including knowing which is the current version of a document and providing appropriate levels of access to sensitive documents to a wide variety of participants. If a secure and easy-to-use system is available, this creates value for all participants. Any member of the team could provide the collaboration system, and in fact this represents a relationship opportunity.

Another form of collaboration is discussing complex ideas with clients. In the world of financial markets, I believe that what I call "collaborative trade and portfolio analytics" will be a significant aspect of changing relationships between the "sell-side" investment banks and brokers and the "buy-side" fund managers and corporate treasuries. A good example of this is given by a product offered by Credit Suisse First Boston named Locus. This provides sophisticated analysis of derivatives strategies as a basis for discussion with clients. Salespeople can present their clients with a live view of a trading strategy they are proposing, and as they both view the analysis each can change assumptions in the models, see what the implications are from the client's perspective, and if necessary adjust the strategy to suit the client's perspectives and portfolios.

Given that the execution of financial markets transactions is swiftly becoming commoditized through institutional online trading tools such as TradeWeb and FXAll, this type of highly collaborative knowledge-based interaction with clients will become increasingly important. If banks cannot clearly demonstrate that they can create superior value for their clients in their interactions, clients will not waste their time speaking with salespeople, and the bank's key relationships will suffer.

---

### Infosys InTouch

Infosys Technologies, based in Bangalore, India, is one of the country's largest providers of technology and consulting services to clients worldwide, with over 32,000 employees and $1 billion in revenue in 2004, while growing at a pace of over 40 percent annually. As the global technology outsourcing industry matures, clients are increasingly demanding transparency and designing very detailed contractual relationships. In this environment, Infosys seeks to build partnerships with its clients. Its clients are usually located in different continents, so Infosys needs to create a high level of comfort, and shift relationships so that value is created jointly. A critical foundation for this is having highly developed internal processes, so that clients have an extremely consistent framework for seeing what is happening in the course of the project, and a firm context for any issues that may arise en route. Infosys, as many of its Indian peers, has made it a priority to achieve certification on its process excellence from bodies such as the Software Engineering Institute. To leverage its process maturity into client value creation, Infosys has implemented a client portal named InTouch. This is designed to give its clients complete transparency of the work process, and to enable effective client collaboration and shared development.

InTouch provides extremely detailed ongoing status reports to clients, including information on all project activities, schedule changes,

*(Continued)*

productivity levels, potential risks, quality measures, performance on service-level agreement indicators, and so on. This is available in a browser view. However, immediate alerts are provided to clients if any indicator is out of expected ranges. The level of detail in the reports provides a sound foundation for discussion with clients on project progress, and how any issues are being dealt with. The portal also covers client responsibilities in the project, which could include providing resources, project elements delivered in-house, and sign-offs. All information on the project is summarized in a dashboard made available to the client's chief information officer, which indicates in red any areas for concern, with clear visibility of the source of the issue. Other client staff can choose to drill down into as much detail as they choose on project activity and performance. The client portal also contains all documents, models, and process descriptions for client projects, as well as glossaries that can be used by both client and Infosys staff. Visibility is also given of key executives, project staffing, contact information, and people turnover.

Very often technology outsourcing involves shared development projects that are undertaken across both the outsourcer and the client. For this to be effective, a common technology infrastructure is essential. This will include a shared platform for source code control, issue logging, project metrics, and so on. Since Infosys has established mature processes in these areas, it often works with clients to set up or enhance rigorous internal processes, notably by identifying and implementing appropriate metrics for project monitoring as a foundation for establishing quality processes. In these cases, Infosys provides "quality consultants" that are based at its clients' premises to help implement these processes. The degree of integration between operations that clients expect is reflected in some of Infosys' contracts. In some cases clients are asking for Infosys' performance to be measured on indicators such as the improvement in productivity of the clients' in-house programmers. They clearly expect that engaging Infosys will help enhance their own processes and capabilities.

Distributed Workflow

Prudential Property Investment Managers is the United Kingdom's largest institutional property investment manager, spending up to £10 million a year on legal fees for about 2,000 highly varied transactions. In early 2003, it expressed concerns to its panel of legal services providers on the cost of these services. Prior to one of Prudential's regular reviews, Robert Kidby, relationship partner and head of property services for Lovells, the sixth largest international law firm in the world and one of Prudential's service providers, floated an idea with the head of Prudential's legal services department, Robert Allen. He suggested that when Prudential sent its legal work to Lovells the firm would separate the complex sophisticated transactions, which it would allocate to its top lawyers, from the mundane commoditized work, which it would send out to be performed by low-cost regional law firms. It would then reintegrate the work performed by other firms and complete quality control before passing it back to the client, ensuring both a single client interface and an optimized cost structure.

Prudential had instituted a formal review panel to assess proposals from its law firms, including business line executives as well as members of its legal team. Some panel members were reticent on the potential problems of this highly novel approach, including accountability. Kidby, working with other key members of his relationship team for Prudential, engaged with the panel members to address their concerns. Internally, Kidby worked with his partners at Lovells to help them to recognize the value of the innovative business model, and to pull together the resources and expertise to make the project happen.

In July 2003 Prudential announced that it would drop the other main members of its legal panel, and award the bulk of its legal work to Lovells. The platform to deliver services to Prudential was named *Mexican Wave*, to illustrate how each team member stands up and sits down at the right time to create a collaborative outcome. The new approach to service delivery has significantly changed Lovell's relationship with this key client. On the one hand, Prudential has constant access to all lawyers performing the work, as well as a tailored extranet that gives it complete visibility of all work in progress. However, Prudential is also substantially more open with Lovells in disclosing its strategic directions and internal processes, which enables continually greater customization in service delivery.

Most importantly, Prudential finds that the service fulfills its needs so well that it has sacked its other major legal services providers, and allocated all of its property transaction work to Lovells. The Mexican Wave service has since been rolled out for two other Lovells clients, Prudential Plc and Aviva. An additional two clients have signed up for MexNet, which is the web site Lovells uses to give transparency to clients and monitor work that is outsourced.[5]

There are several lessons from this story. One is that modularization, discussed in Chapter 2, as a key driver in professional services is a reality recognized by major clients. Another is that professional firms need to be increasingly aware, how they allocate work not only between themselves and their clients but also potentially with external services providers. If elements of professional services functions are provided outside the firm, which is increasingly the case, firms need to become highly effective at sourcing suppliers, managing external processes, performing quality control, and integrating external work into their internal processes.

It is interesting to note that Prudential Property chose to ask Lovells to run the entire process of receiving the work, selecting and managing the outsourcing firms, and performing quality control. It could have chosen to run this all itself, allocating work to different firms as it saw fit, but it has allowed Lovells essentially to run part of its processes. This is a powerful positioning.

Many new possibilities are afforded through the use of technologies, and professional firms need at the very least to think through the potential implications before their clients do. The greater flexibility can allow clients to select which elements of the professional work required they wish to perform in-house, considering the resources they have on hand or the depth of relevant knowledge they have. They can then hire an external firm to perform the other elements, and integrate them seamlessly. The work process has immediately become allocated between the client and its services provider.

Firms need to think through how their clients could participate in their current work processes. On the one hand there are risks, in that parts of the work currently performed for clients could be lost. However, there is a very strong upside, in that if you work with your client to establish joint integrated processes you have effectively achieved client lock-in. Your client will have to work considerably with other firms in order to be able to create a joint system with the same degree of efficiency. As you saw in Chapter 1, you will have created positive lock-in by embedding yourself in your clients' processes.

## CUSTOMER COMMUNICATION CHANNELS

It is valuable for professional services firms to examine perspectives on customer communication from industries that have a broader range of low-value relationships, where efficiencies are critical. The same lessons on allocating resources effectively apply equally to high-value services provision, especially as professional firms touch more people across their client organizations, and potentially broaden their ambit to provide services to new client sectors.

In the heyday of the dot-com era, many believed that the old laws of business and relationships had been revoked. In their highly influential book *Blown to Bits*, Evans and Wurster proclaimed that there was no longer a trade-off between "richness" and "reach" and that henceforth companies could reach as many customers as they wished without sacrificing richness of interaction.[6]

Indeed, this is one of the best ways to understand the power of communications technologies on customer relationships. However, the reality is that critical trade-offs remain in customer communication. In the case of high-value customer relationships, expensive customer service representatives can be supplemented but not replaced by sophisticated web sites. Managing the trade-offs between various customer communication channels well is at the heart of effective customer relationship management.

People still have a role in building lasting, profitable customer relationships. There is much power in performing automated interaction, data capture, and marketing analysis well. However, the most valuable customer relationships must be nurtured by a mix of human and digital channels that draws on and integrates the strengths of each. Those that achieve this balance as both technology advances and customer attitudes shift will reap the rewards as we move into the future of customer relationships.

## The Trade-off Between Efficiency and Relationship Strength

Not so long ago it was pretty straightforward: you could interact with your customers in shops, by telephone, or by mail. Other options were not available. Any communication from customers had to be responded to by a person who had the capabilities and training to provide effective service. Today, we still have those same choices available. In addition, a plethora of new ways of communicating with customers has sprung up.

Efficiency in customer communication is a critical driver today. Companies want to achieve low costs and to have systems that can be scaled to work effectively for as many customers as they wish. With increasing competition and price pressures, this is fundamental to doing business profitably. On the other hand, companies also need to nurture the strongest possible relationships with their customers, which means keeping them loyal, having rich personal interaction, learning more about them all the time, and closing transactions. Connectivity and relationship technologies are helping to make these two aims more compatible, but there remains a trade-off between them. As illustrated in Figure 7–1, there are three key domains for customer communication.

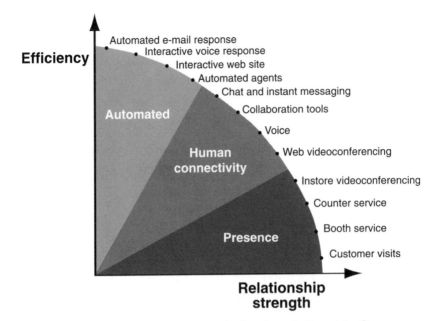

FIGURE 7-1  *The spectrum of customer communication channels.* Copyright © 2004 Advanced Human Technologies. Reprinted with permission.

- *Presence:* There is no substitute for people being physically present in the same place, which allows them to sit down together, converse, relate as humans, and discover more about each other. Shop fronts and meetings will always have their place in customer interaction. However, increasingly physical venues will also incorporate other media for accessing customer service.
- *Human connectivity:* The majority of customer service is provided by people, connected to customers via telecommunications. Until recently this has been done solely by voice over the public telephone system. However, this is now supplemented by e-mail, chat, video, and other emerging channels that allow richer interaction.

- *Automated:* Since the introduction of interactive voice response (IVR) systems, customers are growing steadily more accustomed to interacting with computers. Technology is continually enabling broader and more effective systems to provide automated customer service.

## Summary: Relationship Channels and Communication

Knowledge-based relationships depend on communication, so we must actively manage the range of channels we use to communicate with our clients. There are five key enablers of knowledge transfer: interactivity, bandwidth, structure, reusability, and customizability. Each of the range of channels available has different characteristics in terms of facilitating knowledge transfer, which affects how these should be used and combined to build an effective portfolio of communication channels.

Communication technologies are transforming professional services/client relationships. High-value information is provided digitally, services are being delivered online, collaborative technologies are changing the professional/client relationship, and workflow is sometimes becoming distributed across organizational boundaries. In implementing communication channels to customers, we need to consider the trade-off between efficiency and relationship strength.

Communication is the foundation of any relationship. Yet for any major client we need to go beyond individual relationships. Chapter 8 covers how to create and structure true firm-wide relationships.

## Notes

[1]   Richard L. Daft and Robert H. Lengel, "Information Richness: A New Approach to Manager Information Processing and Organization Design," in *Research in Organizational Behaviour*, B. Staw and L. L. Cummings (eds.), vol. 6, Greenwich, Conn.: JAI Press, 1984; and "Organizational Information Requirements, Media Richness and Structural Design," *Management Science*, vol. 32, no. 5, May 1986, pp. 554–571.

[2] Daft and Lengel (1984), p. 194.

[3] See, for example, the *Journal of Computer-Mediated Communication*, at *www.ascusc.org/jcmc*.

[4] See *www.globalbestpractices.com*.

[5] Tim Newbold, "More Clients Ride Lovells' 'Mexican Wave'," *Legal Week*, September 16, 2004.

[6] Philip Evans and Thomas S. Wurster, *Blown to Bits: How the New Economics of Information Transforms Strategy*, Boston: Harvard Business School Press, 2000.

# 8

# Firm-wide Relationship Management
## Structuring Client Contact

One of the key issues for any professional services firm is moving its client relationships beyond single points of contact at the firm and the client to true firm-wide relationships. The most obvious problem with contact being focused on individuals on each side is the vulnerability of the relationship. All it takes is the relationship manager or your key client contact to leave or be transferred and the relationship can easily founder. Moreover, a true knowledge-based client relationship cannot be implemented through an individual. It requires broader contact across both the firm and the client, bringing together the unique expertise of the firm in a way that creates superior value for the client.

How to structure client contact is a vitally important theme for professional services firms. However, understanding that the desired outcome should be powerful knowledge-based relationships provides valuable guidance on how to design interactions. In Chapter 9 I will examine in detail the issue of forming and leading relationship teams. This chapter covers the broader issues of structuring knowledge-based client relationships.

## DEVELOPING POWERFUL KNOWLEDGE-BASED RELATIONSHIPS

Our primary objective is to develop sustained and highly profitable relationships with organizational clients. You have seen throughout this book that adding value to clients with knowledge is critical in achieving that. This offers us a key reference point in developing strategies for relationship management. The following are some of the specific outcomes we should keep in mind in designing the structure of client contact.

- Maximum value added to clients as perceived by key client executives
- Continuously deeper knowledge of every aspect of clients
- Close contact with and high "share of mind" of key decision makers
- Ongoing generation of mutually profitable business
- Learning from the client and getting high-value feedback

Focusing on developing knowledge-based relationships, specifically in the context of creating ongoing profitable business and positive client lock-in, is a sound foundation on which to base relationship management strategies.

### Industry and Client Differences in Structuring Contact

It is difficult to generalize about how to structure client contact, since what is most effective will depend on the style and capabilities of the professional service firm, the client industry, and the client's culture and organizational structure. Variables between industries and engagements with the greatest impact on the most effective structure of client contact include

- Services delivery models
- The nature of client-perceived value creation

- The organizational function and level in the client where knowledge outcomes are created
- The time frame and scope of the engagement

Professionals will recognize what is most common in their industry and firm for each of these issues, and the implications in terms of modifying the design of relationships. Beyond the more general issues that determine how different firms will tend to manage their relationships, it is important to recognize when different types of engagements or clients demand variations in the usual approaches, and to maintain the flexibility to modify these easily.

## Client Culture

The culture of the client organization can have a dramatic effect on the most effective approaches to relationship management and knowledge transfer, and indeed to what degree knowledge transfer will be valued. One of the most important dimensions is how autocratic or participatory the client culture is. This will have a major impact on the design of relationship management and interaction, most obviously in the degree to which contact and knowledge transfer is concentrated on top management — or sometimes even an individual — as opposed to being distributed throughout the organization. A related dimension is the degree of centralization or decentralization of the client organization, especially in decision making.

Another significant factor affecting the design of knowledge transfer is the degree to which the client culture is "expert" based. This is usually evident in the status accorded to experts or knowledge specialists. Most professional service firms clearly fall into this category. Client organizations may or may not mirror this. One implication of dealing with an expert-based client culture is the importance that must be placed on interacting with and getting buy-in from the experts, who are the arbiters of the value of knowledge within their organizations, and can hold sway far beyond that suggested by their titles or positions.

Taking into account national cultures is also critical in knowledge sharing and transfer. A U.S. professional service firm attempting to apply its usual approaches, for example, in Japan, Brazil, or France would likely have limited success. Knowledge is not only personal but has a strong cultural basis, especially in its creation and sharing. These cultural divides in regard to knowledge transfer can be bridged, but they require close attention and respect for cultural differences.[1]

## Institutionalizing Knowledge Transfer

Since knowledge is an attribute of individuals, it is a real challenge to "institutionalize" knowledge transfer, in the sense of embedding it in the client organization beyond a few key staff members. Many consultants wax lyrical about knowledge transfer in their brochures and proposals. Where most fail to deliver, however, is in truly institutionalizing the knowledge transfer, rather than providing a few documents, presentations, and workshops that make select individuals in the client organization feel they are more knowledgeable. Gary Hamel notes the crucial distinction between firms gaining access to skills and actually internalizing those skills.[2]

To achieve this degree of knowledge transfer demands a deep understanding of organizational dynamics and knowledge flow. Knowing the client organization extremely well is just as important. People within an organization usually do not need formal training to understand what is happening internally and how to exert influence effectively. A similar depth of understanding is needed on the part of outside professionals in order to achieve knowledge transfer that is effective at an organizational level. Again, the strength of the relationship and the degree of knowledge of the client organization are critical in achieving this objective.

Since institutionalizing knowledge transfer depends on internal knowledge flows within the client organization, sensitivity to political factors is crucial. In closer client relationships, the service provider often starts to become part of the internal political landscape, which can be both a benefit and a hindrance. In fact, one of the very valuable roles external professionals can play is in acting as a bridge or even mediator between different client divisions and groups. There is often limited or ineffective communication within client organizations, so that the position of a professional service firm can allow them to assist and develop internal knowledge flows, which adds substantial value in itself and is intrinsic to ensuring the institutionalization of the knowledge it offers.

## Establishing Knowledge Transfer Outcomes

A key element in achieving effective knowledge transfer is establishing and agreeing on specific knowledge transfer outcomes with the client. This step is very important for four reasons. First, it establishes whether the client truly values knowledge transfer. If it does not, that clarifies and simplifies the client engagement. Second, it provides a specific link, both in the formal agreement and in the client's mind, between knowledge transfer and value. Third, it provides a specific and presumably top-level endorsement of knowledge transfer, which can help overcome organizational politics. Fourth, it provides a way of charging the client on a value basis as opposed to a time basis. This theme is developed further in Chapter 11, which covers the pricing of knowledge.

Knowledge transfer outcomes can be defined on the individual level in terms of development of personal knowledge or skills, while on the organizational level capabilities can be measured in terms of change in productivity, quality, or similar yardsticks. Most high-value knowledge transfer outcomes are difficult to assess or quantify for the purposes of formal agreements. Even so, to the degree they can be stated as objectives it is valuable to do so. In some cases it may be preferable not to link them to specific performance or payment targets, because of the difficulty in accurate measurement and the impact of other variables, although it is usually worth at least stating them in order to establish client recognition of value.

## Managing Knowledge Gatekeepers

All organizations contain people who play the role, usually informally, of knowledge gatekeepers. In a positive context, they are often centers of influence in the organization, provide usefully filtered information and knowledge from the business environment to the organization, and greatly facilitate the impact of professional service providers. On the downside, they can use their positions of influence to control information and knowledge flow according to their own priorities and agenda.[3]

In most professional services engagements there are one or two designated contacts at the client organization, and their propensities as knowledge gatekeepers will play a key role in the success of any knowledge transfer in the project. It is rarely appropriate to "go around" the primary client contacts, even if it would result in better outcomes for the client organization.

In many cases the heart of the issue is in positioning your primary contacts as the heroes of the engagement, rather than claiming all the glory of success for yourself. If in their roles as knowledge gatekeepers they are able to provide real value to others in the organization, they will facilitate the knowledge transfer process. If, however, they want to maintain strict control over contact within their organization, the restriction on interactivity, bandwidth, participation, and flexibility will strongly impact the knowledge transfer outcomes.

## Project Ownership

One of the greatest barriers to knowledge uptake is what has been called the Not-Invented-Here syndrome.[4] Many organizational cultures, particularly in industries driven by innovation, believe that they come up with the best ideas, and if it is from outside it is suspect and probably not as good. Addressing this is an important management issue, as in an increasingly interconnected economy no single company can compete on its own ideas alone.

From the perspective of a professional services firm, a culture in the client organization that is suspicious of outside knowledge can easily doom a project, whether or not it depends on knowledge transfer. In any engagement with limited scope, it is probably unrealistic to attempt to change the corporate culture, which means that success will depend on the people who are centers of influence in the client feeling that they have ownership of the project. Getting client buy-in must be a key objective in all professional service engagements. However, it is particularly critical where knowledge transfer is essential to the project.

The essence of getting clients to feel and act as if they have ownership of the project is clearly in participation. All stages of the project, from setting objectives and designing the process to execution of a plan, should include the broadest possible involvement from the client consistent with its culture. Selecting the key players who act as centers of influence in the organization to participate is critical. This strategy starts to cast the role of the professional service firm increasingly as one of knowledge elicitation rather than knowledge communication. If indeed the client perceives that its knowledge and capabilities are being enhanced rather than external knowledge delivered or imposed, the likelihood of success of the project will be greatly improved. Once this perception has been established, it provides a far greater opportunity for service providers to apply their own methodologies and content knowledge. Of course, in some client cultures the issue of ownership will not be major, and it may instead be specifically looking for an outside expert to provide knowledge leadership.

## Project Handover: Leaving a Legacy

One of the most critical junctures in all professional services engagements, and especially those in which knowledge transfer is an issue, is that of project handover. How professional services firms approach this reflects whether they truly wish to transfer knowledge, or just talk about it. Effective project handover will result in the client experiencing a large degree of completeness (and presumably satisfaction) with the project, while ineffective handover will mean the client may need to come back for more work on the same issues. This is often what is intended. Although this may generate more business in the short run, the client will be highly inclined to change to a new supplier when the next significant project comes up. It is increasingly common for sophisticated clients to expect and demand effective project handover specifically in order to achieve greater self-sufficiency as an outcome of engagements.

There are two essential outcomes to address in ensuring successful project handover: the knowledge of staff members and access to codified knowledge or information. Both are essential for the client's knowledge to be usable on an ongoing basis, and neither is sufficient by itself. In addressing the people side of project handovers, the issues that must be addressed include the following.

- What knowledge and skills are required by which client staff members
- Where in the organization these staff are likely to be posted
- Whether they will have the time to address ongoing project issues
- What will happen if key staff members leave the company or are transferred to new roles

A strategy must also be in place to ensure that the necessary information is available to the client. This will often include documentation on methodologies, as covered in Chapter 5. Even if individuals at the client organization have learned experientially, they will still want to refer to documentation, and this can be used to develop skills in other staff members.

Information can and certainly should be provided in documents and additions to the client's knowledge base. However, far greater value can be provided by providing access to dynamic information, such as a continually updated web site. One advantage of this approach is that it helps to strengthen the relationship and the "share of mind" of the client; that is, the share of awareness and thought about the service provider by key client executives. Building in an ongoing knowledge transfer component to all significant engagements can play a major role in developing relationships.

Often a key element in successful handovers is specifically training the client to run its own internal programs to develop the skills and knowledge of a broad range of its staff after the service provider has left. This can include providing training manuals and "train the trainer" courses for specified client staff. Providing knowledge in a generative form, which means the client can develop skills further on its own, allows the use of licensing fees, which can be a healthy complement to the usual fee structures. This subject is covered in more detail in Chapter 11.

Particularly where knowledge transfer is a key objective, project handover should be formalized, rather than just letting the engagement end. In addition to the issues of staff skills and codified knowledge, other issues that should be addressed include circumstances in which the supplier may need to be called back in to work on or further develop the same project or issue. Establishing that contingency clearly in advance means that if further work is necessary the service provider will not be seen to be "freeloading."

HP Consulting has often run what it calls a "project snapshot" with clients. This began as a way of identifying lessons for itself from projects it had run, though it is now extended to be run as a similar process with clients. It can be done at any time in the project, though it usually occurs at the conclusion. HP Consulting allocates to every project what it calls "knowledge consultants," who are responsible for designing the process for the engagement by drawing on the firm's previous experience, and for deriving lessons from the current project. Part of their responsibility is to facilitate the project snapshot workshop, which is commonly run over a few hours.

The team seeks to identify what has worked in the project, what has not worked, what useful knowledge has been created, and what lessons are applicable in other parts of the client organization. It also identifies what documents or other materials are needed for the client to reuse the lessons from the project in other ways and places. HP Consulting also uses a process it calls "knowledge mapping," which involves drawing a map of knowledge at the firm and at its client. The map traces what knowledge needs to flow to which people at the client group and in what form. This is used as a basis for planning effective knowledge transfer to the client.

## KNOWLEDGE RELATIONSHIP ROLES

Several distinct roles are played in professional service firms in achieving knowledge outcomes for clients. Managing and coordinating these roles and the way they work together is at the heart of developing an effective structure for client contact and relationship management. This requires understanding the roles, the skills they require, and the ways in which they interact and complement each other in building client relationships.

In the traditional style of professional services, partners were selected from those that demonstrated the ability to cover the full spectrum of professional activities, including business generation, client relationship management, specialist knowledge, and staff management. Now there is far more flexibility in the roles that need to be fulfilled, and the overall relationship is commonly run by teams rather than a single individual.

The primary knowledge relationship roles are senior representative, relationship coordinator, knowledge specialist, and knowledge customizer. Clearly any one individual can play all or any combination of these roles. However, it is unusual to find the necessary skills for all of these roles in one person, and it is increasingly common for the roles to be separated. As we will see, the essence of what distinguishes different models for relationship management in knowledge-based relationships is the configurations in which these roles are combined and applied.

## Senior Representative

In most relationships, the professional service firm has a senior representative who acts as the face of the firm in top-level client contacts, and sometimes assumes overall responsibility and supervision of the account. The function of the role is essentially to establish credibility with the client, often in the selling phase, and also at critical junctures in the project and relationship, particularly when access to the top client level is required. This role does not play an important part in knowledge transfer per se. However, it is often central in the initial framing of the relationship between the companies, and its ongoing development.

## Relationship Coordinator

The person who assumes the role of relationship coordinator is often called a relationship manager, account manager, or project manager. However, we have avoided these terms to more clearly distinguish the role of coordinator from the other knowledge relationship roles. A relationship coordinator is responsible for orchestrating the resources of the service provider to achieve the desired outcomes for the client.

This is often fundamentally a project management task, which includes defining the project objectives with the client, and establishing and guiding a process that achieves those. This is particularly the case where there is a specific engagement, when the relationship coordinator is most commonly called a project manager.

More generally, particularly in ongoing relationships, the function involves furnishing access to the relevant resources of the service provider. Effectiveness as a relationship coordinator depends on rich knowledge of both the client and the service firm. The coordinator must not only know what resources are available within the service provider and have the influence to access those but also understand the client's organizational culture, processes, and people. Without this knowledge, the complex relationship processes necessary for knowledge transfer are unlikely to succeed.

## Knowledge Specialist

Knowledge specialists are the source of the knowledge and expertise on which the provision of services is based, so they are the heart of professional service firms. In many ways they are the key resource of the organization, and are usually treated as such. Depth and richness of knowledge is critical in order to add significant value to the client. However, knowledge specialists are not always skilled at communication. A significant implication of the growing importance of knowledge transfer is that knowledge specialists can often no longer work only in their field of specialization with peers, but increasingly must communicate with a broader audience.

Knowledge specialists often work with their peers internally in order to perform black-box services for clients. In addition, they increasingly communicate with their peers at client organizations in knowledge sharing and transfer. Clearly, some knowledge specialists have the skills necessary to communicate their knowledge effectively to nonspecialist clients, and in any case professional service firms should specifically focus on developing the knowledge communication skills of their knowledge specialists. However, where knowledge transfer is required in a broader context, specialists may need to work with others to help communicate their knowledge effectively.

## Knowledge Customizer

The fourth major role in knowledge relationships is that of knowledge customizer. This role comprises two related functions: customizing information and knowledge for the specific requirements of the client and communicating that knowledge effectively. As noted in Chapter 3, the customization of information is one of the most highly valued activities. It includes filtering, synthesizing, and presenting information so that it is directly relevant to the client. Professional service firms generate an enormous amount of high-value information and knowledge. However, the final step of customizing that base of knowledge to meet the client's specific situation arguably adds the greatest value.

Effectively performing the role of knowledge customization requires in-depth knowledge of the client, including what information and knowledge adds the greatest value, the client's decision-making processes and capabilities, and the cognitive preferences of key individuals in the client group. The role is often nominally a "sales" function, which is largely consumed by customizing and packaging specialist knowledge to make it most useful to clients.

With its large global auditing and consulting clients, Ernst & Young suggests to the client that it incorporate the role of "knowledge steward" on the consulting team. This person is based at the client, and his or her sole function is to understand the state of the client's industry and its competitors, tap Ernst & Young's resources in the field, compile this input in a usable format, and provide it to the appropriate people in the client group. The role is commonly taken by a senior team member, and is rotated every few months, though usually supported by dedicated resources at Ernst & Young. This is largely a role of knowledge customization, combining adding value to information mainly by customizing it to a single client and tailoring communication to give the greatest value for the specific audience.

Swiss financial institution UBS is one of the five largest banks in the world by market capitalization. Its private banking division is the largest operation of its kind worldwide, holding over $400 billion of the assets of high-net-worth individuals. The investment banking arm of UBS generates an enormous base of knowledge and recommendations on investments in international financial markets for its corporate and institutional client base. These are customized for each institutional client by the institutional sales team, which knows their clients' interests and investment parameters. UBS's research is designed for institutions, however, and is often not appropriate or directly useful for its private banking clients.

The UBS private banking group has instituted an Active Advisory Team (AAT), which adapts the investment banking arm's research to make it relevant for its own client base of high-net-worth individuals. In turn, each private banking relationship manager again tailors the research further to provide directly applicable knowledge and advice for their individual clients. The AAT function is a pure example of the role of knowledge customizer, taking existing knowledge and customizing it for a specific market segment.

## Portfolio Sales Model

Another example of the knowledge customizer role is in the relationships of financial market sales and research groups of investment banks with their portfolio manager clients, illustrated in Figure 8–1. Here the knowledge specialist role is represented by the research function, while different aspects of the sales function can be equated to the roles of relationship coordinator and knowledge customizer.

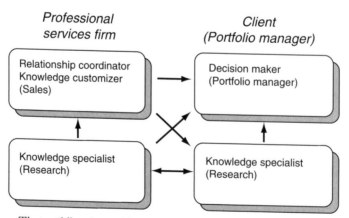

FIGURE 8–1    *The portfolio sales model of relationship management.* Copyright © 2004 Advanced Human Technologies. Reprinted with permission.

The relationship coordinator, who is effectively the relationship manager for the overall account, coordinates the array of specialists available within the firm, ranging from bond analysts to equity underwriters. The large investment banks are prototypical virtual organizations, with fluid movement of resources that must be brought together to be applied to specific client issues.

Within each product area, a salesperson will have responsibility for servicing the client. Often the most important function of the salespeople is that of knowledge customization. They take the more general research generated by the analysts and adapt it so that it adds value to their clients, for example by being formulated as specific recommendations relevant to their current portfolios. In addition, they will monitor available sources of information in order to filter and customize it to provide value to their client base.

## Senior and Junior Roles

There is an important distinction in knowledge relationship management between senior and junior staff. The most commonly heard criticism of professional service firms is that the senior "rainmakers" who secure and close the business are never seen again, and junior staff are allocated to execute the project. In a knowledge transfer context, clients note that the juniors — frequently fresh out of business school or other postgraduate studies — may have a lot of process knowledge but very little industry-specific or other content knowledge they can transfer.

This does not mean that junior staff should not be involved in these projects. Indeed, as David Maister points out, profitability and staff development in professional service firms depend to a significant degree on not having senior staff perform work that junior staff can do.[5] It does mean that the roles of junior and senior staff in knowledge transfer projects must be well thought out. In most cases, senior professionals should perform the lead for each knowledge role, with junior members playing a supporting role.

## Client Knowledge Roles

Just as different knowledge relationship roles exist within professional service firms, there is a range of distinct roles in client organizations that relate to assimilating knowledge and value from suppliers. Understanding these roles and how they are structured in your clients is fundamental to designing an optimal approach to relationship management. To a large degree the client roles mirror the roles at the professional service firm.

The senior representative role on the client side is critical. Often clients nominate certain senior executives to be responsible for particular groups of professional service providers. They act as access points to the organization, but are usually not involved in the details of projects. They will play a key role in determining the style of the engagement.

An important group of roles is that of decision makers at the client organization. Adding value at the strategic decision-making level usually provides the greatest value in knowledge transfer, so that having the richest possible interaction with this group is very important. The senior representative — although often also a decision maker — can act as a filter to the decision-making group, which can either impede or facilitate effective knowledge transfer at this level. Line decision makers are often accessed in groups, or through information channels including electronic media. Service providers usually have ongoing access to portfolio decision makers, and can focus on them as individuals, as well as considering them as participants in portfolio management committees.

In project-based engagements, there will often be a project manager on the client side, who is the counterpart of the project manager or relationship coordinator at the service provider. In a similar way, client knowledge specialists often play important roles, mirroring those at the professional service firm. In knowledge transfer the knowledge specialists commonly prefer to deal with other specialists, and can have little patience for nonspecialists. Another important role is that of knowledge gatekeeper, as discussed earlier. This role can be played by the same people in any of the roles mentioned above, notably the senior representative and project manager, though there can also be other more junior gatekeeper roles that are relevant in ongoing interactions.

## MODELS OF RELATIONSHIP MANAGEMENT

There are many possible models for relationship management. In designing relationship structures, it is very useful to start from the intent of building knowledge-based relationships. Different models can be created by using diverse approaches to how the four primary knowledge relationship roles combine and relate. These knowledge roles can be woven together in many different ways, each of which is appropriate at different stages of the relationship development process.

### Guru Model

In the guru model, most high-value client contact is concentrated on an individual or small number of individuals, as represented in Figure 8–2.[6] They play the roles of senior representative, knowledge specialist, and large parts of the relationship coordinator and knowledge customizer roles. In reality, as much as possible of the supporting work behind each of these roles is performed by more junior staff. However, client contact is largely channeled through the "guru," who can command premium prices for his or her time, and justify the very high support levels required. The ratio of support staff to partners is often substantially higher in the guru model than in a typical professional service firm. Examples of the guru model in a standalone firm include the professional service firms run by high-profile consultants, such as Gary Hamel's Strategos or Robert Kaplan and David Norton's BSCol.

This model also represents the reality of the manner in which many professional services engagements begin, and of how they are run over

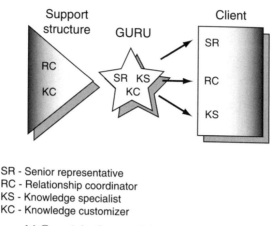

SR - Senior representative
RC - Relationship coordinator
KS - Knowledge specialist
KC - Knowledge customizer

FIGURE 8–2    *Guru model.* Copyright © 2004 Advanced Human Technologies. Reprinted with permission.

the long term. It is often appropriate to begin to engage with clients using the guru model, as it establishes credibility and offers clarity to the client. However, it is all too common for the lead professional to act as a gatekeeper, failing to introduce new professionals from the firm and remaining as the primary contact for the client for all issues. This limits the scope of the relationship, keeps it vulnerable to executive changes, and usually places constraints on the ability to create superior value for the client.

## Expansion Model

In the expansion model, illustrated in Figure 8–3, contact begins to expand beyond the key contact at the firm. The relationship leader initiates contact with a more diverse range of people on the client side, and begins to introduce professionals and others from the firm. These may be support staff, junior professionals who are performing work, or professionals from other service lines or areas of practice.

The important issue is that this is specifically a transitional model, linking the guru model relationship to a more comprehensive firm-wide relationship. The expansion model does not represent a steady

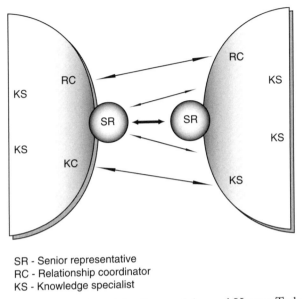

SR - Senior representative
RC - Relationship coordinator
KS - Knowledge specialist

FIGURE 8–3 *Expansion model.* Copyright © 2004 Advanced Human Technologies. Reprinted with permission.

state, but characterizes the process of making new client contacts that move the relationship toward the desired structure.

## Mirror Model

The mirror model for client relationships, as illustrated in Figure 8–4, was developed and refined by 3M (Minnesota Mining and Manufacturing), under the name of the diamond model.[7] The core principle is that people communicate directly with their peers, as opposed to communication being channeled through a relationship manager. Since the roles on the service provider side reflect those on the client side, this style of relationship structure can also be called the mirror model. Research shows that the ability of a firm to learn from another firm is determined by the similarity of their knowledge bases, organizational structures, and ways of thinking.[8] This suggests that the mirror model can be a particularly powerful model of relationship management.

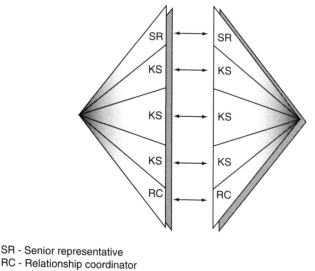

SR - Senior representative
RC - Relationship coordinator
KS - Knowledge specialist

FIGURE 8–4    *The mirror model.* Copyright © 2004 Advanced Human Technologies. Reprinted with permission.

In the mirror model, the senior representative liases with client senior management, knowledge specialists communicate with their peers at the client group, and the relationship coordinator or project manager works with the client project manager and organizes the rich array of client contact, as illustrated in Figure 8–4.[8] In this case, knowledge customizers or communicators will come into play when there is contact across groups between the service provider and client, for example, when specialists need to work with or communicate to client staff in other areas. A hallmark of this type of relationship is that there is often so much ongoing contact between different people that it cannot be managed in detail. Relationship coordinators can never know everything that is happening with a large client organization, and can only orchestrate resources on a broad basis, and when requested by specialists. This strategy usually results in far more dynamic relationships.

To establish a mirror model you need to identify the roles of executives on the client side that you will be dealing with, and the issues they will be dealing with. The first stage is to identify the people at your firm who are best suited to engaging with someone in this specific role, and preferably with the individual at the client. In some cases (as in Arc Worldwide; see "Arc Worldwide" following) the firm can actually specifically hire people who have experience in the particular job role and industry as the client executive they are dealing with, so as to maximize common understanding and the ability to work effectively together.

---

### Arc Worldwide

Arc Worldwide is a global integrated marketing firm headquartered in Chicago, and is part of the Publicis network. Since 2000, four companies merged to form Arc Worldwide: Arc, Frankel, iLeo, and Semaphore Partners (which was previously Giant Step, profiled in the first edition of this book). Arc uses a mirror relationship structure for its major projects, and in fact is even more focused on implementing this structure than it was previously, according to Arc's Director of Client Services Margaret Douglas. Developing interactive, broad-based marketing programs requires the participation of a diverse array of client functions, ranging across programming, design, strategy, planning, marketing, and more.

To address these issues, Arc forms joint project teams with the client. The overall project managers on the agency and client side work together in guiding the project, and every specialist group at Arc is allocated a counterpart at the client, to establish what is effectively two project teams linked in a mirror image. Arc has established teams that specialize in each of the areas that would be represented on the client side in projects, specifically in order to be able to mirror those roles. It has also found that hiring people who have experience in their clients' functions means they can communicate effectively with their peers, and explain online marketing issues by relating them to the client team's existing expertise.

*(Continued)*

This structure can also be valuable if there is insufficient communication within the client group, say between IT and marketing, as team members can help bridge those communication gaps, and if necessary provide cross-training so that each of the client teams is familiar with the other teams' issues. One of the shifts in making this structure even more relevant today is that most clients have developed significant capabilities in many of the relevant functions. Although they want work to be performed externally they also want to be able to maintain self-sufficiency after projects are developed. The pairing of client and Arc staff enables one-on-one training, as well as the development and hand-off of specific deliverables such as style guides and templates to enable these to be used effectively by clients. Projects begin with a one-day kick-off workshop, which includes role definitions on each side, how they match and work together, deliverables, resources required, and the joint work plan moving forward.

Because knowledge and skills transfer is often an explicit component of client deliverables, client training is embedded in project design. In addition to the one-on-one relationships in the mirror model and classroom training programs as required, projects may include what Arc executives describe as "co-mentoring," in which team members provide highly interactive guidance to the client on their expertise, and are simultaneously mentored by their client on its industry. The concept is introduced in the kick-off workshop. Part of the quarterly assessment for project managers relates to how successful they have been at "client mentoring."

Arc used to publish a glossary of interactive marketing terminology to ensure a common understanding of jargon between its staff and clients. It is now taking a more visual approach, creating pictorial representations of the project strategy, activities, and technologies. This is used with all people they interact with at the client, to form a common perspective and bridge communication from technologists through designers to business strategists. Online project rooms are implemented for each client, with open access on both sides. These are designed to provide visibility of projects across the client and the scope for general feedback and discussion on the work, as well as to host details of all project activities.

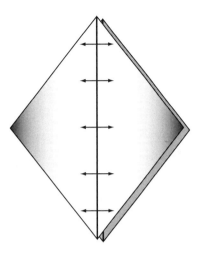

FIGURE 8–5   *Integration model.* Copyright © 2004
Advanced Human Technologies. Reprinted with
permission.

## Integration Model

The final relationship model is the integration model, shown in Figure 8–5, at which stage the boundaries between the firm and the client have blurred beyond recognition. It is not clear precisely where one company ends and the other begins, with shared project teams, staff reallocated for periods to the other firm, and usually joint contribution of resources, potentially including financial capital and equipment. This is where the client relationship becomes a true partnership, with each party working together to find ways to maximize value within a shared space. This can require redefinition of job roles to allow for reporting lines across organizations. In the case of the relationship between Transfield and the Shell refinery described in Chapter 1, performance reviews of staff are sometimes done by executives in the other company if the work done is substantially across organizational borders.

## Evolution of Relationship Models

In most cases the relationship models will progress through the four stages described above. It is not possible, for example, to begin a

TABLE 8–1   *Evolution of the relationship models.* Copyright © 2004 Advanced Human Technologies. Reprinted with permission.

| Relationship Stage | Relationship Model |
| --- | --- |
| Engaging | Guru |
| Aligning | Expansion |
| Deepening | Mirror |
| Partnering | Integration |

relationship with a mirror model style of engagement. The sets of individual relationships that make up a firm-wide relationship need to be formed over time, and built within a broader organizational context.

Chapter 1 introduced the four stages of relationship development: engaging, aligning, deepening, and partnering. These coincide with the four relationship models, as shown in Table 8–1.

The client should be clear from the beginning where the relationship is going. There should be discussion with the client and agreement from the outset on how the relationship will progress. As the relationship models progress, there should be no surprises for the client on how things are shifting and why.

The essence of the evolution of the relationship models over time is the staged introduction of new professionals into the relationship, and forming ties with new contacts at the client. For every professional introduced into the relationship, the client should be clear on why she is being introduced, how she creates value for the client, and her roles and responsibilities in the relationship team.

Not every client will progress through the relationship models to an integration model. This depends on both the client's interest in doing so and on the potential value of the client to the firm. For smaller clients, a guru model may well be appropriate, or there may be no reason to go beyond the expansion model, with a few contacts on each side. The investment in creating a mirror model is only justified when it is a highly valuable client. It is critical to allocate resources where they will yield a strong return.

## Designing Relationship Management Models

Ultimately all models are caricatures that cannot express the detailed shape of client interaction, and the range and variety of client organizations. Service providers must design approaches to their client relationships that stem from their understanding of how they add value to clients, and are flexible enough to be readily adapted for different clients.

Particularly when knowledge transfer is an explicit or implicit objective, considering knowledge roles of the service provider and the client can be very helpful in the design process. This provides a ready tool to map the allocation of responsibilities and who should be interacting with whom at the client group in order to maximize knowledge transfer, added value, and deeper relationships.

## Client Postings and Staff Exchanges

Since interaction and dialogue are the heart of knowledge transfer, what better way to develop rich knowledge transfer than either posting staff at the client's offices or having client staff work in your offices? It is fairly common practice among law firms to post staff at their major clients, sometimes only charging the client the salary of the lawyer rather than the usual hourly rate. This is an excellent example of the conjunction of rich two-way knowledge transfer and relationship development. The client learns both content and process knowledge through ongoing interaction over a period of months, while it builds a deep personal and business relationship and becomes far more inclined to choose that law firm over others it knows less well.

In any large project it is common for professional service firms to post staff at clients, however at computer services giant EDS effectively all professionals assigned to client projects are based at the client site. Some clients specifically ask their service providers for exchanges to promote knowledge transfer. Nicholas Applegate, an investment manager based in San Diego, California, which manages over $30 billion worldwide, has a formal analyst exchange program that brings analysts from the major stockbrokers that service it into its offices for a month at a time.[9]

## TECHNOLOGY IN RELATIONSHIP MANAGEMENT

The rapid rise in the use of technology in all client communication is fundamentally changing the dynamics of relationships, as I began to explore in Chapter 7. Communication with clients changes, and new service offerings become possible. However, there are also specific issues within the relationship management process. One of the most important of these is how to introduce new communication channels and technology-based offerings to clients. Another critical issue is how to implement internal systems that support effective relationship management.

### Introducing Online Channels to Clients

As firms introduce new online channels for client interaction and service delivery, there needs to be a very clear structure and process for introducing them to clients. A common example is an extranet that gives clients access to relevant documents and information from the firm. This may have been introduced by the professional firm, or in some cases requested by the client. The first objective is simply to make clients aware of the new channels and their possibilities. However, at least as important is having them used by clients in the ways you would like. The risk is that clients start to use new channels in ways that do not further your relationship objectives. In some cases, banks have introduced online foreign exchange trading services, substantially to increase efficiencies for smaller clients. However, larger clients have taken to the services in a big way, meaning that they speak far less frequently with the foreign exchange salespeople and the relationship starts to atrophy.

For any new channels, it should be the responsibility of the relationship manager to introduce the new channels to the clients. It is a mistake to let technical staff show your clients the systems, as their focus will be the systems' capabilities rather than how they should be used within the relationship.

Many firms now have the capabilities to roll out a customized extranet for clients virtually on demand. For instance, the 1,300-attorney firm Piper Rudnick Gray Cary and the United Kingdom arm of Deloitte both have systems whereby an extranet site can be set up for a client very rapidly, including a relevant structure, client logos, and permissions for internal staff and client executives to access information appropriately. A clear, streamlined process should be established to enable these sites to be set up with minimal effort and resources. In other cases, it is almost standard to provide the client with a workspace that allows professionals and client staff to gain visibility of the work process and share information as required.

One of the most important aspects of establishing these systems is setting up permissions for different parts of the system. If, for example, you are allowing your client to see the project management process, you will need to specify who at the client can have access to which information. In the case of Ernst & Young working with its advertising conglomerate audit client discussed in Chapter 7, at both the national and global level each individual at the client side had customized permissions to see the financial reporting information as it was consolidated back to the head office. Similarly, at the professional services firm there may be sensitive client information that should only be available to professionals who are specifically responsible for that domain. Significant thought needs to go into establishing a permissions system. There are often gray areas in what should be made visible. In general, in fostering knowledge-based relationships you should err on the side of showing clients more rather than less.

## Manpower

Manpower Inc. is the second largest employment services company in the world, in 2003 earning over $12 billion and placing 2.3 million workers on temporary assignments. It has recently diversified from its core business of providing temporary employees to move into outplacement, consulting, audit, compliance, and related employment services.[10]

Manpower has provided select clients since 1999 with a Virtual Account Management (VAM) system, which presents real-life stories about how Manpower has successfully worked with the client, as well as information on internal procedures for dealing with Manpower. In identifying and writing these stories for the client, Manpower wanted to make them relevant, useful, and interesting, without appearing to be obvious advertising. The VAM systems are designed specifically for each client, drawing on stories from that account. In addition, the "look and feel" of the site is tailored to fit into the client's intranet, and suit its corporate culture. These customized extranets require substantial resources from Manpower, so they are provided only to large national or global accounts, although the relationship benefits are sufficient to allow them to be currently free of charge to clients.

Manpower is a decentralized organization, with no attempt to restrict field contact with the client unless it prefers a more focused relationship style. One intention of the extranet sites is to make them as easy as possible for clients to identify and contact the appropriate manager or specialist at Manpower, so internal directories are provided on site. As the site is done in collaboration with the client, internal approval processes for hiring staff through Manpower are also posted.

One key aspect of the service is that it is based on stories, which is one of the most powerful ways of communicating knowledge. The stories represent real case studies from within the client organization, so they are perceived as directly relevant to users of the system. Account directors gather these stories by tapping the experiences of all of its representatives. Manpower's intention behind VAM was not only to add greater value to its clients but also to build partnership relationships and weave itself deeper into its clients' operations, which is reflected in the way the stories are gathered.

Manpower wherever possible works as a partner with its clients, rather than as a black-box provider of staff. To assist its initiatives, it has implemented an internal knowledge-sharing system called COGNIS, which is focused on making all of its client-facing executives aware of best practice across the firm, and connecting them to the people with the relevant experience. In one case, Manpower jointly developed and implemented an innovative program with the manufacturing plant of a major automotive company. The plant is located in a rural area, and the manufacturer was finding it difficult to find well-educated and skilled staff.

Manpower established a program in which it provided initial training to job seekers, rotated them for a year across the plant's operating functions, and then moved them into a customized internal mentorship program. After two years the client had the option of hiring the temporary staff into full-time positions, and elected to do so for 70 percent of the trainees. Relevant executives across Manpower's global operations were made aware of this case, among many other examples of innovative client work. The intention is for interested parties to contact the relevant executive directly, following certain rules of engagement, including first reading everything written on the case.

Since 1999, Manpower has run a "Global Learning Center," a virtual university providing over 3,600 online interactive courses to develop the skills of its temporary staff and clients' employees, including a wide range of business and technology skills delivered in multiple languages. Providing this training in an easy-to-access format means it not only adds greater value to its corporate clients by providing more skilled staff but also directly develops the skills and knowledge of its other customer base, which is its temporary staff. These courses are available free of charge to all internal and Manpower-registered temporary staff.

## Client Relationship Management Systems

The term *customer relationship management* (CRM), like many other management concepts, has been appropriated and debased by technology vendors and implementers. The practice of CRM arose primarily in retail and call-center environments, meaning that it requires significant adaptation to be applicable in the context of enduring corporate relationships in which high-value services are delivered.

For professional services firms, there are two important — and distinct — perspectives on systems to help them manage their client relationships. The first is that of contact management, which aligns most with the traditional view of CRM. This allows professionals and firms to capture information about key contacts at their clients and about communication they have had with different people at the firm. The second view is enabling relationship team collaboration. On the one hand, this allows client plans, strategies, and activities, as described in Chapter 6, to be captured and available to everyone in the team. It also provides a forum for exchange of information on client activities. This is described further in Chapter 9. Most firms focus on the first perspective of contact management, while fewer provide spaces for teams to work effectively together. Ideally, these two frames will be combined. This is often done by using portal technology to provide professionals with a client-specific view of communication and activities across the firm relating to a client. Several software vendors offer ways of integrating e-mail communication into these client views, so that all e-mail to and from the client is available in the one space, together with relevant documents.

Investment bank JPMorgan Chase has implemented an intensely customized version of CRM-vendor Siebel's system, which it calls "The Relationship Exchange." This is specifically designed to provide for each client — which are primarily complex global organizations — a comprehensive view of contact information, client communication, and service delivery activities. More than 10,000 bankers in over 50 countries use the system.

JPMorgan Chase's CRM was driven substantially by the recent merger between JPMorgan and Chase Manhattan, which resulted in disparate client databases. This was compounded by the fact that much client information was held on different systems across company divisions, and sometimes even down to departments or individuals. One institutional bank I have consulted to counted over 120 separate client information systems within its walls. This means that any professional firm endeavoring to implement "one view" of its clients will have a massive effort in integrating disparate systems. Not only that, but there will be substantial duplication of information, often in slightly different formats. Many organizations find that the "cleansing" of data required to create a single CRM system across the firm is so challenging that the entire effort is abandoned.

I believe one of the most under-addressed issues in CRM is having the systems directly enable value creation from the client's perspective. Systems need to be designed in order to customize information and facilitate knowledge transfer. To do this, CRM systems should include information about client decision-making processes, cognitive styles, culture, and other factors that will assist in effectively adding value with knowledge.

Even at many prestigious professional service firms, it is surprising how often the relationship manager does not know their clients' investment approval processes or other basic and extremely valuable information. Staff should be explicitly guided in developing on an ongoing basis richer information on their clients' individual and organizational propensities in assimilating knowledge, which will assist more effective knowledge transfer. Moreover, information that will allow automated customization of service delivery should be gathered. This requires starting with what information or processes you want to customize for the client and working backward to find out what information in what format you require to do this, and then proactively gathering this information.

## SUMMARY: FIRM-WIDE RELATIONSHIP MANAGEMENT

To create true firm-wide relationships with clients, an array of issues needs to be considered. A key challenge is institutionalizing knowledge transfer. Some of the key skills required to achieve this include managing the knowledge gatekeepers and implementing practical approaches to project handover.

Effective structuring of relationship management is based on defining the key knowledge roles at the professional services firm and the client, and structuring the relations between these in ways that allow interaction and knowledge exchange to flourish. In the course of developing client partnerships, professional are likely to lead their clients through the guru, expansion, mirror, and integration models of relationship structure. Throughout this process, keeping the client clear on the intent and detail of the progress of the relationship structures is critical.

Technology is beginning to play a key role in client relationships. Relationship leaders need to consider how to introduce technology into the relationship. Customer relationship management software is an increasingly important internal tool.

Following on studying relationship structures, we need to understand how the individuals involved in client work can collaborate to achieve optimal results. In Chapter 9, I will examine how relationship teams function, and the role of relationship leaders.

## NOTES

1   O'Hara-Devereaux and Johansen offer valuable frameworks and suggestions for bridging cultural gaps. See Mary O'Hara-Devereaux and Robert Johansen, *Global Work: Bridging Distance, Culture, and Time*, San Francisco: Jossey-Bass, 1994.

2   Gary Hamel, "Competition for Competence and Interpartner Learning within International Strategic Alliances," *Strategic Management Journal* 12, 1991, pp. 83–103.

3   Cohen and Levinthal discuss the role of gatekeepers in assimilating external knowledge. See Wesley M. Cohen and Daniel A. Levinthal, "Absorptive Capacity: A New Perspective on Learning and Innovation," *Administrative Science Quarterly* 35, 1990, pp. 128–152.

4   See, for example, Cohen and Levinthal (p. 133) or Leonard (p. 159).

5   Maister, Chapter 4.

6   The guru model was suggested by Göran Roos of Intellectual Capital Services, London, U.K.

7   From Stewart (1997).

[8]  Peter J. Lane and Michael Lubatkin, "Relative Absorptive Capacity and Interorganizational Learning," *Strategic Management Journal* 19, 1998, pp. 461–477.

[9]  "Nicholas Applegate: Where It's Research with a Sense of Urgency," *Investor Weekly*, December 14, 1998, p. 7.

[10]  Part of the information on Manpower can be found in Susan Elliott, "Manpower Creates Customer Loyalty through Shared 'Stories,' Information," *Knowledge Management in Practice*, no. 3, Houston, TX: American Productivity & Quality Center, 3rd Quarter, 1998.

# 9

# Leading Relationship Teams
## Creating Consistent Communication

**A**ny significant client relationship will entail a number of people at the firm who communicate with the client: sometimes dozens; sometimes as many as hundreds. The diversity of these client contact points creates both opportunities and challenges. More contact provides the potential for deeper client knowledge, greater value creation through the direct engagement of your knowledge specialists, and the ability to identify additional ways to create value for the client. Yet the reality of a diverse and distributed client relationship team is that communication is rarely optimal. Not only are these opportunities often neglected but ineffective teamwork can rapidly expose to the client your organizational weaknesses and lack of communication.

It is also important to remember that any professional firm of more than one person is predicated on being able to deliver the applied knowledge of diverse specialists to the client. If a corporate client is serviced by an executive from a firm of 10,000 professionals, the assumption is that the client can access all of the resources of the firm. If it cannot, it might as well go to a sole practitioner who is not burdened by the massive overheads of the large firm. The ability to build effective connections among the firm in order to be able to provide clients access to relevant knowledge is critical.

The reality is that knowledge specialists tend to identify most with their own discipline. The barriers between different segments of professional firms can be minimized, but rarely abolished. Unless firms are extremely specialized, there are almost always issues of meshing different professional cultures in creating effective internal communication.

In essence, the relationship team comprises everyone at the firm who has any contact with the client. Each professional has his or her own set of contacts at the client. Building effective communication and collaboration between the professionals on these relationship teams is at the heart of developing powerful knowledge-based relationships. However, it is also important to recognize that every individual at the client is implicitly part of a team that deals with your firm, the company's professional services provider. How they communicate internally — or fail to do so effectively — will be central to how you are able to engage with them and create value. There are three primary objectives for building communication and knowledge sharing within client relationship teams.

- *Consistent communication to client:* The client gets aligned messages from across its contacts at the firm, and understands the full scope of the firm's capabilities.
- *Deeper client knowledge:* The firm learns more about its client across its divisions, locations, and activities, including recognized and unrecognized opportunities to create value.
- *Client leadership:* The firm demonstrates better communication within its relationship team than there is between executives at the client, resulting in professional credibility and additional opportunities to create client value.

There are two possible situations when relationship teams deal with significant clients. If the members of your team communicate more effectively among themselves than the executives at your client do, you look great. You are able to tell client executives what is happening in other parts of their organization, to make introductions between them, and demonstrate that you work professionally and effectively. The other possibility is that client executives communicate better among themselves than your team members do, in which case your firm appears unprofessional, uncoordinated, and ineffective.

The ability of professional firms to consistently create teams that can achieve the previously mentioned objectives will be a key determinant of success. Building effective client relationship teams is at the heart of powerful knowledge-based relationships.

## RELATIONSHIP TEAM LEADERSHIP

Relationship teams require effective leadership to achieve their objectives. In almost every case, this leadership role needs to be allocated for each major client, and clearly established as a significant role within the firm. This relationship leadership role is dual facing. The relationship leader needs to provide leadership both internally to the relationship team and externally to the client, as illustrated in Figure 9–1.

The selection of the relationship team leader needs to be done with great care. Traditionally partnerships have required that all partners

FIGURE 9–1   *Dual-facing relationship leadership.* Copyright © 2004 Advanced Human Technologies. Reprinted with permission.

are capable of running large client relationships. However, an increasing number of firms are establishing two or more categories of partners, distinguishing between those that are good at client relationship management and those that excel at their domain expertise but are not as effective with clients. This distinction helps to avoid professionals ending up in roles to which they are not suited, to the detriment of the firm and the client. Very similar issues are at play in firms that are not partnerships.

Most commonly, when relationship leader roles are formalized the senior professionals who have had the most contact in the past with the clients are selected. In some cases this works best, as they have the greatest client knowledge and personal relationships. However, if they do not have the requisite aptitudes and attitudes that support relationship leadership they can block the development of a relationship. Relationship leaders need to embody the following four key qualities.

- *Strategic thinker:* Far too many professionals placed in a relationship leader role act simply in a maintenance role, performing client contact and service duties to maintain the current relationship. The relationship leader needs to be able to envisage the potential of the relationship, and creatively explore the many options that could allow it to continually deepen and progress.
- *Collaborative:* Having a gatekeeper as a relationship leader strongly limits value creation for both the firm and its client. A leader must be open in introducing new contacts from the firm to the client. The effectiveness of a relationship team depends on a high degree of collaboration. This attitude and behavior must be clearly and consistently demonstrated by the team leader.
- *Clear communicator:* The heart of any client/supplier relationship must be clear communication. Matching expectations on both sides of the engagement is essential to mutual happiness and success. The paramount responsibility

of relationship leaders is guiding and framing communication to and from their clients, so they must be effective at creating rich, unambiguous communication.

- *Effective influencer:* Relationship leaders will rarely have direct responsibility for all members of their relationship teams. As such, they must be effective at influencing team members and their supervisors, going beyond their formal responsibilities. Clearly the ability to influence is equally valuable in working with client executives.

There are many possible ways of defining the relationship leader role. However, it is critical that it be clearly defined and that everyone in the firm understands what the role does and does not entail. Beyond having primary responsibility for client communication, the leader is responsible for the relationship team, including forming and leading it. One of the important variables is whether the relationship leader role includes the "relationship coordinator" role described in Chapter 8. The relationship coordinator role is more involved with coordinating contact between organizations, identifying the right resources internally, and facilitating communication within the relationship team. This can be a relatively junior role. Where possible, the relationship leader should be able to delegate these coordination activities to someone else, in order to concentrate on the key leadership activities. In Chapter 12 I will cover key issues in skills training and personal development for relationship leaders.

Deutsche Bank, one of the world's largest financial institutions, has for some years had a relationship management program in place across its banking divisions. One of its priorities for the program is providing a clear definition of the relationship manager role. This is particularly important, in that he or she needs to bring together people from across various divisions and locations of the bank. The formal relationship management function until recently had not had a well-established history in the organization. Relationship managers are selected who understand and have access to the key client, are familiar with a broad range of the bank's products rather than simply one specialist area, and have the ability to work collaboratively both inside the bank and with the client.[1]


## TEAM FORMATION

Relationship teams are often formed by default, with new professionals brought in when clients request additional services, based on who has free time in their schedule. The formation of relationship teams should attract significant attention, as the right team will enable effective knowledge-based relationships.

The first issue is one of representation. Since one of the key objectives is to identify opportunities to create value for clients, it is important that every significant practice area of the firm be represented on the relationship team. If there is no current or forecast need for that practice area by the client, the team membership may in some cases entail as little as occasional updates on client activity. However, it is important that there be broad representation, in order to be able to recognize latent or emerging opportunities.

The team selection process is based on getting an effective fit between the team member, the team, and the client. The following are some of the key factors that need to be addressed in selecting a high-performance team.

- Specialist knowledge required
- Delivery skills required
- Industry knowledge
- Client culture
- Existing client contacts and chemistry
- Communication styles
- Team compatibility

There will always have to be compromises, particularly based on availability of the right professionals. However, the relationship leader must strive to bring together the best possible team, in which its members can respect one another, work effectively together, and bring together the expertise in the firm that is most relevant to the client.

## Personal Chemistry

As knowledge-based relationships require rich, dynamic interaction between people, how well individuals interact and understand each other is an important factor. The personal chemistry between people can make a significant difference to the business results achieved. Many professional service firms allocate clients to relationship managers specifically on the basis of how good their chemistry is with the key contact at the client. Chapter 10 examines how contrasting rather than matching personality styles can be valuable in knowledge creation. However, in relationship team selection the ability to communicate effectively and to build a relationship of personal trust with key client executives and other team members is a more important factor.

## TEAM COMMUNICATION AND KNOWLEDGE SHARING

Effective communication and knowledge sharing is at the heart of a relationship team being able to achieve its key objectives of consistent client communication, deeper client knowledge, and client leadership. It is one of the most important responsibilities of the relationship leader to create the environment and processes that enable this. This begins by helping the entire team to gain clarity on their objectives. Certainly this includes the group's objectives for the client and any specific projects. However, it also requires the relationship leader to work with all team members to help them understand how working within this client team aligns with and supports their personal career objectives. This is a critical aspect of building collaborative behaviors.

## EFFECTIVE KNOWLEDGE SHARING

One of the most important aspects of knowledge-based relationships is getting effective knowledge sharing between relationship team members. The primary knowledge that needs to be shared is about the client organization, all client contacts and activities, and any resources or expertise in any other parts of the firm — or beyond — that could be of value to the client. The microcosm of the relationship team reflects the same issues of knowledge management across the enterprise. However, as the team is part of the organization it depends on the organization's existing capabilities. In Chapter 6 you saw how strategy, structure, processes, skills, and culture need to be aligned in order for a firm to progress its client relationship capabilities. However effective a relationship team and its leader, it will be extremely difficult to achieve effective knowledge sharing without a company culture that supports it.

Meetings are a critical element to knowledge sharing in the team. Below I discuss in more detail some of the key team meetings and how to run these. In fact, an enormous amount is possible simply in getting clear definition of roles and responsibilities within the relationship team. If each individual is clear on what his or her responsibilities are for knowledge sharing, and how to go about these, this is a very solid foundation.

Most firms have made some attempt to implement customer relationship management (CRM) systems over the last years, with fewer successes than failures. Traditional CRM systems are usually glorified contact managers, providing information on individuals and firms and to the degree they can be captured, any interactions with them. These types of systems are definitely valuable if implemented well, but are not oriented to relationship teams, which are the heart of high-value client management. What is required are systems focused on individual client organizations that provide a consolidated view of what is known about the client and all activities and communication. In effect, these are portals that provide single-point access to these resources.

Some implementations allow all e-mail communication to and from the client from anyone in the firm to be seen in one screen (subject to confidentiality restrictions).

This client portal should also contain the current team agenda and responsibilities, so that these are visible and can be readily tracked. Usually it will also provide access to any specific client projects, though in many cases it is important to distinguish between projects and the overall relationship.

One approach that can be very useful is implementing a regular client update. The relationship leader will usually delegate to someone in the team the responsibility of producing a regular update to all team members, that consolidates all relevant developments with the client. This will include the more obvious elements such as significant project activity, major client meetings, and new contacts at the client and professionals introduced from the firm. However, it should also include more general knowledge gleaned from the client that could disclose opportunities, and influence client strategy. Examples are any projects under consideration, emerging strategic issues for the client, and any other possible signals of opportunities, such as industry or regulatory developments, concerns or issues expressed by the client, observed deficiencies, and so on. Team members should be instructed to forward any relevant information to the person responsible for compiling the update. This is usually far more efficient than sharing this in face-to-face meetings. One major law firm that has a strong relationship with a global investment bank, including over 30 partners in the relationship team, compiles a regular newsletter just for key executives working on the relationship. As the client is highly decentralized, the newsletter allows the partners to know what is happening across the relationship, and to identify opportunities for additional services.

It is not just the relationship team members that need to have clarity on the team members and activities. The client should also be kept informed about the relationship team, its members, their responsibilities, and reporting lines. Client executives should know who they should speak to at the firm about specific issues.

It is critical to keep the client fully informed about changes to the relationship team. The client should not find out team changes by accident, but be kept informed as there are any changes. This is particularly important in the case of the relationship leader. One audit firm engaged in succession planning for the retirement of the relationship leader of one of its major clients, finally selecting a distinguished partner for the role. When the client was informed that its relationship partner was leaving the firm and being replaced, senior client executives expressed their very strong displeasure at being kept in the dark and not consulted about the transition and the appropriate successor. The relationship was jeopardized, whereas keeping the client informed through the process could have had a strong positive impact on the relationship and might have helped to transition it from an individual focus to a true organization-wide relationship.

Buckman Laboratories, a specialty chemicals company based in Memphis, Tennessee, with global operations, has established relationship teams to deal with its top-tier clients. While it provides products to its clients, a significant aspect of its market positioning and differentiation is in providing knowledge-based services to its clients, and it has on a number of occasions been named in the annual Most Admired Knowledge Enterprise (MAKE) awards. The company has established teams for its top 17 existing or desired clients, with team leaders named for each target company. Based on Buckman's experience in successfully building knowledge sharing in the company, each team is asked to establish a team charter. Team leaders are provided with a standard charter form, and lead the team through a process of defining their mission, expectations, scope, goals, deliverables, resources required, and each team member's responsibilities.

Teams are required to meet at least five times each year, though most meet more often. Since all teams are global, where necessary this is done by voice, usually eschewing web conferencing because the Internet is not always available to salespeople who are always on the move. Information updates are done before the calls, and any issues discussed in the meeting that help identify possibilities for team members to help each other are dealt with one on one after the call. Buckman has rolled out an intensive four-day training program covering the entire suite of relationship tools Buckman has developed over the last years, including the After Action Review to gather lessons learned in client projects, and the Transition Workshop to assist clients in switching from their existing supplier to Buckman.[2] Staff must have completed the training program in order to join a global team, which is perceived as a prestigious role in the organization.

## RUNNING KEY RELATIONSHIP TEAM MEETINGS

Throughout the relationship process, there are a range of key relationship team meetings that enable the effective progress of the relationship. It is the responsibility of the relationship leader to run these meetings. Acquiring the necessary skills to do so should be a key part of the development of professionals as they mature to take on leadership roles. There are a number of relationship team meetings through the various stages of the relationship development process. Some of the key meetings are shown in Figure 9–2.

### Launching and Managing Relationship Teams

The most important step for the relationship team process is the launch meeting. Whenever there is a formal relationship team, there should be a launch meeting, with as many people as possible physically present. The regularity of subsequent face-to-face meetings will depend on the importance of the client, but the launch meeting is critical in achieving team alignment.

A key element of the launch meeting is for all team members to gain clarity on their roles and responsibilities in the team. There are four key responsibilities that should be defined for all members.

- *Professional and project activities:* Activities within the client engagement

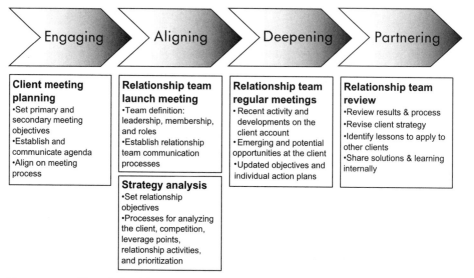

FIGURE 9–2   *Key relationship team meetings in the relationship development process.*
Copyright © 2004 Advanced Human Technologies. Reprinted with permission.

- *Client communication:* Primary client contacts, and what is communicated with whom at the client
- *Relationship action items:* Action items from the overall client relationship strategy agenda
- *Internal communication:* What is communicated, and how and to whom, within the relationship team

These responsibilities do not need to be defined in minute detail for each individual. However, each member should have a clear understanding of their role within the team.

The relationship leader also needs to use the relationship team launch meeting to establish the team's collaboration and communication processes. As discussed above, there are no hard and fast rules on how the team should communicate. Every relationship and team will be different, and require an approach that balances effective communication with the investment of time and resources required. The intention is absolutely not to tie professionals up in meetings for all their productive time, but only to enable the communication that allows relationships to be optimized. One of the key choices is how regularly teams meet, either face-to-face or online. This is unlikely to be less than semiannually, and for some major clients this could be as often as weekly.

These regular team meetings need to be run to be as effective as possible. This is the responsibility of the team leaders, whether they run it themselves or delegate it to an expert facilitator. If you have been to many team meetings in which everyone at the table in turn says what they have been doing with the client, you will appreciate that this is not usually very efficient. As much as possible should be shared before the meeting in briefing documents, specific issues should be dealt with by subgroups, and the plenary team meeting should be focused on highlights and joint decision making. In the case of substantial client projects with dedicated resources, however, knowledge sharing and problem solving are critical issues, and may merit more open-ended exploration.

Either during the team launch meeting, or for significant clients possibly as a separate meeting, the team needs to develop the client strategy. The client strategy development process is described in detail in Chapter 6. The key issue here is that the team should be involved in the development of the strategy. Not only will the team members have a greater commitment to the strategy if they are involved in the formulation process but also they often have valuable insights or perspectives on the client and its key executives that can be applied in building a solid client strategy.

Ross, Dixon & Bell, a 100-lawyer firm with four offices across the United States, wanted to help its attorneys to understand its clients' businesses better. In preparing for an offsite meeting for the firm, the marketing department found that Harvard Business School had written a case study on the strategic issues of one of its long-lasting clients. This triggered the idea of writing its own case studies on its key clients. This led to the development of what it calls its "Lawyer's

Business School." Groups of lawyers are given live client case studies to read beforehand, and then at the retreat they work together to discuss and analyze the client's key issues. The teams were constructed across practice groups and offices, specifically designed to identify potential opportunities at these major clients. In the months following the offsite meeting, revenues from two of the clients that had been covered in the exercise had risen substantially.[3]

## Critical Client Meetings

In the same way that there are a number of internal meetings that need to be run in the process of developing client relationships, there are critical client meetings at each stage of the relationship development process, as illustrated in Figure 9–3.

One of the most important client meetings in developing knowledge-based relationships is that of strategy alignment. This involves sharing your strategy with the client as a key element of building rich two-way communication and aligning the two companies' objectives. Professionals are often reluctant to share their strategies with their clients, but those I know who have done so have invariably experi-

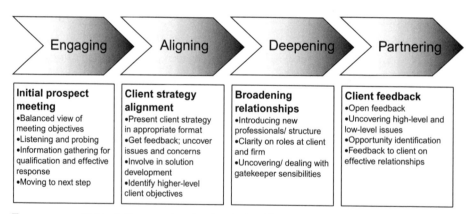

FIGURE 9–3  *Critical client meetings in the relationship development process.* Copyright © 2004 Advanced Human Technologies. Reprinted with permission.

enced positive results. In one case, a law firm was working with a major telecommunications company. After developing a clear client strategy, including objectives, responsibilities, and action items, it shared the strategy in full with its client.

The firm was in fact the number two provider of legal services to the telecom company, and it recognized its client's extremely strong ties to its number one law firm, including the general counsel being an alumnus of that firm. As such, its strategic objectives for the client included an increase in client spending, but not supplanting its competitor as the number one law firm. This recognition of relationship realities made the client far more comfortable in extending and broadening its relationship. In this case, client preferences were a sensitive issue, and difficult to discuss directly, but in presenting a strategy document to the client this paved the way for broaching the topic in the context of their own relationship.

Clearly there will sometimes be limits to what you share with clients, for example sometimes on pricing or competitive strategies. However, in most cases it is better to err on the side of sharing more with clients. Gaining deeper client knowledge is central to building knowledge-based relationships, and the more you share with clients the more likely they are to be open with you. In some cases, sharing your client strategy with client executives can be the trigger point that will suddenly deepen the relationship.

Another key client meeting is broadening relationships, particularly in asking client contacts for internal referrals. This is an essential action in extending relationships, yet many professionals are uncomfortable with this process, and it is important for them to become more practiced in this type of meeting.

Indeed, identifying these meetings provides an effective focus for skill development for relationship leaders. One very effective approach is to use professional actors to allow executives to rehearse specific client meetings. If well briefed, the actors can create very realistic situations in which executives can gain familiarity and comfort with what is likely to work or not work in a real-life context.

## CSC Value Delivery Teams

Computer Sciences Corporation (CSC) is one of the world's largest technology consulting and outsourcing firms, employing 91,000 employees in 80 countries. In order to deliver projects for its clients, it brings together teams from multiple operational divisions. Specifically to address the challenges of dealing with highly complex projects with its largest clients, which are often multinational, CSC has developed what it calls a value delivery team (VDT) methodology. There are three key functions CSC includes in its major client projects: client management, work management, and solution management. Executives with specific roles and backgrounds are allocated on a full-time basis to each function, depending on the type of engagement. An account executive is usually responsible for client management. A program manager will often cover work management, and in outsourcing projects a service delivery manager may also be involved.

The third element, which is part of what makes CSC's approach distinctive, is that of solution architect. This role is responsible for addressing the complexities of the project and reducing uncertainty in the structure of the engagement, before handing it over to technical specialists. One of the key elements of the VDT is that reporting responsibilities shift to the account executive. Usually program managers, service delivery managers, and solution architects report within their operational divisions. However, when they are allocated to a VDT on a full-time basis their primary reporting line is to the team account executive.

The VDT methodology is founded on a training program that potential VDT members must attend. This begins with web-based learning to cover key concepts, and then shifts into a complex three-day case study involving all VDT members. The case study was created through extensive research on critical project and team issues in CSC's U.S., European, and Australian operations, identifying challenging real-life situations that tend to recur in client engagements. It positions the participants in a hypothetical client engagement that covers all of CSC's major service lines, six months into the project when problems have arisen. The case study participants must work together to get the engagement back on track.

One of the early issues covered in the workshop is gaining clarity in defining team roles and their intersection. As the team works together the members are observed by coaches, and given very open feedback at the end on how they have performed. Based on how the team has worked together in the case study, a final team is selected for the client engagement. Since team definition is required early in client engagements, the team workshop may be run during contract negotiations or even earlier. CSC has also used the VDT approach to develop the cohesiveness of existing teams.

## BUILDING CLIENT FEEDBACK LOOPS

One of the relationship functions performed poorly by many professional firms is gaining and applying client feedback. Many firms have instituted surveys of their major clients. However, these are a very narrow and ineffective channel to get client input. These are often essentially satisfaction surveys, which denote how happy the clients are with various aspects of the service they receive. This is useful insofar as it allows professionals to identify problem areas, as long as the client is honest in its responses. However, the survey results usually give no information about what to do to remedy the situation.

Client feedback processes should be embedded into every major client relationship. This will include regular invitations for specific and open-ended feedback during the engagement process. It will also include dedicated feedback sessions, which are purely for clients to express their views on the relationship and the service they are receiving. Firms should have an institutionalized feedback process that provides clear guidelines on how feedback should be gathered from major clients. However, it should have significant flexibility in its implementation, so that the approaches that will work best with the client and relationship leader can be implemented. In many cases the relationship leader, together with key team members, will meet with client executives for a specific client feedback session.

One of the challenges with this approach is that the client will often not be forthcoming with their feedback, especially with regard to the relationship leader. It is important to acknowledge that clients themselves are often uncomfortable giving negative feedback, and even given the opportunity they may not do so if the conditions are not right. As such, some firms have implemented the policy of feedback sessions being conducted by a partner or senior executive who has no direct responsibilities for the relationship. This allows clients to be more open in their feedback. In other cases third-party consultants are engaged to gather feedback from clients. This can sometimes result in less constrained feedback. However, the intermediation through another party can result in loss of clarity and relevance in the feedback.

The most important aspect of client feedback is that the client sees that action is taken. The loop must be closed, so that feedback is not just acted on, but clients can see demonstrable action and results. Client feedback can be applied in two ways: specifically within the client relationship or more broadly across the organization, if warranted. In either case, it is essential to communicate back to the client on the practical response to its feedback, preferably in such a way that the client can observe a difference in how it is serviced.

Feedback should be a prime source of innovation. All client feedback should be analyzed to see whether there are ways in which the firm can enhance its processes. In addition, formal feedback should be a key source of customization. In Chapter 1 you saw how customization of client communication and service delivery is one of the four key elements of the virtuous circle of knowledge-based relationships. Deeper client knowledge to enable that customization should be gathered at all points in the relationship. However, formal feedback sessions should be designed specifically to gather information that will allow you to customize your relationship efforts further.

Another key issue is capturing the knowledge gained from the client. Good internal knowledge management practices, including providing the ability and motivation to capture and store valuable information, are necessary for this process to occur. However, there is rarely a specific focus on capturing knowledge from the client. Better firms have some type of "lessons learned" system for each engagement, but it is often not structured to identify feedback for specific purposes.

## SUMMARY: LEADING RELATIONSHIP TEAMS

Significant client relationships usually involve many professionals who have contact with the client. These constitute a relationship team, which needs to communicate and collaborate effectively to provide a consistent interface to the client, and continuously build deeper client knowledge.

The dual-facing role of relationship leader is critical, both in leading the client into richer, knowledge-based relationships and in leading the relationship team into cohesive and effective behaviors. The relationship leader needs to take the relationship team through a series of key team meetings and processes, including relationship team launch, strategy setting, and applying client feedback.

The ultimate intention of building effective relationship structures and relationship teams is to engage more deeply with the client. In Chapter 10 I will look at how professional services firms and their clients can move toward the co-creation of knowledge and value.

## NOTES

[1] Peter Mathias and Juergen Fitschen, "Managing Global Client Relationships at Deutsche Bank: Management Discipline, Process and Technology," *Focus: Europe*, vol. 1, no. 1, 1st Quarter, 2001, pp. 1–5.

[2] Ross Dawson, *Living Networks: Leading Your Company, Customers, and Partners in the Hyper-Connected Economy*, Upper Saddle River, NJ: Financial Times/Prentice-Hall, 2002, pp. 70–72.

[3] Paul Vitrano and Helen Bertelli, "B-School for Lawyers," *Legal Times*, May 10, 2004, p. 24.

# 10

# Cocreating Value
## Building Partnerships and Developing Knowledge

The logical outcome of knowledge-based relationships is the creation of true partnerships, in which the client and the professional firm bring together their unique knowledge and capabilities to generate value. As you saw in Chapter 1, relationship leadership is all about shifting your clients' perspective on the relationship to one in which you can create a partnership. One of the key aspects of this type of relationship is knowledge cocreation, in which new knowledge and capabilities are jointly generated in the course of the engagement.

## BUSINESS MODELS FOR COCREATING VALUE

Creating value jointly with clients does not fit the traditional business models of most professional services firms. The direction of the flow of value between clients and suppliers has already blurred substantially over the last decade, and the explicit cocreation of value blurs it yet further.[1] This evolution means changes are often required in ways of thinking about relationships, and the business models on which they are founded. Value cocreation is in many cases a shift toward fundamentally different conceptions of the nature of business and value in professional services relationships.

Knowledge Cocreation

A significant aspect of client partnerships in professional services is the cocreation of knowledge. In this case, each party allocates resources to a project, and expects to generate valuable knowledge as an outcome. This makes the relationship far closer to a collaboration or alliance than a traditional client/provider relationship, and the client could ask why it should pay for this nature of collaboration.

There are a number of possible answers. Commonly a large part of the value created by the service provider stems from its expertise in structuring the collaboration so that it produces valuable results for the client. However, it often also brings content knowledge to the project, taking its value creation to a higher level. In the professional services models described in Chapter 2, "outcome facilitation" describes a firm that helps a client develop useful knowledge for itself. However, if the professional firm has deep content expertise that is complementary to that of its clients, it shifts to the "collaborative solutions" positioning, which is essential for the true cocreation of value.

In many cases the nature of the knowledge on the client and provider side is substantially different, which results in the value of the collaboration. Some industries well suited to knowledge cocreation bring together process knowledge from the professional firm regarding how best to create valuable outputs, company and industry-specific knowledge from the client, and creativity from both sides. Examples of disciplines in which these types of structures are common include advertising, engineering, design, and strategy consulting. However, these approaches can equally well be applied in other industries.

Clearly, the exercise must add value to the client over and above what it could achieve on its own. The ability of the professional firm to achieve added value gives it the right to receive payment for what could be seen as a collaboration. If the service provider obviously also receives substantial value from the project in its own right, the client may be justified in trying to renegotiate the relationship to more of an alliance-based approach.

## Client Relationships in Value Cocreation

Value cocreation suggests a nontraditional, more symmetrical client relationship. Mutual trust is essential for these types of partnerships, so they most commonly evolve over time from existing professional service relationships. As you saw in Chapters 1 and 6, much of the design of relationship development is focused on moving toward partnerships with those clients that merit it. In these cases, the relationship structure is likely to shift from that of a classic client/supplier relationship in which services are rendered and fees charged to different approaches such as multiclient projects or even establishing joint ventures as a vehicle for collaboration. Some other approaches to business models for collaborative relationships are given in Chapter 11, from the perspective of pricing knowledge.

## Multiclient Projects

It is increasingly common for professional firms to work with a group of clients on a single knowledge-based project. The genesis of this structure was found in independent think tanks that sought funding for research projects from a range of organizations that would benefit from the likely outcomes of the research. The most common format for multiclient projects remains very similar, with a fixed contribution allowing entry into the syndicate. The members participate throughout the process of knowledge creation, receive customized briefings and reports of the findings, and usually join in facilitated sessions that bring together all members. One example is Babson College's Working Knowledge Group, which brings together an array of companies to participate in research in knowledge management. The Institute for the Future in Menlo Park, California, runs a variety of multiclient engagements.

In the multiclient project model, commonly much of the knowledge generation is expected to come from the professional firm or research institute. However, there is also usually substantial input from the participants, especially in group interaction. The value of a group of complementary organizations working together on an issue of common relevance can be immense. Again, part of the value the supplier provides lies in its skills in structuring and guiding knowledge flow and development, as well as its relationships, which allow a diverse group of organizations to be brought together in a mutually beneficial format.

One important issue is whether the clients involved in the project are competitors. Often multiclient projects are designed to have only one client from any given industry, although with careful design projects can provide opportunities for competitors to be involved. Global Business Network has many clients in industries such as energy and chemicals, and finds that much of the value perceived by clients is specifically in providing a forum in which they can engage in constructive interaction with real or potential competitors.

---

### Mother

London and New York-based advertising agency Mother is commonly referred to as "the world's hottest ad agency."[2] Founded in London in 1996, it has grown to 125 staff while turning away many potential clients, and has won the coveted U.K. "Agency of the Year" in both 2001 and 2002, as well as racking up over 50 creative awards. Clients include an array of major brands such as Coca-Cola, Unilever, Orange, and Boots. In the first five years of its existence it won 14 of the 16 pitches in which it participated, with many other clients simply electing to work with them rather than go through an initial beauty parade. The chief executive of Egg, the world's largest pure online bank, credited its Mother-created advertising campaign for creating 205,000 new customers in the space of three months.[3]

Mother has implemented what is for the advertising industry a very unusual approach to working with its clients, which allows it to engage in highly collaborative relationships. There are no account executives (known in the industry as "suits"), and thus clients work directly with creative and other agency staff. There are three primary roles that liaise directly with the client. Strategists are responsible for achieving business outcomes for both the firm and client. While they will often have the most contact with the senior client executives, they do not have formal responsibility for the relationship, which is distributed across all team members working on the client project. Creatives play their traditional role of generating creative ideas for the client, though usually engaging directly with the client rather than working in the background. The third key role is that of "mothers," who are senior executives responsible for logistics and ensuring that all things are done on schedule. In addition, production staff deal directly with clients whenever necessary. The intention of the approach is ensuring there is no middleman and that at all times there is direct communication from relevant agency staff to the client as best suits the client, the project, and the desired outcomes.

In the advertising industry, account executives are usually the liaison between the client and the creatives. Mother gets the creatives involved from the outset, and actively engaged with the client through the creative process. Interaction usually begins by defining the client's problem, and ensuring it can be addressed with a communications solution. The intention is then to bring together the unique expertise of Mother in generating useful creative ideas and the client's knowledge of its business and industry in order to create a solution. The premise of Mother's work with clients is that it is okay to be wrong, says partner Andy Bellass. Accepting that failure is the route to success frees up creativity and the ability of clients to participate actively in selecting and refining the ideas that will solve its business problems. This requires putting the issue and potential solution at the center of discussion, and bringing together a focused team of experienced people from both Mother and the client to explore potential solutions, combine the best of these, and generate a final product that meets the client's objectives. Mother eschews creating a "brief," which intermediates between the account planner and the creative staff, preferring direct communication and a model of cocreation.

## Establishing Joint Ventures

The ultimate implementation of knowledge cocreation is establishing a joint venture or alliance to develop and exploit knowledge. This puts both partners on a more obviously equal footing, and addresses the issue of remuneration in line with the value of contribution, as discussed in Chapter 11.

Universities tend to prefer licensing the technology they develop rather than entering into partnerships, although Stanford University has taken innovative approaches for developments that merit the effort. When an inventor at Stanford developed a new music synthesis technology, it created a trademark, Sondius, which would have a life and revenue potential beyond the patent expiration for the technology. Stanford then established a partnership with Yamaha, combining the music company's intellectual property with its own to form a portfolio of more than 400 patents. A range of products developed using the joint intellectual property has been released onto the market.[4]

## DESIGNING KNOWLEDGE COCREATION

As you have seen, the expertise in the *process* of cocreating knowledge usually comes from the professional services provider. Having responsibility for this justifies the fees charged by the service provider. Effective management of the process of knowledge cocreation depends on understanding the issues in designing processes for working with knowledge collaboratively, and then managing the ongoing dynamics of the process. I will first cover some of the structures of knowledge creation that will help us design successful processes, and then examine the dynamics of cocreation.

## Knowledge Development Loops

The development of knowledge is an iterative process, in which experience and lessons provide a basis for deeper understandings in

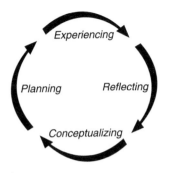

FIGURE 10–1  *The learning cycle.*

ongoing feedback loops. A loop-based framework for understanding learning and knowledge development was developed by David Kolb. This still provides a foundation for much of the field of adult learning.

Kolb suggested that there are four phases in the learning cycle. The first is experiencing, which stems from doing an activity. The second phase is engaging in reflection on the experience, which is followed by conceptualization, through interpreting the events and the relationships between them. The fourth stage is the planning of further action based on the learning, which brings it full circle back to engagement in further experience.[5] The entire process is illustrated in Figure 10–1.

Knowledge feedback loops are at the heart of knowledge creation within organizations. Although knowledge creation is by its nature iterative, how the loop functions will be different between organizations. Which part of the cycle is emphasized and the linkages between each phase will vary substantially. Understanding the nature and detail of this feedback loop provides insights into how to structure all knowledge-based work with clients.

Since knowledge cocreation involves at least two organizations, it is very valuable to understand the dynamics of the knowledge creation loop, not only within the client but also within your own organization. Figure 10–2 shows how the knowledge development loop within two individual organizations can be combined to become a shared

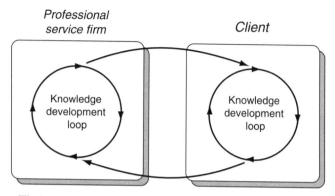

FIGURE 10–2  *The knowledge development loop within and between organizations.*

process of creation and development between two organizations. This framework can be a valuable tool to help design effective collaboration processes. Once the differences and relative strengths of each phase of the knowledge development loops in each company are understood, they can then be combined into an interorganizational knowledge development loop that best encompasses and uses the loops and strengths within each organization. This larger loop focuses attention on and helps define which elements of the knowledge creation cycle should be performed by each organization, and specifically what communication channels and content will maximize the richness of feedback and development.

## DYNAMICS OF KNOWLEDGE COCREATION

Knowledge is almost always created in some form of collaboration rather than by individuals working alone. Fostering the types of motivation and interaction that result in valuable knowledge creation within a company is a complex challenge, and some organizations are clearly more successful at this than others. Taking this collaboration to a multi-organizational situation makes it far more complex and difficult again, with the boundaries between organizations creating major challenges in facilitating collaborative knowledge creation. On the other hand, one advantage of having organizations jointly engage in knowledge creation is that it forces a more explicit model for collaboration, and clarity in the constituent processes, which in themselves can create substantial value.

## Process Management

In collaborative knowledge creation, it is usually preferable for one organization to hold primary responsibility for managing the creative process. The professional services firm will usually take this role, and in any case should position itself to take this responsibility, as this is arguably the major source of value and typically the primary success factor in the project.

Part of this role is essentially project management — ensuring that the resources are brought together to make happen whatever is necessary. This is still a subsidiary to managing the process of knowledge creation, which includes consideration of all of the dynamics of this volatile undertaking. Managing the creation of knowledge is certainly far more of an art than a science, a key part of which is finding the delicate balance between directing the process and letting it happen.

## Facilitation

The primary process in knowledge creation is facilitation. It is not only critical in cocreation but in all knowledge-rich situations. This skill should be deeply embedded in every professional services firm, for its own internal knowledge creation and for adding value to clients. Facilitation can be described as the process of bringing together disparate knowledge in a complementary and useful way. It is intrinsically unstructured, to best allow the most useful interaction between participants in ways that will achieve a valuable combination of knowledge.

Facilitation is a very high-level skill that to be accomplished successfully must draw on a rich understanding of people, groups, knowledge, paradigms, and business. It is often applied within the frame of knowledge elicitation, in getting clients to make the most of the latent knowledge within their organization. However, it is even more fundamental to knowledge cocreation, in bringing together knowledge and ideas that have probably been developed from substantially different perspectives.

## Brainstorming

Brainstorming has become a core tool in business facilitation since the process was developed by Alex Osborn.[6] The original principles of putting forward all ideas, not criticizing, looking for quantity, and combining and improving the initial suggestions are still used by organizations worldwide. While generating a large number of ideas is the avowed intention and basis of the brainstorming methodology, the greater value is in the subsequent combination of those ideas, and the dynamics created by the situation. It is typically just one element in the overall process of knowledge creation, but can play an important role, particularly in setting a frame for the desired dynamics of knowledge interaction.

IDEO of Palo Alto, California, the largest product design consulting firm in the United States, bases a significant part of its reputation on its brainstorming ability. It has found that in addition to generating valuable ideas and knowledge internally, and assisting in the sharing and development of knowledge, it also produces useful ideas and knowledge for clients, and helps generate business for the firm.[7]

Projects at IDEO routinely start with the client explaining the problem or situation to a brainstorming group of designers. Clients are taught the basic principles of brainstorming, and are reminded of the rules if they break them when participating in workshops. One of the perceived benefits of running a brainstorming session is simply that it is an efficient way for clients to get ideas compared to individual meetings or reports. While brainstorming is used in essentially all projects as part of IDEO's core methodology, some clients choose to hire IDEO just to run brainstorming sessions.

Creative Abrasion and Matching People

One central issue in running successful projects involving the co-creation of knowledge is the effective interaction of staff from both organizations. Dorothy Leonard suggests that "creative abrasion" is one of the most important elements for the generation of knowledge.[8] If people with similar ways of thinking are brought together, there is far more likely to be groupthink than the generation of the sparks that results in volatile knowledge creation. Knowledge often emerges from the collaboration of people with very different ways of looking at their field. Indeed, Nissan Design International, for example, deliberately puts together teams by hiring people with contrasting cognitive styles.[9]

This suggests that joint knowledge creation teams should be designed to provide this level of creative abrasion. Building in this abrasion does require very strong facilitation and supervision skills, however, as interpersonal abrasion can clearly also result in less pleasant outcomes. Deliberately matching professionals with client staff having different cognitive styles is certainly risky, but it can also result in far richer knowledge creation for the client, both on individual and organizational levels. One way of reducing risk is discussing with the client beforehand the deliberate introduction of this creative abrasion, and the potential wrinkles on the way. This purposeful use of creative abrasion in knowledge creation projects should be contrasted with knowledge communication-based engagements and sales relationships, which are more likely to succeed if cognitive styles are matched.

Developing External Communities of Practice

Since the idea of "communities of practice" was first introduced — probably by John Seely Brown, the chief scientist at research and development institution Xerox PARC — it has emerged as one of the key concepts in knowledge management. A community of practice brings together practitioners within a field of specialization in order to share high-level knowledge and experience.[10] These communities have always existed and are an intrinsic part of all knowledge development, as knowledge specialists will always seek out their peers in order to develop their own knowledge.

The issue is how to assist these communities to develop in ways that are useful for all participants. Since knowledge specialists are usually eager to establish interactions with their peers, it can come down to making it easy for people to share knowledge and ideas, which is often a technology issue of connecting people in easy and useful ways.

Communities of practice commonly exist within a single organization, or across highly specialized fields of science or engineering. In many cases knowledge specialists have greater loyalty to their field of knowledge than their organizations. It is possible for professional services firms specifically to create communities of practice either with single clients or groups of clients.

Linking a professional services firm's knowledge specialists with their peers in clients in a community of practice will certainly add substantial value to clients through the useful sharing of knowledge, as will assisting clients in creating and developing their own communities of practice. Many professional services firms have developed expertise in building these communities in the process of leveraging their internal knowledge, and can pass on this expertise to their clients. Another perspective is considering the knowledge relationship roles introduced in Chapter 8, and seeing the building of communities of practice as taking the richness of interaction between knowledge specialists at the service provider and their peers at the client as far as it will go.

Taking the concept a step further, professional services firms can add significant value by building communities of practice among groups of its clients. This adds value by providing the technology infrastructure for them to share knowledge, bringing together a group with common interests, and sometimes facilitating the interaction.

## World Bank Institute

The World Bank Institute (WBI) is the arm of the World Bank charged with being a catalyst for generating and sharing the knowledge necessary to alleviate poverty and foster development; in short, developing capabilities in poor countries. Its clients include national and local government bodies and nongovernmental organizations with development objectives. However, it works primarily with partners, with 60 percent of its activities developed and delivered jointly with external organizations. Historically, the WBI provided classroom training. Now it has diversified to provide extensive online e-learning programs, videos, and training in other formats, as well as facilitating many external efforts.

The World Bank helped establish the Global Development Learning Network (GDLN), which is a partnership of distance learning centers and other organizations that are committed to poverty reduction. This was born out of an internal World Bank initiative that it recognized would be more effective if it became part of a broader network. There are now over 60 GDLN centers around the world, with many of the activities focused on direct forum-based sharing of knowledge and experiences on issues such as education reform and HIV and AIDS prevention. WBI itself has provided over 100 courses and seminars to GDLN on a range of development topics.

The World Bank has been very active in developing communities of practice, both internally, where they are called thematic groups and number more than 80, and externally among its clients. One of the client communities of practice it has helped to establish is the Latin American Urban Network (Ayuda Urbana), which was created by the mayors of 10 cities in Central America to link their municipal government staff in sharing knowledge and experiences on common issues they face. The group combines face-to-face meetings, an interactive web site, and online discussion to help create more effective local policies and implementation. Similarly, the municipal staff of 40 cities in the Philippines have come together to share their knowledge, facilitated by a World Bank grant. The group is linked by a web site that includes bulletin boards and video conferencing. More recently the group has established a

*(Continued)*

marketplace to match community projects with potential donors and resources across the 40 cities. As challenges arise for member cities, they are able to link directly to people who have been dealing with similar issues. The China Association of Mayors, an existing network of more than 600 cities, established a knowledge-sharing system based on the Filipino initiative.[11]

## Conferences and Roundtables

While bringing communities together online provides a valuable forum for exchange, it does not have the same power in terms of exchanging and creating knowledge as bringing people together in the same place. Conferences are a wonderful time-tested way of bringing people together. Many attendees find greater value in the informal exchanges and discussions with other delegates than in the formal presentations. While it is "old technology," bringing together people in this way will always be immensely valuable. Many organizations host conferences that bring their clients together, providing benefits such as knowledge exchange and formation of communities of practice among their users.

Roundtables are more focused, and provide a forum for exchange of views, information, and knowledge among participants. Fannie Mae operates in the secondary market to provide home financing targeted to low-, moderate-, and middle-income people. It is the largest source of funds for home mortgages in the United States. While its end customers are primarily families, it deals directly with lending institutions, and has other stakeholders, including local government and business. Fannie Mae regularly hosts regional roundtables and forums, bringing together lenders, business leaders, local politicians, research organizations such as universities and think tanks, and other parties. The participants' objectives in making home ownership more accessible are highly aligned, and thus the forums provide them with the opportunity to create solutions together, drawing on their complementary knowledge and helping Fannie Mae to develop new products and services appropriate for evolving markets.

Montgomery Watson Harza (MWH) is a diversified professional services firm with over $1 billion in revenues, specializing in water, wastewater, and power issues. The firm regularly runs focused client roundtables on a variety of topics, to create value and build relationships. Many of its U.S. clients have extensive operations in Asia. MWH has organized a series of roundtables, held in the United States, for its clients to discuss how best to do business in Asia. These are run on a quarterly basis, each half-day session covering the issues in one Asian region, such as India, China, or Southeast Asia. MWH executives begin by providing a brief introduction to some of the issues they have seen and dealt with, and then use an experienced facilitator to guide discussion and knowledge sharing between the roundtable participants. The firm runs other roundtables on issues of strong interest to its clients, always designed to foster knowledge sharing between participants.

## Knowledge Capture

As discussed in Chapter 5, a substantial proportion of the value gained by clients can be found in the capture of knowledge in a usable form. In addition to the knowledge capture that would be part of the engagement anyway, in the context of knowledge cocreation it is very valuable to document the actual process by which the knowledge is generated. This documentation can allow the client to gain not only the knowledge content but greater facility in the creation process.

Since the process of knowledge creation usually generates a broad array of ideas that are then refined to produce specific outcomes, a great deal of latent value often remains in the ideas left behind on the way. These can be revisited later to solve other issues or simply to mine for gems. The spin-offs from NASA space research have been as diverse as better pillows and detecting cherry pits in cherry pie filling. However, commercializing the research behind these advances required both capturing the lessons from the steps in the process and choosing to follow up on them. Wherever possible, recording the process of knowledge cocreation and providing it to the client in a usable format, and possibly making that a specified outcome of the project, can greatly increase the value proposition for the client.[12]

## ISSUES IN KNOWLEDGE COCREATION

There are significant issues and potential problems in knowledge co-creation, not least of which is the ownership of any intellectual property created. The complexity of these issues can prove to be a strong disincentive for organizations to engage in knowledge cocreation, and illustrates why trust is critical even in the initiation of knowledge cocreation projects.

### Mutual Trust

The most fundamental rule in cocreating knowledge is working from mutual trust. If it is not present to a sufficient degree at the beginning of an engagement, the project is not likely to be viable. The trust must be reciprocal; that is, it is equally important for the service provider to trust its client as the other way around.

Researchers who have studied joint ventures have concluded that however much participating firms try to cover all potential issues in contracts success ultimately depends on trust.[13] This is not to suggest that legal agreements should not be used, but that there is no way for agreements to cover all contingencies and that there is no substitute for trust.[14] The bottom line is that the benefits of the cocreation of knowledge are severely limited without significant mutual trust. These types of projects are therefore more likely to stem from an existing strong relationship than to be a starting point for collaboration.

Even given reasonable levels of mutual trust, it is still critical to discuss and agree from the outset how the most important issues, such as ownership of intellectual property, will be handled. While it is impossible to foresee all eventualities, the more possibilities that are discussed the more likely that situations can be handled in a way that benefits all parties and builds rather than destroys relationships.

Confidentiality is already a bedrock of professional services engagements, and thus should need no further emphasis. The depth of client information and knowledge obtained in the process of knowledge cocreation can be a significant step beyond that shared in other styles of working, and therefore requires a greater degree of confidentiality and strong mutual trust.

## Ownership of Intellectual Property

Knowledge is a valuable asset, and if two or more parties create knowledge together the issue of the ownership of that knowledge will inevitably arise. Intellectual property is essentially knowledge or intellectual capital that can be legally protected. This definition includes, for example, documents that can be copyrighted, inventions that can be patented, and process names that can be trademarked. Most ideas or processes themselves cannot be patented, however, and while formal documentation of this knowledge can be legally protected the knowledge itself cannot. As such, much of the actual valuable knowledge generated in a project will be extremely difficult to protect, and thus is not intellectual property in the legal sense.

When intellectual property in the form of patents and copyrights is generated from a project, it can be relatively straightforward to allocate ownership and benefits, as long as this eventuality has been discussed and agreed upon beforehand. The way in which this is approached will depend on the nature of the collaboration, and will vary from vesting all intellectual property with the client to sharing ownership or licensing rights or occasionally vesting ownership with the professional services firm. Professional services firms often seek to specify that they and the client both have the right to use processes and methodologies developed during a project, as most of these innovations are generated in the course of client engagements. The ability to use this knowledge can be restricted in ways that make sense to both parties. For example, consulting firms can be permitted to apply methodologies developed in any industries other than that of the client. Clearly, whatever is agreed upon regarding the allocation of eventual intellectual property should be established contractually.

Trade secrets or confidential information law protects ideas that have not entered the public domain or that cannot be protected by copyright or patents. This is often more relevant than intellectual property law in the cocreation of knowledge, and agreements should usually contain confidentiality clauses. Of course, whenever there are potential legal or contractual issues you need to seek specialist legal advice.

## SUMMARY: COCREATING VALUE WITH CLIENTS

The strongest form of a knowledge-based relationship is one in which the professional services firm and client create value together, often by jointly developing knowledge. This implies different business models from the usual experts-for-hire approach, including the possibilities of establishing joint ventures and running multiclient projects.

To add value in knowledge cocreation, services firms must have expertise not only in their specialist fields but also in the dynamics of knowledge collaboration, including effective process management, facilitation, and brainstorming. Developing external communities of practice creates real value in allowing clients to share knowledge on an ongoing basis. Mutual trust is a prerequisite of effective knowledge cocreation projects, partly in order to be able to negotiate and work with issues such as the ownership of any intellectual property created.

Building far closer relationships with clients — including implementing knowledge cocreation — means that the boundaries between organizations blur and traditional approaches to pricing services begin to become ineffective. In Chapter 11 I review some of the more common approaches to pricing knowledge-based services, and examine a range of ways of implementing pricing models that reflect the value created for the client.

## NOTES

1   Davis and Meyer explore in detail the theme of blurring in the direction of flow of value. See Davis and Meyer, op. cit.

2   Stefano Hatfield, "Mother Loves Your," *Creativity*, March 2002, pp. 30–31.

3   Anonymous, "Creative Agency of the Year: Mother," *Marketing* 12, December 2002.

4   See Lawrence M. Fisher, "Technology Transfer at Stanford University," *Strategy & Business*, 4th Quarter, 1998.

5   David A. Kolb, *Experiential Learning: Experience as the Source of Learning and Development*, Englewood Cliffs, NJ: Prentice-Hall, 1984.

6   Alex F. Osborn, *Applied Imagination*, 3rd rev. ed., New York: Charles Scribner's Sons, 1963, pp. 151.

7   Information on IDEO is drawn from Robert I. Sutton and Andrew Hargadon, "Brainstorming Groups in Context: Effectiveness in a Product Design Firm," *Administrative Science Quarterly* 41, 1996, pp. 685–718.

8   Leonard, op. cit., pp. 63–65.

9   See Leonard, op. cit., pp. 79–81, and Katharine Mieszkowski, "Opposites Attract," *Fast Company*, no. 12, December 1997, p. 42.

10  John Seely Brown and Estee Solomon Gray, "The People Are the Company," *Fast Company*, no. 1, November 1995, p. 78.

11  Don Cohen and Bruno Laporte, "The Evolution of the Knowledge Bank," *KM Magazine*, March 2004.

12  See Gary Abramson, "Their Pain, Your Gain," *CIO Enterprise*, October 15, 1998.

13  See Kathryn R. Harrigan, *Strategies for Joints Ventures*, Lexington, MA: Lexington Books, 1986, as quoted in Gary Hamel, "Competition for Competence and Interpartner Learning within International Strategic Alliances," *Strategic Management Journal* 12, 1991, pp. 83–103; and Leonard, op. cit., p. 174.

14  Ring and Van de Ven suggest that in high-commitment relationships informal agreements will increasingly replace legal contracts, as their experience with each builds trust. See Peter S. Ring and Andrew H. Van de Ven, "Developmental Processes of Cooperative Interorganizational Relationships," *Academy of Management Review* 19, no. 1, 1994, pp. 90–118.

# 11

# Value-Based Pricing
## Implementing New Revenue Models

How do you price knowledge-based services? This thorny problem still has no clear answers, and while there have been many developments in professional services pricing over the last years there is still much change to come. The nub of the issue is that information and knowledge behave in very different ways to most products or simple services. Applying knowledge to client's problems does not reduce your knowledge resources. In fact, it is more likely to increase them as you learn from the engagement. There is often little relationship between the cost of inputs and the value created. Much attention has also been paid to how knowledge is often subject to increasing returns rather than diminishing returns: it can increase in value the more it is shared.[1]

All of these characteristics suggest that the pricing of knowledge-based services should be very different from that of more traditional products and services. Yet still many of the same approaches to pricing are used. One important reason is simply the immense difficulty of valuing and pricing knowledge. In particular, the value of knowledge depends on its context and the client.

The organic, fluid nature of knowledge means there is no easy way to price it, and no neat, glib answer as to how professional services firms should charge for their services. Certainly, however, professional service firms need to reexamine the basis on which they charge, and at least experiment with different approaches to pricing. This chapter aims to cover many of the most common approaches to pricing knowledge. As with much of this book, the intention is to provide practitioners across the professional industries with lessons from their counterparts in related fields.[2]

## BEYOND TRADITIONAL PRICING MODELS

Over the past decade new pricing models have started to emerge, often as a result of deregulation and the competitive forces covered in Chapter 2. Legal and consulting firms historically have tended to charge according to the time they spend working on a job, irrespective of the quality of the knowledge going into the engagement and the value to clients. Stockbrokers and advertising agencies have traditionally charged a percentage of the transactions in which they are involved.

While these approaches are still common, and will continue to be used in many situations, new models and approaches are emerging. Innovators will experiment with new forms and find what works and what does not, leading the way for professional services industries to move on from the traditional approaches. In the coming years, clients will be confronted with a far broader choice of pricing models as well as services, and ultimately will choose the offerings that give them the greatest value for the price they pay.

One easy way of making prices relate to client-perceived value is to charge high fees, and the clients you get are those that perceive higher value than they are charged. Textbook pricing theory can be used to find a profit-maximizing pricing level. However, in reality a more flexible system will result in greater revenue, as the nature of knowledge-based services is far more fluid than the products on which most pricing theories are based.

In an environment in which services have been unbundled, one of the key issues is distinguishing between the commoditized and differentiated elements of the offering. There will always be elements of the range of services offered that are commoditized, and competitive pricing strategies must be applied in these cases. However, the differentiated elements of the offering should be priced as much as possible based on the value to the client. When an offering is differentiated, it is throwing money away and devaluing the offering to price it in the same way as a commoditized offering. Another key issue in developing pricing models is that of client relationships. Certainly you wish to maximize revenue for work performed. However, if the quality of the client relationships suffers long-term profitability could be affected.

## TRADITIONAL PRICING MODELS

Here I will examine the more traditional approaches to pricing knowledge and knowledge-based services, which include time-based pricing, fixed fees, and commissions. In the following section I will cover approaches to pricing that attempt to link price more directly to value. The fact that the approaches covered here are more traditional does not mean that they are not necessarily useful or appropriate in many situations. However, they have distinct limitations that mean the use of alternative pricing models often proves valuable.

### Time and Cost Pricing

The most common method for professionals to charge is based on their time. In most organizations this is fairly closely related to their cost in terms of salary, overhead, and unbilled time. Professional practice management is largely focused on managing these factors.

Most professional firms pay as salary in the order of 20 to 50 percent of the overall service revenue generated directly by their nonpartner staff. When there are substantial costs involved other than salaries and basic overheads, such as major infrastructure or capital requirements, as in the case of investment banking, this proportion can be substantially less. Because the major cost of most professional service firms is their staff, time-based pricing is essentially a type of "cost plus" pricing, which takes the costs of providing a service and adds a margin.

While billing by time spent is easy, convenient, and relatively transparent to clients, it may have very little relation to the value to the client. Should a brilliant innovation generated in a minute's inspiration be charged out for a fraction of the cost of drafting a standard letter? Expertise and usable new ideas in a particular field may take months or years of unbilled time to develop. Should these then be available for the price of an hour's time, or less, if some of the core lessons have been distilled and made explicit in a document that can be forwarded by e-mail? Some professional service firms are experiencing significant problems with these issues.

Time-based charging will always have a role, however, because of its simplicity, and in the end the hourly or daily rate can be adjusted to meet market demand. One key factor is that clients are used to paying by time in many industries. This means it can initially be difficult to wean clients off these approaches. Perhaps the most important problem with time-based charging is that there is not necessarily a direct relation to value generation for the client.

## Fixed Fees and Retainers

Many professional service firms charge a fixed fee to carry out a specified project, without the client seeing how the fee is made up of the time and cost of staff required. There has been a strong shift to fees from time or commission measures over the last years, notably in consulting and advertising. In reality the fee is almost always calculated on a time and cost basis, with possibly an additional premium if the client is likely to bear it. Even so, project-based pricing increasingly provides the opportunity for professional services firms to price their work and knowledge transfer based on the value they believe the client is likely to accrue, and to convince their client that the value they will receive from the project is greater than the price they will pay.

Cambridge Technology Partners, a U.S. software implementation firm, built annual revenues of over $600 million in the first eight years from its birth in 1999 before being acquired by Novell. This impressive growth was largely driven by what was at the time its novel approach of setting a fixed time and fixed price for large projects. The precedent forced many other technology services firms into adopting fixed fee models. This approach has rapidly shifted into other professional services domains, with consulting and legal services firms now often proposing fixed fees for client projects and matters.

Hybrid models, which involve combinations of fees and time-based pricing, are becoming more common. These include charging a fixed fee for pre-specified services and charging on a time basis for any additional work, or time-based charging up to a pre-specified limit.[3] These essentially represent types of risk-sharing arrangements, which are discussed later in this chapter.

## Commissions

A related approach to pricing knowledge is charging a commission or percentage on the value of transactions. This has traditionally been the case in a range of professional services industries, although deregulation and the associated competitive forces have resulted in major strains on the system, and substantial changes in commission-based charging. For example, a fixed percentage commission on share transactions is increasingly rare, and in the advertising industry the traditional model of charging a percentage of the cost of media billing was long ago overtaken by new pricing trends.

A fixed commission system still holds in some fields, such as equity underwriting. In all industries, however, this approach is under continued pressure from new entrants who offer more attractive pricing structures. While measuring value added by a professional services firm as a proportion of the dollar amount of the transaction involved is a rather crude approach, it does provide a yardstick, and allows competitive advantage to be determined by the quality of services and other value added by the service firm.

## Retainers and Membership Fees

Retainers in their most basic form provide access to a firm's services. Commonly they include the provision of a pre-agreed (often time-based) amount of services, beyond which further fees are charged. This is, of course, essentially another variation on time-based pricing. META Group, a market research and consulting firm based in Stamford, Connecticut, offers its retainer clients several levels by which they can access a wide range of services. This starts with the provision of written research, which can be delivered on paper, over the Internet, through Lotus Notes, or in other digital forms. The next level brings in participation in teleconferences run by industry analysts on topical issues. Retainer clients also get access to META Group conferences, which cover either broad directions or specific topics in the IT industry, and briefings, including both morning seminars and roundtable discussions that allow clients to get together and share experiences. Individualized services that are part of the package of retainer service include a review of the client's strategic plan, and a customized half-day briefing, which can be used however the client wishes. To cap it off, the client receives unlimited telephone consultation with META Group analysts.

Since knowledge-based value creation is best based on ongoing conversations and interactions, it can be appropriate to charge clients a membership fee to join these dialogues. This approach can either provide access to professionals at the service provider in informal ways such as telephone conversations, or participation in broader communities including other clients. Global Business Network's core services, including conferences, subscriptions, and access, are all covered with an annual membership fee. Generally, membership fees can be used to provide access to high-level dialogue in a range of ways, notably in conferences or private online forums.

## Tenders

Knowledge-based services are often subject to tendering, where the client specifies its requirements and asks for the lowest price and best performance within its specifications. The use of tendering implies that the services are commoditized, and that they are driven purely or primarily by price. Unless service providers can differentiate themselves within the tender process, which is difficult, there is little or no opportunity for premium pricing. As much as possible, firms need to establish their differentiation with the client before tenders are called, and build relationships that avoid direct price-competitive situations.

## PRINCIPLES OF VALUE-BASED PRICING

The Holy Grail of professional services is to find a way of charging based on the value received or perceived by the client. Of course, in order to get business in the first place the client must perceive substantially greater value than the price charged. Some firms have a policy of only taking on assignments that give a demonstrable value-to-price ratio. Global management consulting firm Proudfoot PLC-states that the firm will only take on work it can demonstrate will add value equal to at least three times the cost of the project. McKinsey & Company and many other major consulting firms have a similar tacit policy, sometimes specifying far higher multiples.

One of the most important aspects of implementing value-based pricing is that it helps to align the objectives of clients and service providers. If both sides benefit when projects are successful and suffer when they do not go well, they have clearly made a strong move to a true partnership-style relationship. This means that while service providers are eager to establish value-based pricing in order to earn larger fees than they could otherwise there is also a strong incentive for organizations to reward their service providers in ways that mean they will be highly motivated to ensure successful outcomes.

Implementing value-based pricing is deeply tied to developing knowledge-based client relationships. The types of agreements and disclosure of information required by many models and approaches requires strong mutual trust. They are far more likely to happen once there is already a deep level of familiarity. Such disclosure, along with the alignment of objectives that is intrinsic to many of these approaches to pricing, helps to develop intimacy and far closer relationships.

## Measuring Value

Ideally in establishing knowledge-based pricing models we would be able to measure value created for clients as a result of engagements or relationships, and many new pricing models attempt to do this. The problems are legion, however, which means that except in cases such as contingency fees for litigation few firms have implemented these broadly.

The greatest difficulty is in isolating the contribution of the professional services firm from the many other factors that impact performance. If a consultant assists a client in refining its strategic positioning, and sales go up 30 percent, is that a result of the consulting engagement, or because of an upturn in the economy, or production problems at a competitor?

The key issue in determining whether value-based measures are likely to be usable in any given circumstance is the scope of the project or relationship relative to the scope of what is being measured. There is no way of completely isolating the value impact of external professional services. However, if this factor is sufficiently large, both sides can agree to share in changes in performance.

If what is being measured is narrower in scope, it is easier to believe that the engagement is responsible for enhanced results. Work with smaller companies or divisions, or at the product level, is more likely to impact revenue and profitability. It is possible for an engagement with a large multinational corporation to significantly impact group profitability, but it would have to be on a massive scale.

These issues also mean that cost, revenue, profitability, shareholder value, and share price represent increasing orders of difficulty for use as measures of value. The variables that impact costs are usually far more under control than those for revenue, and these can often be identified so that the impact of the engagement can more easily be measured. In addition, costs can usually be fairly readily measured or allocated down to a departmental basis, which is not possible for revenues. Profitability includes both cost and revenue variables, while shareholder value and share price are affected by a wide variety of macro issues. These can be used for executive compensation, but there would usually have to be a very close relationship with an external service provider, or for the client to be a relatively small organization, to link these variables to fees.

Mutual trust is a critical issue in these types of measures of client value. Cost figures and other accounting measures are easy to fudge, so unless the service provider trusts the client's assessment of the figures, cost-impact charging will not be implemented.

## Risk Sharing

The concept of risk sharing is central to all value-based pricing. Sharing the rewards of a project between a service provider and its client — essentially getting participation in the value created — means there must also be more sharing of risk. Clients have little reason to give away bonuses to their service providers without the provider also sharing some of the potential downside. With clients that have a low tolerance for risk or cost, it represents an opportunity for the service provider to take on some of that risk in exchange for a larger portion of the benefits. Since organizations' tolerance for risk varies substantially, risk-sharing arrangements must be negotiated on a case-by-case basis.

As suggested above, implementing risk-sharing pricing arrangements — whether or not they are formally articulated as such — means that the service provider and client share in both the upside and downside of the success of projects. This alignment of objectives can be contrasted to the win/lose stance in which each is trying to get the most out while putting the least in. The way in which risk sharing is most commonly implemented is by charging clients a base fee that represents the service firm's labor and overhead costs, plus perhaps a nominal margin and sharing in the value created by the engagement.

## Agreed Objectives

When final value creation in terms of profitability or related measures is difficult to relate directly to the work performed, other yardsticks can be applied that represent indirect value to the client, but over which the service provider has more control. Among many others, these can include results of surveys of client or product awareness or image for advertising agencies and public relations firms, changes in quality or failure rates in production for consultants, or time for project completion for construction firms or software developers.

In a knowledge transfer-based engagement, the agreed objectives can be knowledge outcomes specified at the outset, as discussed in Chapter 8. These can include skill levels of client staff and the effectiveness of capabilities. The core issue is being able to demonstrate that greater knowledge or capabilities exist in the client at the end of the engagement.

## Client-Perceived Value

In cases in which it is impossible or impractical to measure the impact of services performed, assessing client perception of value can sometimes be used. This is perhaps particularly relevant in adding value to others' decision making, where it is impossible to separate the various inputs to the final decision, and only the decision makers can judge what was valuable to them in their decision. There are clearly many difficulties in using client perception of value. In many situations it becomes simply a subjective bonus, which is rarely satisfactory to both parties. One of the most important conditions for client-perceived value to be used effectively as a basis for or component of pricing is that the client indeed believes it receives substantial ongoing value from its suppliers, and is highly motivated to reward excellent performance. One of DDB Worldwide's major clients has chosen to provide it with an annual discretionary bonus. Based entirely on its own judgment, without any consultation or disclosure of reasons, it makes a bonus payment to DDB.

Client-perceived value is very difficult to implement in isolated engagements that are not part of ongoing relationships. It also tends to be more effective if the client uses a limited panel of service providers with which it has ongoing relationships. This means that the client can determine an approximate fee pool to be shared among its panel of service providers, possibly linking this to its own performance by various measures and then allocating this pool between the panel on the basis of perceived value added by each over a period. This type of approach has been most fully implemented in the institutional stockbroking industry, and is described later in the chapter.

---

### DDB Worldwide

Advertising network DDB Worldwide, with 206 offices in 96 countries, was named "Most Awarded Agency Network in the World" for 2004, on the basis of the creative awards received by its operations worldwide. Chairman Keith Reinhard has long been an innovator in promoting the "agency of the future," and has been an active proponent of pay-for-results approaches to fees for much of his career.

In 1991, DDB Worldwide began by offering to guarantee results on its advertising campaigns under certain conditions. This first initiative did not work as well as had been hoped, in part because although the CEOs of client organizations were enthusiastic about the concept the brand managers preferred to have control over the relationship and were sometimes reluctant to share information. The agency then shifted from offering a guarantee to making part of its compensation based on results. This involves a basic fee structure that allows the agency to cover its costs plus a basic margin, with bonuses paid based on the results achieved by the client.

*(Continued)*

The key issue in establishing the bonuses is agreeing on measures for results that are aligned with the clients' marketing objectives, and are as directly as possible attributable to the agencies' efforts. Some measures used include sales and profit of the client as a whole or for the relevant division, media or production savings, and survey measures of brand or advertising awareness and intention to purchase. If the objective of the client were to increase distribution, this would represent a different type of assignment that could be measured, for example, by number and diversity of distribution channels.

By 2004, about half of DDB's compensation agreements included pay for performance elements. A common criterion is copy test scores, which measure how ads are received by focus groups. Achieving predetermined sales objectives is frequently used to trigger specific incentive payments. However, the most common single method currently used is agency evaluations, in which client staff subjectively grade the agency on a variety of criteria, which could include creativity, responsiveness, results, or any other issues meaningful to the client. Usually the assessment is transparent, with both the criteria and points awarded shown to the agency, and DDB given the opportunity to respond. The assessment is then used to determine payments to the agency, based on differential commission rates, bonus levels, or agency profit margins. Some clients use all three of these inputs, whereas others use just one or a combination of these. One major client applies only the agency evaluation system, using it to award a profit margin to the agency of between 5 and 15 percent.

Since a core element of DDB Worldwide's business is developing brands, it actively seeks to create its own brands and license these to clients, thus keeping the intellectual property in-house. In one example, it created the brand H2OPE. It licenses this for an annual fee to the Stockholm Water Foundation, which on-licenses it to companies. DDB has also recently created a series of cat beverages it is seeking to license, including an energy drink called Tigerwater and salmon-flavored drinking water going by the name of L'eau de Chat. Reinhard says he wants his business to become more like the music industry, in which the creators do not sell their ideas for a fixed price but license them to generate ongoing revenue.

## IMPLEMENTING VALUE-BASED PRICING MODELS

Since in professional services every engagement is customized, it presents a marvelous opportunity for creativity and experimentation in developing and implementing value-based pricing models. There is no one solution, and within professional services each industry and even each client may merit a different approach. While for smaller clients or engagements the effort of negotiating a tailored arrangement may not be worthwhile, any significant project or relationship offers the potential for client and service provider to align their interests in the way they agree on pricing. Consenting adults can choose to engage in whatever form of pricing structure they believe meets their respective objectives. The survey of approaches given here is by no means exhaustive, but covers a range of useful and innovative structures, with examples of firms that have successfully implemented these.

### Cost, Revenue, and Profitability Impact

Developing pricing models based on measuring the impact on cost, revenue, and profitability can only be done effectively in certain conditions, as discussed above. Implementing these is essentially an issue of nominating an appropriate measure, and determining how this will be linked to the service provider's remuneration. Both sides have to agree that whatever measure is used — be it cost, revenue, or profitability in a given domain — is substantially linked to the contribution of the professional service firm. The link to fees can be structured in many ways, including taking a percentage of value created and bonuses for achieving specified targets.

In one recent example of cost-impact pricing, Booz Allen Hamilton negotiated an agreement with its client to allocate a proportion of the fees for a cost-reduction reengineering project to the success in achieving the targeted savings. Together they established a scorecard of measures, including the number of people, costs associated with functions, new processes established, and so on across several divisions in the organization. The initial project and implementation lasted several months, with regular meetings over the following six months to review progress, to take remedial action where necessary, and at specified milestones to establish the achievement of agreed indicators on which further payments were based. The regular follow-up meetings also served to establish a deeper and richer dialogue and relationship with the client.

The most common situations in which revenue-related measures can be used are individual products, particularly new products, where the service provider creates or co-creates the entire marketing strategy or campaign, or even the product itself.

### Contingency and Success Fees

Contingency fees, which are fees payable depending on success, are effectively a variation on revenue-based fees. They are most commonly used in litigation, where an agreed proportion of the possible winnings goes to the law firm. This is clearly also a form of risk sharing, since often no other fees are payable and thus the law firm risks getting no return on its efforts. Contingency fees in law have always been standard practice in the United States. However, they were only made legal in the United Kingdom, Australia, and New Zealand in the late 1990s, and are not accepted practice in most other jurisdictions. Success fees are also routine in investment banking, where fees can be payable depending on the success of a range of outcomes, including acquisitions, protection from takeover, or share price increase.

### Licensing

Licensing is an important vehicle used in charging for knowledge and knowledge-based services. In its basic form, it provides an ongoing payment for the use of specified knowledge. This is most often applied to intellectual property such as patents, trademarks, or copyrighted material, where organizations pay a fee for use of the intellectual property. These licensing fees often include a basic annual payment, with an additional payment per use or as a proportion of revenue.

Consulting firm Intellectual Capital Services (ICS), based in London, uses a licensing approach in charging for its services. ICS applies proprietary research and models within its clients to develop company-specific performance and intellectual capital models, or to value intangible assets. A fixed fee is charged for this initial process, and any subsequent processes in developing the systems and models. Clients then pay 18 percent annually of the cumulative fees paid through the relationship for the right to continue to use the systems and models. This fee is invested in further research and development. For their fee, the client receives an annual quality review of the systems or models in use as well as an option on the use of further research results.

Training courses are a good example of a knowledge "product" that can be licensed to clients to generate ongoing revenue as they derive ongoing benefit from knowledge development in their organizations. These can be sold for a single fee that depends on the size of the organization, or an up-front fee supplemented by a licensing fee for each trainee or time the course is run.

## Idea Fees and Licensing

A large proportion of value creation comes from good ideas, yet in general ideas cannot be protected by law as intellectual property. Any way of charging for ideas — which are often flashes of inspiration based on years of experience or remarkable creativity — is a big step toward more effective knowledge-based pricing. Rainey Kelly Campbell Roalfe/Y&R, a young advertising agency in London that was acquired by global communications group Young & Rubicam in 1999, has since its inception based all of its charging on idea fees.

The agency charges a monthly fee based on the resources needed to manage the client account, which is intended simply to cover costs and break even. In addition, it agrees up front with the client a value — and therefore price — for the idea that will achieve the client's objectives. This pricing is established before the idea is created.

However, it is only payable if and when the agency generates an idea the client believes meets its needs. All terms are agreed upon and established contractually at the outset, so that the ideas are protected by contract law rather than intellectual property law, which would be of little use in these circumstances.

The value given to the idea is different for each client, and is intended to reflect the likely impact on client revenue rather than be related to costs such as spending on media. If it is difficult to identify a relationship between advertising and sales revenue, the agency may take a percentage of the budget of the marketing initiative the idea will drive. No commissions are charged on any production or research, so there are no vested interests in increasing costs to the client.

In most cases the ideas are intended to be used over the long term to build brands. If so, there is usually an ongoing annual payment — resembling a licensing fee — as long as the idea is used. If the client changes advertising agencies but wants to continue to use the idea, there is a buy-out charge specified in the contract. Chairman M. T. Rainey acknowledges that it is easier to implement these principles from the outset of client relationships, but emphasizes that the agency's intention is to be in the business of ideas, and as such wants to charge for the ideas it generates.

## Equity and Stock Options

The dot-com boom and bust saw big shifts in the perception of equity and stock options as payment for services. In principle, these are a viable form of payment when companies are small, and effective knowledge-based services can impact the value of the company. Industrial design firm Palo Alto Design Group (PADG) frequently sought out clients that were prepared to offer stock options, warrants, or royalties in return for its services. PADG helped design the enclosure for Palm Computing's Palm Pilot at the concept stage in return for a small fee and warrants in Palm stock, which paid off handsomely when Palm Computing was subsequently bought by U.S. Robotics.[4] In other cases, larger firms have offered fees to their professional services providers that are linked to their share price. However, most professional firms that took equity or stock options in their clients in the late 1990s ended up massively out of pocket after the NASDAQ stock exchange tanked, to the point that some of them went out of business. This has resulted in a climate in which equity is now not often part of professional services compensation.

On the other hand, venture capital can be regarded as knowledge-based services in exchange for equity. The venture capital firm provides capital as well as knowledge of the process of developing a firm through its initial stages, and applies and transfers that knowledge to the firm in which it is investing. In return it takes equity in the firm.

Joint Ventures

Joint ventures can be an ideal vehicle for the commercialization of knowledge cocreated by two companies. They can also be established explicitly for the joint development and subsequent exploitation of knowledge. As suggested in Chapter 10, these approaches truly establish the two firms as partners, and represent very powerful means of aligning their goals and objectives.

In 1997, EDS won what was at the time the largest financial services IT outsourcing contract in the world from the Commonwealth Bank of Australia (CBA), essentially taking over its information technology operations for a minimum of 10 years, with an expected contract amount of $A5 billion. At the same time, CBA took a 35-percent stake in EDS Australia for $A240 million. This has resulted in an immense alignment of interests and objectives of the two parties. Both risks and rewards are shared in a true partnership relationship. As part of the ongoing relationship, EDS and its management consulting subsidiary A. T. Kearney establish "Value Discovery" teams to identify ways in which they can create value together with CBA. The fee structure for each initiative is discussed and negotiated on a case-by-case basis, wherever possible being based on measurement of the value created. The closeness of the relationship allows the ready implementation of innovative pricing structures.

## Institutional Stockbroking Pricing Model

The institutional stockbroking industry provides an excellent model of pricing based on client-perceived value. This has arisen due to industry dynamics, in which institutional investors are highly motivated to reward adequately the stockbrokers who provide timely information, insights, and ideas that improve their investment performance. Since portfolio decisions are ultimately made by the fund managers, however, only they can judge how much value the brokers added to their decision making. Previously this was handled in an ad-hoc way by awarding transactions to the broker who had contributed the most to the investment idea or had been helpful recently, but this informal system was not clear enough in rewarding the brokers for what was most valuable to the fund managers.

It is now the norm for institutional investment managers worldwide to use a formal quantitative value-based voting system for allocating commissions to their stockbrokers. In Europe, for example, about half of all major fund managers use this type of system, with many more using a similar informal system. Typically, investment managers calculate how much brokerage commission they would generate in a year, and then allocate that among their panel of stockbrokers on the basis of the value they perceive has been added to their decision making. This is calculated by quarterly or semiannual voting by every individual fund manager and analyst who has contact with the brokers.[5]

Merrill Lynch Investment Managers (MLIM), a subsidiary of Merrill Lynch, manages almost $500 billion in assets worldwide. Its U.K. operations have a formal system for evaluating and paying its stockbrokers. Every six months it formally reviews the performance of its panel of stockbrokers in adding value. The three primary functions of their stockbrokers that are reviewed are research, sales, and execution. MLIM's fund managers rank the top five analysts in their field of specialization, looking for the broader perspectives they offer rather than more generic number-crunching ability. These ratings are then weighted according to the importance of the sector. Fund managers also allocate votes on sales service by the brokers, focusing on the originality of their ideas and their speed of reaction to market developments. The dealers at MLIM whose responsibility is to get orders executed also vote on the brokers' quality of execution of trades. These votes are then combined to yield an overall ranking of brokers and a rating on a scale of 1 to 50. The results are discussed with the brokers, focusing on the areas in which they can improve their added value and rankings. While actual commission allocation is not necessarily exactly aligned with the ratings, MLIM ensures that over time the business executed with each broker is in line with its established ratings of perceived added value.

It is possible that similar arrangements will arise in other industries in which comparable dynamics are evolving. While these are more likely to be initiated on the client side, they can also be proposed by service firms. As long as sufficient value is created by the service providers, this style of system can benefit all parties.

## SUMMARY: IMPLEMENTING NEW PRICING MODELS

Knowledge-based services have very different characteristics from products and simple services, and require different approaches to pricing. Traditional pricing models, such as time and cost pricing, fixed fees, and commissions, have both advantages and disadvantages, but fail to address many of the important issues surrounding knowledge-based services.

A key objective of professional services firms is to implement ways of pricing based on the value added to clients. Some of the principles of value-based pricing include attempting to measure the value created, sharing both upside and downside risk with clients, agreeing on measurable objectives for engagements, and assessing client-perceived value. Some specific approaches being implemented include measuring cost and revenue impact, licensing, idea fees, equity and stock options, and the institutional stockbroking model.

Having covered some of the key issues of implementing knowledge-based client relationships — managing communication channels, structuring firm-wide relationship management, cocreating knowledge, and applying new pricing models — we now need to pull these strands together to establish an overall action strategy. Chapter 12 examines the issues professional service firms need to address in implementing these principles. Ultimately, knowledge and relationships are connected by people and effective communication between them, so I propose practical approaches to these critical enablers of knowledge-based relationships.

## NOTES

[1]    See, for example, Brian W. Arthur, "Competing Technologies, Increasing Returns, and Lock-In by Historical Events," *The Economic Journal*, no. 99, March 1989, pp. 116–131; Kevin Kelly, *New Rules for the New Economy: 10 Radical Strategies for a Connected World*, New York: Viking, 1998; and the treatment of positive feedback and lock-in in Carl Shapiro and Hal Varian, *Information Rules: A Strategic Guide to the Network Economy*, Boston: Harvard Business School Press, 1998.

[2]    For further ideas on knowledge-based pricing, see Karl-Erik Sveiby's article "Fourteen Ways to Charge for Knowledge," at *www.sveiby.com.au/Twelve Ways.html*.

[3]    Geoffrey James, "Methods of Payment," *CIO Enterprise*, October 15, 1998.

[4]    Eric Ransdell, "Redesigning the Design Business," *Fast Company*, no. 16, August 1998, pp. 36–38.

[5]    Benjamin Ensor, "European Brokers Survey: Pulling Away from the Pack," *Euromoney*, November 1997.

# 12

# Taking Action
## Leading Your Clients in the
## Knowledge Economy

**V**alue in the global economy is shifting strongly to the application of highly specialized knowledge. Professional services firms are the archetypical vendors of knowledge, and well positioned to do extremely well in the years ahead. However, that does not mean life is easy for professionals. As you saw in Chapter 2, the forces of commoditization are intense, with price and other competitive pressures often putting firms on the back foot. Throughout this book I have made the case that the only sustainable escape from these pressures is to implement what I describe as "knowledge-based" relationships with your clients. In fact, a professional firm in which the principles and practices of knowledge-based client relationships are embedded will be able to create a virtuous circle in which it can lock in clients through superior value creation, and extract an increasing proportion of that value for itself.

In Chapter 6 I described how firms can enhance their client relationship capabilities by implementing initiatives across five levels: strategy, structures, processes, skills, and culture. In this chapter I examine some of the practical issues of implementation. Getting a broad understanding of the concept and importance of knowledge-based relationships through the firm is a valuable first step. However, ongoing action on multiple fronts must be taken in order for initiatives to bear fruit and position the firm as a market leader.

## CREATING AND IMPLEMENTING STRATEGY

The strategic failures of professional services firms are legion. Two prime reasons are the difficulties of gaining strategic clarity and coherence in a diverse partnership and the fact that the most senior executives in many firms are so often still engaged in client work, and swamped by the demands of managing the firm internally. There is rarely time and space for the apparent luxury of thinking about the future and how to shift the organization to meet a rapidly changing environment. When times are good — as they mainly have been in most sectors for a long time now — there is little willingness to believe that what works today will not continue to work forever forward.

The starting point has to be the implicit or explicit strategic decision-making structures of the firm. If the firm is a public company, strategic responsibilities are vested in the CEO and board, usually with assistance from a strategy unit. The structures for setting strategy are absolutely clear. In a partnership, the situation is usually very different. A managing partner or chief executive is there by the grace of the partners. In some partnerships, particularly large, global firms, the authority is strongly vested in top management, and while they must take input from their shareholders — that is, the partners — they have the ability to set and enforce firm directions. However, in many other partnerships strategic decision making is effectively done collectively, with the managing partners not being awarded independent authority to set firm strategy. This decision-making structure is inherently highly conservative, as a large proportion of partners must agree on change in order for it to happen.

The most effective approaches to developing strategy in a professional services firm will depend substantially on the firm's idiosyncratic strategic decision-making structures, including not only formal processes but also the individuals involved and their influence in the firm. Where the decision-making process is less centralized and more devolved, there must be a specific emphasis on getting broad involvement throughout the strategic process. The exploration of the drivers of change, competitive pressures, and emerging opportunities for the firm should include professionals from across the organization, so that all executives can become aware of what may impact their future earning potential.

Scenario planning, discussed in Chapter 4 as a tool for client engagements, is a powerful approach in achieving alignment and common understanding among disparate groups, and in driving effective and robust strategies. The process can be designed specifically to get broad involvement in examining firm pressures, opportunities, and strategic options, without requiring significant demands on fee earners. However, effective implementation of scenario planning requires a high level of expertise. Firms without substantial experience in this area should not try to do this without help from consultants that specialize in these approaches.


## Business Models

There are many obvious strategic issues that need to be addressed by professional services firms, such as what industries and types of clients they target, the scope of services provided down to the specific practice area level, styles of service delivery, whether or how services are packaged into products, and so on. In Chapter 6 you saw some of the issues involved in gaining strategic clarity at this level. However, the most fundamental issue firms need to examine and revisit is that of their business models. The majority of professionals implicitly believe that they will live out their working days charging clients for their time by six-minute increments. This may turn out to be true for many of them. However, it is important to question this and to make a decision whether this is indeed the best path forward.

One of the best starting points is to examine the impact of commoditization on the firm. The simple framework for dealing with commoditization described in Chapter 2 can give valuable insights into whether there are elements of the array of services currently provided that should not be provided to clients by billing for professionals' time. As soon as you start recognizing that some elements of your services fit that profile, you either have to discard them or find new ways of pricing them. These new service models will include process-based services, such as performing or facilitating simple transactions, and online services, which can cover an entire range of offerings from providing access to information to sophisticated expert systems that provide advice within defined parameters.

At this point, the key issue to address is how the new business models sit relative to existing time-billing approaches. Are they distinct offerings, or are they offered by the same professional to the same client within a single engagement? In the case of Deloitte UK and London law firm Berwin Leighton Paisner, they brought together their expertise to establish an interactive online compliance service targeted to small businesses. Since this was outside the core market of both firms, they elected to establish a new company called Be-Professional to provide the service. This enabled both firms to leverage their existing knowledge and systems into new markets, while keeping the venture independent from existing clients and structures. In many other cases the new offerings will be relevant to existing clients of the firm. This means that all front-line professionals that deal with clients have to understand how new offerings complement traditional service delivery, and how they can be combined to create a compelling integrated client offering.

Other revenue models may arise on a case-by-case basis. Recognizing opportunity, firms will start to engage in these on a more consistent basis. For example, developing intellectual property with clients and sharing licensing revenues can become a significant aspect of high-value client relationships, and an important mechanism in creating true partnerships.


Technology

Technology strategy is even more important for professional services firms than for most other industries. For manufacturers, for example, technology helps them to be more efficient at sourcing supplies and in the manufacturing process. In professional services, technology is changing both the way firms work internally and the way they create and deliver value to their clients.

In a sense, the issues of business models and technology are inseparable, as any thorough analysis of how technology will impact the firm will involve reexamining the firm's business models. Commoditization has been a key theme throughout this book. Another perspective on the same issue is simply to ask what current professional services processes can be or might be automated by technology. If these processes can be automated and you choose not to do so, you had better have a very good understanding of how you will compete with firms that have automated those processes.

Shifting to client collaboration brings up a host of strategic issues. It is not difficult to implement collaborative technologies in the client relationship. However, immediately questions start arising of who is playing what role in the value creation process, and as a result how the professional services provided should be priced. These are difficult questions, but the very fact of them arising indicates that you have a deeply embedded relationship. It is far better to face these challenges than to be perceived as a black-box commoditized provider.

One of the most critical issues is that of technology disintermediation. If more of your services are delivered online, does this result in less personal contact with your clients, the erosion of mutual knowledge, and decay of the relationship? Any technology strategy needs to address this eventuality. Of course, as you saw in Chapter 6 there are plenty of clients with whom you do not want to be in constant contact, and this means technology implementation in the client relationship must be done differently across client segments.

The most important aspect of technology strategy, however, is the people and culture involved. When technology is introduced, it changes how people work and their working relationships. Unless people like these changes — and often even if they do — there will be massive challenges in making them happen. The potential of technology to transform professional services — mainly for the better — is extraordinary. It is those firms that succeed in taking their people with them on that journey that will reap the greatest rewards.

### Point B

Seattle-based project management consulting firm Point B has grown from three people at its inception in 1995 to 170 people in four states in 2004, despite being selective about the work it takes on. In the process, it has garnered an award as one of Washington State's best companies to work for.[1] Point B's positioning is unusual for a professional services firm. It focuses on what it calls "project leadership," in which it provides experienced project leaders to its clients as individuals or in very small teams, to help companies run projects and bring problem situations under control. Their mission is to help their clients get from where they are to "point B," where they want to be. They do not take on work as external project managers, and only work with clients who want to retain ownership of the project but who require assistance. The client's internal resources and project management capabilities are utilized as much as possible, with key roles being filled as necessary by Point B to help lead projects to success, working closely with a project leader or sponsor at the client. Unusual for a firm that deals extensively — though not solely — with technology-based projects, Point B has no reseller agreements, vendor alliances, or other external relationships that could jeopardize its clients' perceptions of its objectivity.

While the firm's executives are technically very competent at the mechanics of project management, they often find that a significant part of the value they create is in identifying and resolving interpersonal issues. To obtain results inside organizations, very often human issues need to be addressed. Tim Jenkins, cofounder of Point B, says that the firm hires for, among other criteria, high emotional intelligence and the ability to form relationships with a broad range of people. Being able to work tactfully inside a client and draw out issues and potential roadblocks is frequently at the heart of maximizing the chances of project success.

This positioning means the firm is far less vulnerable in the face of clients' increasing interest in outsourcing and offshoring solutions.

When Point B is engaged to get an existing project back on track, its professionals may use the excuse of updating the project plan and issues log to interview the people involved in the project, and identify hidden issues. They deliberately take advantage of being outside the client organization to work across the company, for example bringing two departments together to resolve hand-off issues, or even informally creating opportunities for people in different parts of the company to meet when they do not know each other as well as they should. In one client engagement, Point B consultants discovered that there was one staff member who was critical to the organization and had knowledge vital to a key project's success, yet who was not even known to the company's senior executives. Point B was able to make him visible internally, and place him in a central role in the project. The external perspective provided by Point B helped bring to fruition some of its client's latent capabilities.

In one case, Point B worked with Microsoft's IT Group on a major project to consolidate the support vendors that provide call center and deskside support to the organization into an integrated global help desk. In collaboration with Microsoft IT, project leaders provided by Point B designed and implemented a transition plan to ensure a successful transfer with minimal interruption to Microsoft staff.

## PROFESSIONAL AND LEADERSHIP DEVELOPMENT

The role of relationship leader is at the heart of firms' ability to create valued knowledge-based relationships, as I have emphasized throughout this book. Their roles as leaders are dual facing: leading their clients into richer, more collaborative relationships, and leading internal relationship teams to bring together the firm's expertise and create true firm-wide relationships with their clients. The qualities required of these types of relationship leaders, as described in Chapter 9, are certainly not in oversupply. On the one hand, firms need to identify those of their professionals who have the capabilities to act as relationship leaders. The reality is that many senior experienced professionals may be outstanding at their practice areas but lack either the interpersonal skills or collaborative orientation essential in a relationship leader. However, it is critical also to provide ongoing leadership development programs both to those that are already capable of working in those roles and to those who are best equipped to move into those roles with appropriate support and development.

Not all professionals are or will become relationship leaders, yet they will all work within relationship teams and interface with client executives. They too require structured development and support to become effective, not just as expert professionals but as effective members of teams that can create knowledge-based partnerships with clients.

## Staged Development Programs

One of the key challenges of professional services firms is that their professionals begin work with deep specialist knowledge acquired through extensive education, yet with almost no exposure to issues of managing clients. Through their careers they progress by developing their knowledge and capabilities, and gradually acquiring more responsibilities in running projects and working with clients. However, this is often done primarily in the area of pure service delivery. When they finally become partners or senior professionals, client responsibilities are suddenly thrust on them, with many ill prepared for this.

Too many professional development programs focus solely on expertise, with little or no attention paid to relationship issues. All development programs should focus on two key domains: the internal and the external. Internal skills include issues such as time management, managing interpersonal conflict, delegating, and staff coaching. External skills encompass managing client expectations, business development, thought leadership, and similar issues. Certainly for professionals new to the workforce, the balance will be to the internal rather than external relationships. However, even from the outset neophyte professionals should be inculcated into an enabling set of attitudes and behaviors in their client interactions and work. As professionals progress through the levels of the firm's hierarchy, the balance of issues will become more equally divided between the internal and the external.

Workshops will certainly be a significant element of ongoing professional development programs. For more senior professionals, however, these will tend to be more facilitated sessions rather than training. The primary value becomes having the time away from the front line to consider what is more and less effective, to share experiences and lessons learned with colleagues, and to learn new frameworks professionals can apply for themselves in their work. This does require highly skilled workshop leaders that can command respect from the experienced professionals they are working with.

In many firms, much of the professional development process is integrated into the job, in working with more experienced colleagues within client engagements. However, it is important that this truly does enable structured learning by junior staff, which depends on the skills and attitudes of the senior professionals. More formal mentoring programs can be extremely valuable, though again mentors need to have appropriate understanding of what will be valuable both to themselves and the persons they mentor.

## Information and Knowledge Skills

Professionals are quintessential knowledge workers. Every aspect of their work involves dealing with information and knowledge. As such, their skills at effectively working with information and knowledge are at the heart of their capabilities. Certainly they need continual development of the specialist knowledge that enables them to add value. However, their most basic skills, on which their effectiveness and success is founded, are knowledge skills. This domain of human skills was introduced in Chapter 3, where I examined the key areas of enhancing organizational knowledge capabilities.

Information and knowledge skills include assessing relevance and filtering information overload, reading and note taking, analysis, synthesizing information, pattern recognition, and decision making. These are all components of the basic skill set of professionals and are essential to their tasks, so most are already good or excellent at these functions. This level of proficiency does not mean that those skills cannot or should not be developed further, however. In fact, developing these skills is one of the prime ways of achieving differentiation in professional services, and usually provides an excellent return on investment.

All of these skills can be developed in classroom training. However, one of the most useful approaches to developing knowledge skills lies in facilitating knowledge workers in developing their own information strategies — taking them through all aspects of the processes, from accessing and filtering information to decision making and communication. Each professional, with unique job characteristics and his or her own preferences and style for dealing with information, will benefit from a different approach to dealing with information and knowledge. Taking professionals through this process gives them the basic tools they require. It allows them the opportunity to stand back from their work and enhance their personal skills from the perspective of adding value to information and knowledge, especially in the context of how that creates value for clients.

## Knowledge Communication Skills

Knowledge communication skills may be a subset of communication skills, but to be developed effectively they require substantially different approaches to most types of communication training. Most communication training is related to sales functions, gaining a fairly basic understanding of personality types, or such tasks as writing business letters. While these are important skills, these should be considered foundation skills.

Knowledge communication is based on far more than clarity and persuasion. It is about being able to effect in others a changed understanding of sophisticated concepts.

The primary skills and knowledge underlying knowledge communication are an understanding of cognitive styles and the structure of mental models, especially the psychology of decision making. These basic skills can be applied to adapting interaction to individual clients, developing presentations, facilitating meetings, and designing effective written and visual communication.

Knowledge communication skills can be developed in a classroom environment, but must be practiced. For example, training in cognitive styles should include exercises that force professionals to adapt their communication of recommendations and concepts to clients with different styles. Many training courses implement similar approaches for application in a sales environment. However, few do so in a knowledge communication context.

## Facilitation and Knowledge Development

Developing knowledge is a cooperative process largely based on the interaction of people with contrasting mental models. Facilitation is *the* foundation skill for knowledge elicitation and creation. Good facilitation is essentially about achieving the best from a group of people. This involves resolving apparent conflicts resulting from divergence in group members' mental models, and together building a frame or result that respects and builds on the diversity and difference of perspective and experience in the group.

Facilitation is a fundamental skill, which draws on a specific range of interpersonal capabilities that can be developed over time. Many training and development programs are available that focus on facilitation. It is helpful if these are framed specifically in a knowledge development context. Some related skills also central to knowledge creation and development were covered in Chapter 10. These include brainstorming, process management, and the development of organizational and inter-organizational knowledge creation loops.

## Flexibility in Communication

The law of requisite variety, introduced in Chapter 4, suggests that the more flexible your behavior the more likely you are to achieve your desired outcomes. This is very clearly the case in communication. People who have a narrow repertoire of communication styles experience limited success in communicating with others, whereas those with extensive flexibility in their approaches to communication are far more effective. They are able to keep on trying new and different approaches to communicating until they achieve the results they are looking for, rather than simply continuing to try the same approach even if it gives inconsistent results. This is one of the most critical skills in facilitation. A good facilitator has access to a very broad repertoire of behaviors, and is constantly willing to experiment with new approaches in order to allow groups to achieve what they want.

Developing flexibility should be an overriding objective of all training and development in communication. It is an ongoing process, and only over time are people able to broaden their access to different approaches to communicating with others.

## ENHANCING CLIENT COMMUNICATION

One of the most important areas in enhancing the value added to clients is designing the presentation of information so that it can be readily assimilated and internalized as knowledge. The effective presentation of information has always been a major focus in professional services. However, focusing on effective knowledge transfer rather than simple provision of information brings out the value of using more innovative approaches.

## Structuring Communication

Information presented as written documents must be organized effectively to be readily used by clients. This is traditionally accomplished in a hierarchical structure, which enumerates points and subpoints. This is perhaps best encapsulated in the well-known "pyramid principle," which Barbara Minto developed when she was responsible for communications at McKinsey & Company, and which is still the de facto standard for writing at the firm.[2]

This principle proposes that communication should be structured in a pyramid, with the apex representing the purpose or conclusions of the message, and supporting information and ideas providing more detail as you move further down the pyramid, based on grouping ideas logically. The most efficient way to provide concepts to readers is from the top down, which means that they get the essence of the communication at the outset, and can choose how much detail they access in supporting the primary message.

Online communication allows far greater flexibility in the structure of information and communication than afforded by paper documents. Overviews and toolbars on the computer screen can indicate exactly where in the hierarchy and network of documents or concepts one is currently located, giving an inherent sense of overall structure.

## Stories and Metaphors

People learn best through stories, metaphors, and analogies. Supporting evidence for this is presented in the Appendix. Most people will acknowledge that they learn most easily when they are presented with stories having personal relevance, metaphors enabling them to relate their experience to new areas, and analogies between concepts. The richness and open-ended nature of these forms of communication facilitate people in integrating new ideas into their ways of thinking, and developing their own enabling knowledge structures. The process of knowledge acquisition is essentially one of forming relationships between new and existing experience and concepts. Using approaches to communication that intrinsically relate to the relationships and structure of experience allows for the easiest and richest learning. Clearly, these approaches are not only very effective for communicating knowledge but assist people in creating their own knowledge by introducing different perspectives on their existing knowledge.

3M has applied these principles to reform its business planning process around the use of stories, which it calls strategic narratives. These have replaced the traditional "bullet-point" or list-based approach to planning, which 3M found did not evoke the richness of thinking necessary for effective strategic planning.[3] Manpower, as discussed in Chapter 8, has designed its client extranet around stories, giving people concrete examples of how their peers have achieved successful results. This approach not only allows them to integrate that knowledge easily but to create entertaining and accessible information that attracts attention.

## VISUAL COMMUNICATION

Working with visual representations is one of the areas with the greatest scope for enhancement of knowledge communication. The Appendix reviews the evidence that visual representation greatly increases the comprehension and retention of conceptual information when used as a complement to text. In addition, good visuals attract the eye and help to cut through the flood of documents received by busy executives.

While many professionals have emerged from an education process that is very text intensive and focused on linear structure, this does not necessarily match the cognitive styles of their clients. As business becomes more complex, it is important to move beyond linear representations, and use other forms to convey the interrelationships between concepts and activities. The issue is one of using visual representations as a vehicle for representing information and as a tool for discussing and generating ideas and approaches. This immediately creates a knowledge-based interaction.

## Information and Concept Visualization

Data and information visualization are well-developed fields that use graphics to represent and convey large quantities of complex data. Yale University's Edward Tufte has helped take information visualization to an art form with his books *Envisioning Information* and *The Visual Display of Quantitative Information*.[4] The ready availability of advanced software to transform data into graphs and other visual representations has meant these approaches are becoming far more widely used. This is making it considerably easier for people to assimilate large quantities of information, and sometimes the relationships within it, although in general visual representations could still be used far more widely and effectively.

Concept visualization is distinct from information visualization. It seeks to convey conceptual understanding rather than simply information. The precept is to design visual representations — usually as a complement to text — that maximize the effective internalization of knowledge. This can be framed both as knowledge communication in conveying specific conceptual frameworks or as knowledge elicitation in the sense of providing clients with an opportunity to frame and structure their knowledge in a useful way.[5]

## Mind Mapping

One approach to visual representations beginning to be used fairly broadly in the business community is mind mapping, a tool originated by Tony Buzan.[6] It makes use of a visual format to show the relationships between ideas, which for many people is a far easier way to represent their thinking, and allows all the key concepts of a given subject to be visible in one diagram. A simple mind map of some of the concepts illustrated in this book is shown in Figure 12-1. Wherever possible it is valuable to incorporate color into mind maps, as it attracts attention better and can facilitate the assimilation of ideas.

New York-based Inferential Focus synthesizes information about emerging trends in society and business for its client base of major

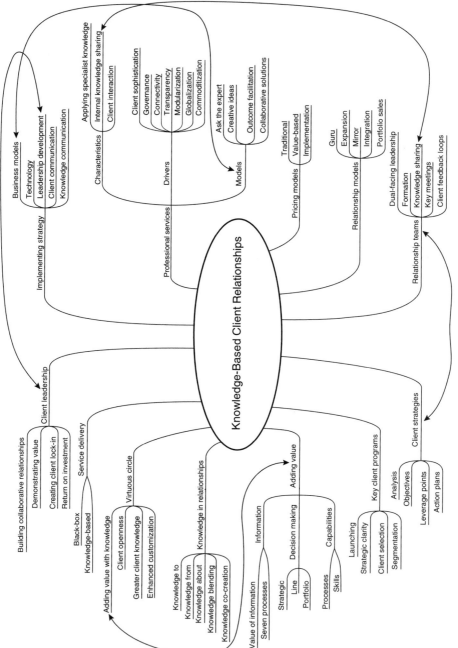

FIGURE 12–1  *Mind map of this book.* Copyright © 2004 Advanced Human Technologies. Reprinted with permission.

corporations and institutional investors. To communicate these trends and ideas to its clients the firm uses mind maps, which help bring together disparate information in a way that clearly shows the relationships and relevance to the user.[7]

## Visual Metaphors

The use of visual metaphors can allow very powerful communication of concepts and ideas. People can directly relate to the concepts presented in visual metaphors, which are broadly accessible and easy to internalize. Root Learning of Perrysburg, Ohio, produces learning maps for its clients based on visual metaphors. Much of its work is in strategic planning and change management programs, in which the issues facing the organization and its strategic directions are presented in a number of detailed four-foot by six-foot graphics. The intention is for staff and executives quite literally to see the big picture.[8]

## LEADERSHIP IN PROFESSIONAL SERVICES

Knowledge and relationships are at the heart of the future of business. Combined into powerful knowledge-based relationships, they provide the only sustainable escape from the driving force of commoditization. Yet these types of relationships rarely arise unbidden. Leadership is required to demonstrate the way forward into these new ways of working.

Professional services are based on highly specialized knowledge, and thus will play an increasingly important role as our world becomes more complex. Yet the education of many professionals has not prepared them to move beyond their domains of specialization. Professional services firms must develop their professionals into true leaders. Dual-facing leadership is required. They must lead their clients into deep, collaborative relationships, and they must lead diverse teams of professionals to create value for clients far beyond what can be achieved by an uncoordinated set of individuals.

Information technology is in the process of transforming business. Yet, ironically, this makes people all the more important. As everything else becomes commoditized, what will remain as a source of differentiation are the things that are most human. There will always be domains in which human knowledge transcends computers. In addition, relationships between people, especially those that bring together unique knowledge and personalities, are at the center of business.

Knowing that the future of professional services is about people, knowledge, relationships, and effective communication, we must work to better understand the process by which people acquire, create, and develop knowledge. Applying this understanding effectively is perhaps at the heart of creating greater value in a knowledge-based economy. The science of cognitive psychology has much to teach us in terms of understanding how people think and work with their knowledge. However, much work remains to be done in applying these insights in practical ways in a business context. The Appendix offers a framework for some of the research that has been done in the field, in a way that can be applied in business.

While parts of business and society will become increasingly mechanized, the opportunity also exists for a far deeper appreciation of people's abilities to create and apply knowledge individually and collectively. Bringing people together in order to jointly enrich their knowledge, perhaps especially across organizational boundaries, will become a finer art and science, and increasingly central to the creation of value in the knowledge economy. I am deeply optimistic about the future of business, because I see people all around the world who believe in their own and others' potential, and want to work more closely with others to create knowledge and build deeper, closer relationships between people. I believe that this is the only way to achieve lasting commercial success, as well as being the pathway to gain the greatest joy and satisfaction from your work. I hope to meet you on the journey.

## NOTES

1   Deidre Gregg, "Preferring Gradual Growth, Consulting Firm Point B Is Selective About Its Projects," *Puget Sound Business Journal*, May 21, 2004.

2   Barbara Minto, *The Minto Pyramid Principle: Logic in Writing, Thinking, and Problem Solving*, London: Minto International, 1996.

3   Gordon Shaw, Robert Brown, and Philip Bromiley, "Strategic Stories: How 3M Is Rewriting Business Planning," *Harvard Business Review*, May/June 1998.

4   Edward Tufte, *Envisioning Information*, Chesire, CT: Graphics Press, 1990; and *The Visual Display of Quantitative Information*, Chesire, CT: Graphics Press, 1992. A less spectacular but useful and exhaustive review of approaches to conveying information visually is given by Robert Harris in *Information Graphics*, Atlanta: Management Graphics, 1996.

5   Richard Saul Wurman has done much to develop the scope of visual communication. He has presented the work of some of the leading practitioners in the field in a beautiful book. See Richard Saul Wurman, *Information Architects*, New York: Graphis, 1997.

6   Tony Buzan with Barry Buzan, *The Mind Map Book*, rev. ed., London: BBC Books, 1993.

7   Mark Fischetti, "Masters of the (Information) Universe," *Fast Company*, August/September 1997, pp. 181–187.

8   See Sherman Stratford, "Bringing Sears into the New World," *Fortune*, October 13, 1997.

# APPENDIX
# The Nature of Mental Models
## How People Acquire Knowledge

The effective transfer of knowledge is predicated on understanding how people acquire knowledge and understanding. Cognitive science is centered on the study of how people learn, think, and communicate, and thus can provide us with valuable lessons in this domain. Here we will review some of the findings from the field of cognitive science — which is comprised of a broad array of disciplines, including cognitive psychology, linguistics, neuroscience, and philosophy — to identify lessons we can apply directly to business. These are rich and diverse disciplines, and our objectives in drawing on them are very specifically to learn how to be more effective at implementing knowledge transfer.

Cognitive science is divided by many arguments over often fundamental issues in the field. Ray Jackendoff, a leading researcher in the field, delicately refers to the "unfortunate sociological problems in cognitive science."[1] Without attempting to resolve any of these arguments, I will draw on the most relevant research and thinking in the field to provide useful lessons for business professionals. Despite the broad diversity of approaches of the scientists working in the field, major progress has been made over the last decades in understanding many of the fundamental issues of human cognition. Delving into the theoretical and empirical background of the foundations of knowledge acquisition will be very valuable in building an understanding of how to design effective client communication and interaction. Unfortunately, this appendix only offers the scope for a brief overview of the field, but I hope it stimulates interest and further study in what I believe is an increasingly critical aspect of leading business practice.

## COGNITIVE STRUCTURE AND COGNITIVE STYLE

The two major topics we will cover are cognitive structure and cognitive style. Cognitive structure deals with the *structures* of the conceptual models on which people base their understanding of their environment. Understanding what is common across the structure of people's mental models is extremely valuable in a variety of ways. Structuring ideas and information in ways that are aligned with the structural forms of mental models means they can be more easily assimilated and internalized. Being familiar with the structure of the mental models of individuals and groups enables far more effective approaches to enriching those models, and adding value to the decision-making processes on which they are based.

While cognitive structure examines what is common across people in terms of their cognition, cognitive style looks at the *differences* between people in how they take in information from their environment, make sense of it, and act on it. As such, understanding cognitive styles is very valuable in customizing presentations to and interactions with individuals and groups in order to result in the greatest knowledge transfer and perceived value.

## MENTAL REPRESENTATIONS

We can never experience reality directly; we must rely on the information provided by our senses. That sensory experience is all we have on which to base the way we think about the world. In some way we must form internal representations of the world from our experiences in order to be able to think about it.

The terms *mental representation* and *mental model* are defined and used in a wide variety of ways by different scholars. To avoid confusion with others' definitions, I will use *mental representation* to mean how people represent their experiences, memories, imaginings, and concepts of the world. These constitute the basic elements people use in thinking. The term *mental model* refers to the models of the world people use to understand their environment and guide how they think and act in order to achieve their objectives. These are constituted from the building blocks of mental representations.

The idea that how people think is based on mental representations is widely (though not universally) accepted by cognitive scientists. Much of the debate is over the nature of the representations people hold in their minds, and how they are used for thinking and knowledge acquisition.

It is worth pointing out that it is very difficult to gain awareness of your own mental processes, and while many will recognize some of the elements of mental representations in themselves they are not likely to perceive them with any degree of accuracy. Still, most of the aspects we will discuss have been demonstrated empirically, and have proven to be useful in the effective communication of knowledge.

## The Nature of Mental Representations

The idea of mental representation has formed the basis for much of the study of cognitive psychology, and there has been heated debate on the nature of those mental representations. The two major types of mental representations that have been proposed are analogical and propositional.

Analogical representations are internal sensory-based representations of external experience, which are effectively analogies of that experience. They are usually taken to mean visual imagery, though they can just as well refer to internally generated or perceived sounds, feelings, or other experiences. Essentially they are sensory constructs, meaning representations based on our five senses.

Propositional representations are abstract in that they are based on symbols and the relationships between them. As such, they are similar to language or mathematical formulae, though they function on a more fundamental level, representing the underlying concepts and relationships people then translate into and from language.

Other researchers have suggested other types of representation. However, analogical and propositional representations — with some variations on these — together cover most of the proposed formulations of the nature of mental representation. Much of the debate in cognitive science has been centered on which of these two types of representation is correct, and the specifics of how they are manipulated in knowledge acquisition and reasoning.

## Dual-Coding Theory

The dual-coding theory, proposed by Allan Paivio, has been perhaps the most influential approach to understanding mental representations.[2] This suggests that people in fact use both analogical and propositional representations in independent but interconnected systems. There has been strong experimental evidence to support the dual-coding theory.[3]

Each of the two representational systems specializes in representing and processing distinct types of information. The propositional system is mainly oriented to language and other tasks requiring sequential processing. The analogical system is usually considered to represent images, and as such deals with visual representations and other tasks requiring spatial or concurrent processing. Each system is proposed to use different units or symbols for representation, but related symbols are linked between the two systems. For example, the mental image of a cat would be linked to the concept and word *cat*. The dual-coding theory is represented diagrammatically in Figure A–1.

This separation of representational systems into propositional and analogical, or more crudely words and pictures, reflects the popular distinction of left brain and right brain. Indeed, evidence suggests that there is correlation between these types of processing and the

Propositional representations          Analogical representations

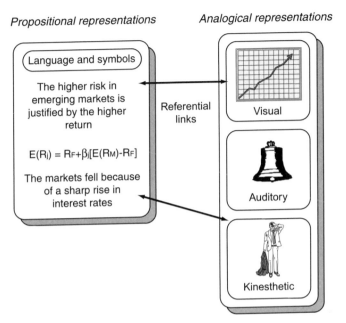

FIGURE A–1    *A diagrammatic representation of dual-coding theory.*

hemispheres of the brain, though it would be a mistake to take these for the same idea.[4]

## Sensory-Based Representations

People use analogical representations based on their senses. People primarily form internal representations that are visual (images or pictures), auditory (sounds), or kinesthetic (physical sensations or feelings), though they can also be olfactory (referring to the sense of smell) and gustatory (referring to the sense of taste, for example when we read a menu and form representations of what we would enjoy the most).

Visual representations are in many situations the most efficient system for information and high-level concept manipulation. An immense amount of information can be contained in a visual representation, often more than in any single propositional representation, and in a way that can be manipulated and processed rapidly and with flexibility. Anecdotally, businesspeople tend to show a preference for visual internal representations.

What are usually referred to as visual representations are better thought of as visuospatial — that is, combining visual representations and the apprehension of spatial relationships. This faculty can be particularly important in conceptual thinking and skills, and has been linked to mathematical ability. Forming internal visuospatial representations does not come easily to everyone. However, these types of images can be extremely effective for the communication of complex concepts to the right audience.[5]

One of the many useful distinctions from the field of neuro-linguistic programming (NLP), originally developed by John Grinder and Richard Bandler in the early 1970s, is the idea of *submodalities*, which takes our understanding of analogical representations to a further level of richness.[6] These introduce further distinctions within each of the major modalities of the representational systems. For example, submodalities or distinctions within internal visual representations could include how bright or dim the representation is, how clear or blurred, how near or far, and so on. The concept was actually first introduced by the American psychologist William James in 1890.[7] However, the field of NLP has found that varying the submodalities of representations can have a significant impact on understanding, emotion, and belief. Later in the appendix we will examine preferences in the use of representational systems as a key element of cognitive style.

Language

Language is the primary structure used for propositional representations, and the basis of many aspects of thought. The topic of language as a basis for knowledge is clearly too vast to address here. However, a few distinctions will help us understand language within the context of mental representations and models.

The great linguist Noam Chomsky in his early work on transformational grammar made the distinction between the *surface structure* and *deep structure* of language.[8] The surface structure is the actual words and structure used in communication, while the deep structure is the structure of the underlying meaning beneath the communication and the relationships between the component concepts. In a simple illustration, the sentences "He gave her the report" and "She was given the report by him" have different surface structures but an identical meaning, and thus the same deep structure. Mental representations of language are formed at the level of deep structure or meaning rather than surface structure or the actual words used.[9] The act of interpreting the meaning of a sentence is the same as that of forming a mental representation of it.

Chomsky's work is largely based on the principle that all humans are born with a "language faculty," which means that we naturally learn whatever language we are exposed to when we are young. However, that language faculty only allows certain rules in the structure and syntax of language. As such, while there are many thousands of languages in the world every one of these has in common the same underlying "universal grammar," which is in fact determined by our biological nature. As such, the mental representations people have access to in understanding language are based on this universal grammar.[10]

## MENTAL MODELS

To review our definition from Chapter 4, a mental model is the model or representation we hold in our mind of the way we believe the world or some part of it works. Mental models are based on mental representations that are either or both analogical or propositional. They provide a framework that helps to give meaning to our perceptions in relation to our previous experiences.

## Mental Models as the Foundation of Knowledge and Understanding

Our working definition of knowledge as "the capacity to act effectively" gives us insight into what it means to understand something. To be able to act effectively within a system requires us to have a model not only of how that system has worked in the past but of how it will act in the future, and a model of our relationship with that system. That is what will allow us to act in a way that will (if our model is useful) achieve the results we desire.

Kenneth Craik, who was the first modern exponent of these ideas, wrote in 1943 that "If the organism carries a 'small-scale model' of external reality and its own possible actions within its head, it is able to try out various alternatives, conclude which is the best of them, react to future situations before they arise, utilize the knowledge of past events in dealing with the present and future, and in every way to react in a much fuller, safer, and more competent manner to the emergencies which face it."[11]

In a similar vein, Philip Johnson-Laird, author of the seminal book *Mental Models*, explains: "If you know what causes a phenomenon, what results from it, how to influence, control, initiate or prevent it, how it relates to others states of affairs or how it resembles them, how to predict its onset and course, what its internal or underlying 'structure' is, then to some extent you understand it. The psychological core of understanding, I shall assume, consists in your having a 'working model' of the phenomenon in your mind. If you understand inflation, a mathematical proof, the way a computer works, DNA or a divorce, then you have a mental representation that serves as a model. . . ."[12]

People's mental models can also be understood as their belief systems. People act on the basis of their mental models, meaning that they implicitly behave as if the foundations and assumptions on which their models are based are true. One way to get insight into people's mental models is to observe the implicit beliefs that guide their attitudes and behaviors.

## Internalization and Integration

Internalization is the process of converting information and experiences into personal knowledge. This is a critical stage in knowledge transfer and all knowledge management. For experience and information to become knowledge, it must be integrated into our existing knowledge and understanding in some form. If there is no integration or connection to what we know already, these are simply remembered facts that do not contribute to our understanding of the world. New experience or information is integrated into our existing understanding by forming connections and associations to existing knowledge and experience, which ultimately means integrating it into our mental models. Since our mental models form the basis of our understanding and chosen action, new information must be integrated in some way into these in order to become knowledge.

The way these connections and associations are formed is based on the intrinsic structure of mental models, which is discussed below. Understanding these principles gives us real insight into not only mental models but how information and experience is internalized into these mental models.

Bower and Hilgard noted that the more objects, patterns, and concepts are stored in memory the more easily is new knowledge about these acquired and used in new contexts. Since learning is associative in terms of making linkages with existing concepts, the ease of acquiring new knowledge depends on the breadth of the categories into which knowledge is organized, the differentiation of those categories, and the richness of linkages across these.[13] This is a critical issue in knowledge acquisition. It means that diversity of knowledge and experience is one of the most fundamental factors in the ability to develop new knowledge, and that people who are overly focused in their experience and knowledge base can be handicapped in further knowledge acquisition.

More generally, the richer the connections and associations we make with our existing experience the more powerful and useful the knowledge gained. If we hear or read some information, and we can relate it only weakly to our existing mental models, it will have limited impact. If we perceive many different associations and perspectives on the new information, it will have a significant impact on the content and possibly structure of our mental models, and result in changed understanding.

This is one of the key reasons dialogue is one of the most powerful sources of changed understanding and richer mental models. Rich interaction between two or more different mental models and perspectives in the process of an ongoing conversation uncovers many potential associations, connections, and perspectives. In presenting information, giving multiple perspectives that relate as broadly as possible to the experience and knowledge base of the client will result in the most valuable knowledge acquisition.

## THE STRUCTURE OF MENTAL MODELS

The basic structures of mental models are common across all people. As noted cognitive philosopher Jerry Fodor states, some of the most fundamental aspects of thought and belief are "grounded in the 'architecture' of mental representation."[14] We can never know the actual representations of the world people hold in their minds, but we can discover some of the structures of their mental models, and how ideas and concepts are related within those. Understanding these structures provides us with a very powerful tool to instruct how we design the communication or elicitation of knowledge, and all interaction with our clients. As Alfred Korzybski pointed out, while a map or model is *not* the territory it represents, its usefulness is based on it having a similar structure to its subject.[15]

Research in the field of cognitive science has allowed us to identify some of the underlying structures and forms of mental models common across people. Johnson-Laird suggests that the structures of mental models are identical to the perceived structures of the situations they represent.[16] What this in fact tells us is that the structures we perceive in our environment are aligned with the structures available to us in building our mental models. The structure of mental models has three central attributes.

- Associative
- Hierarchical
- Systemic

We will go on to apply these principles in examining how stories, scenarios, and metaphors are used in the acquisition of knowledge.

## Associative

Aristotle first proposed that all knowledge is based on associations between ideas. The idea of associations as a basis of knowledge and understanding has played an important role through the history of philosophy. Clearly people form associations between concepts and ideas. This has been modeled in cognitive psychology in the form of *semantic networks*, which describe concepts that are associated mentally, and sometimes the degree of association or similarity between them, which determines how likely one concept will trigger another. Semantic networks have been shown to be good models for predicting some experimental findings in memory and recognition, and they provide a basic framework for understanding the nature of the way associations are formed and used in cognition. A simple example of part of one person's semantic network is illustrated in Figure A–2.

The following are the primary ways in which associations between concepts are formed.

- Similarity and analogy
- Causality
- Contiguity
- Contrast

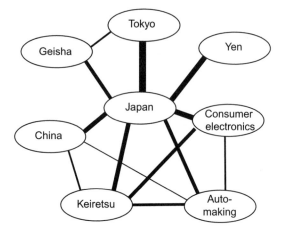

FIGURE A–2 *Part of a person's semantic network.*

## Similarity and Analogy

The most fundamental and important means of association is through perceived similarity. It can be argued that the foundation of thought is how people identify similarity between different things. This issue has been at the heart of much research in cognitive psychology, in an attempt to gain an understanding of how people categorize perceptions and concepts, and thus form associations between them.

Two things are perceived to be similar if they have one or more *attributes* in common. In Tversky's influential model, the degree of similarity between two concepts is based on the attributes they have in common, lessened by the attributes that are different or distinct.[17] Each person will perceive differently what the relevant attributes are, and their degree of similarity. However, the structure of how this is done is common. For example, some of the attributes that Spain and Italy have in common are that they are Mediterranean countries, predominantly Catholic, and speak related Romantic languages, while some of the attributes that are different are the types of food they eat and their political systems. Based on their perception of the importance, and similarity or difference, of these and other attributes, most people see greater similarity between Spain and Italy than, say, Spain and Germany.

Although similarity refers to the commonality of attributes between concepts, analogy refers to the commonality of the relational structure of attributes between concepts. As such, in an analogy the attributes of two concepts may not be common, and in fact usually are not. However, the structure of the relationships between the two concepts is similar. A couple of examples will help to distinguish between similarity and analogy. A mouse is like a rat because they have a number of attributes in common: they look alike, they have whiskers, they both eat cheese, and so on. That is, they are similar. However, an atom is like a solar system not because electrons are like planets but because the relationship of electrons to the nucleus is similar to the relationship of planets to the sun: the solar system is an analogy for an atom.

Dedre Gentner notes that our understanding of analogies "conveys a system of connected knowledge, not a mere assortment of independent facts," and proposes that when people use an analogy the relations mapped across domains are dominated by the higher-order relations.[18] Since understanding is largely based on the relationships between concepts, this mapping across of the high-level structure of relationships shows why analogies are one of the richest tools for knowledge communication.

*Causality*

Causality is a very important element underlying our mental models, and in indicating how different concepts are associated or linked. Our judgments of causality that are implicit in our mental models are critical in determining how we act in seeking the outcomes we desire.

On one level, the basic rules people use to judge causality hold no major surprises, and experimental evidence generally supports what the philosopher David Hume proposed over 200 years ago. For example, whether one thing causes another is often judged according to the time interval and regularity between the perceived cause and

effect, and how physically close the two events are. The covariation
— the degree to which two events occur or do not occur together —
is an important cue to judging causality.[19]

On the other hand, the way people judge causality and probability
has been shown to be subject to many errors and distortions, and an
entire field of study on "cognitive bias" has arisen to research how
people misjudge expectations of events and the relationships between
them. Just one example is the so-called "conjunction fallacy," in which
people often judge the probability of two events happening together
as higher than one of them happening in isolation.[20]

## Contiguity

Association between two ideas is often engendered because they have
been experienced as contiguous; that is, occurring close together in
time or in space. For example, if you heard a particular song on your
first date with your partner, hearing that song again will often evoke
those associations and memories.

## Contrast

In addition to similarity, association can be formed by contrast, in
linking ideas because they are perceived to be opposites or contrasting. In this way, black can be associated with white, and fat with thin.
This is usually less important than other means of forming associations, but is still common.

## Chunking and Hierarchies

George Miller proposed in his landmark paper "The Magic Number
Seven, Plus or Minus Two" that people can only think about approx-
imately seven "chunks" of information simultaneously.[21] This is still
generally accepted as valid. The term *chunk* is used to mean an integrated unit of information, such as a number, word, or concept.
Herbert Simon discovered that the number of chunks people could
hold depended on the complexity of the chunks. He later stated that

in many situations people only hold four to five chunks simultaneously.[22] One of the critical lessons from this is that we cannot expect people to take in simultaneously more than five to seven concepts or ideas. In communication and presentation, we must limit ourselves to this number of concepts.

If you group a number of concepts together on the basis of similarity or any other association, you can then label this group and think of it as a single unit. It has become a single chunk. This frees up our limited thinking capacity to take in additional concepts. For example, if China, India, Thailand, Indonesia, Brazil, Ukraine, and Hungary are determined to be emerging markets for your services, these can then be grouped and thought about as a single concept of "emerging markets."

If the chunks that are formed by grouping similar concepts are in turn grouped with other similar chunks — in this instance "emerging markets" being grouped with say "developed markets" and "minor markets" — a hierarchy of concepts is formed. In this way, the limitations of human thought — specifically on the number of ideas it can hold in the mind simultaneously — automatically lead to a hierarchical structure of thinking.[23] This is shown in Figure A-3.

This process of chunking concepts to form hierarchies is in fact the basis of the development of expertise. Once people have sufficient

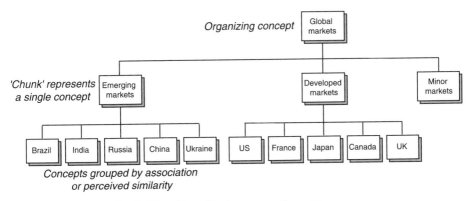

FIGURE A–3    *Chunking builds a hierarchical structure of concepts.*

familiarity with a topic to perceive the underlying similarities between concepts, they can form chunks that are more meaningful in their relationships, and build a hierarchical structure of knowledge relevant and useful in classifying concepts and instances. It is only in building this hierarchy over time that experts can acquire a "big picture" view of their field of expertise, which reflects the structure and relationships of the key relevant concepts.

This has been supported by a range of experiments. One experiment asked novice and expert physicists to classify problems into related groups. It emerged that the novices grouped problems in terms of the surface features evident in their initial appearance, while the experts grouped them based on the underlying principles relating the problems.[24]

## Systemic

In addition to being associative and hierarchical, mental models are also systemic, in the sense of incorporating nonlinear and recursive structures. Systemic thinking is defined by incorporating feedback and self-reference, so the effects of one element of the system can flow through the system to end up influencing and impacting that same element. Douglas Hofstadter in his Pulitzer-prize-winning classic *Gödel, Escher, Bach* developed the theme that consciousness, as well as other phenomena such as imagery and analogies, is based on recursivity (or what he called "Strange Loops"[25]), while cognitive scientists Maturana and Varela have argued that cognition is a biological phenomenon stemming from the intrinsic circularity of the organization of living systems.[26] Pursuing another angle, M.I.T.'s John Morecroft found that the broadly accepted view that decision making is based on bounded rationality, as originally proposed by Herbert Simon and his colleagues, results directly in the feedback structures on which system dynamics is based.[27] Today, cognitive mapping techniques consistently incorporate these recursive and self-referential aspects of mental models.[28]

Systems diagrams have been explicitly designed to represent systemic models and situations, notably in their implicit portrayal of causality, and are a very effective means of communication of complex relationships and principles. A simple example of a systems diagram is Figure 1–2 in this book. Basic guidelines for developing systems diagrams can be found in Senge and in O'Connor and McDermott.[29]

## Scenarios and Stories

People think about and understand the world in terms of scenarios and stories. Neurobiologist Ingvar, by examining the role of the prefrontal cortex in how people organize their cognition of time, proposed that it is through our "memories of the future" — which are imagined scenarios of what may happen — that we perceive meaning in the world.[30] This implies that it is intrinsically human to form scenarios of the future as a basis for reasoning and action.

Research by Tversky and Kahnemann suggests that people will judge the probability of a scenario to be higher if it is more detailed, contains representative events, and is causally linked.[31] Stimulating people's imagination through the presentation of scenarios will cause them to add further detail, thus building richer mental representations of those scenarios, and the attribution of a higher likelihood to them. This has implications in many domains of human behavior. However, it emphasizes the importance of rich and detailed descriptions of possible scenarios or events in knowledge communication.

Many practitioners have emphasized the importance of stories in knowledge acquisition. Part of the reason for this is the way people organize their understanding of causality temporally, as studied by Ingvar. We experience the world as a sequence of events, so it is far easier for us to find similarities and internalize knowledge based on other sequences of events, which we call stories. In addition, stories are rich in the potential for analogies. People will each find their own useful analogies and learnings they can map against their mental models in order to find more effective ways of thinking.

## Metaphors

Metaphors are tools. Metaphors are poetry. Metaphors are bridges to connect our knowledge. Many people think of metaphors as linguistic flourishes, but they are in fact at the very heart of the way we think, and very powerful tools for communicating knowledge effectively. People acquire knowledge by relating it to their existing experience and understanding. Presenting ideas and information with the aid of metaphors inherently provides people with a means and structure for integrating these into their mental models, in a way that draws out the key salient points and enables rich connections to form.

Leading linguists and cognitive scientists George Lakoff and Mark Johnson, in their delightful and influential book *Metaphors We Live By*, explore in detail the nature of the metaphors that guide our everyday perceptions and communication.[32] They find that most of our conceptual system is metaphorical in nature, and they in fact argue that "human thought processes are largely metaphorical." Metaphors are a very valuable resource in evoking conceptual understanding, of course as a complement to more prosaic approaches.

## Applications of the Structure of Mental Models

Understanding the underlying structure of people's mental models is the best possible foundation for designing the communication of conceptual knowledge. The associative, hierarchical, and systemic nature of the structure of mental models suggests that these structures should also be implicit in the information and ideas we present.

Hierarchy has traditionally been a fairly strong feature of much business communication, though it could be used in far more diverse means, particularly in presenting systems of knowledge and in positioning specific communications within a broader context and framework. The "lateral" associations and relationships between concepts are less commonly explicit in communication, partly as this is very difficult to represent effectively and succinctly in text. The failure to address the systemic nature of concepts has been a major weakness in most business communication. However, this is rapidly changing as these ideas become more widely accepted. Systems diagrams, and other illustrations that indicate the recursive nature of causality, are valuable tools. Generally, in order to represent adequately these key structural attributes in communication requires the complementary use of both text and images.

There is strong empirical evidence that scenarios and stories are among the most powerful means of conveying structured information and ideas. Not only should story-based approaches be used extensively in high-value communication but these should involve as broad a range of styles and media as possible, including print, voice, movies, and enactment. Metaphors are one of the most useful tools for conveying conceptual information, and can be presented as words or images. To be effective, however, they must be well thought out, as the complex relationships between two ideas may not always fully support the intended communication.

## COGNITIVE STYLE

The idea of cognitive style recognizes that we all have different approaches and styles to thinking and acting. Cognitive style can be considered a subset of the broader field of personality style, which encompasses all aspects of how a person thinks and behaves. The fields can be difficult to distinguish, and both are useful to us. However, our primary intention and focus here is to understand better the differences in how people go about knowledge-based functions such as taking in information, analyzing it, and making decisions. The idea of personality styles has been applied, for example, to teaching salespeople to adapt their approaches to match the personality and preferences of their clients. However, this is done more commonly as a sales tool than as a way of adding greater value. Much of the value of understanding clients' cognitive styles is enabling you to match their preferences for dealing with information with the way in which you present information and communicate with them, thus building a foundation for rich client relationships.

## Myers-Briggs Type Indicator

The most widely used personality profiling test in business is the Myers-Briggs Type Indicator (MBTI), which was developed in the early 1940s and is now administered to over 3 million people annually. It is based on the original personality distinctions of psychologist Carl Jung, though it has been developed into a more rigorous and testable framework. While it is more a measure of personality style than cognitive style per se, it is useful in many ways, including in engineering the creative abrasion described in Chapter 10. In addition, it does have significant cognitive aspects.[33]

The MBTI categorizes people along four dimensions, each defined by two polar opposites of their primary orientation or preference. These dimensions are Extrovert/Introvert; Sensor/Intuitor; Thinker/Feeler; and Judger/Perceiver.

The dimension of Extrovert/Introvert examines attitudes toward the external world that are reflected in behaviors. Sensor/Intuitor is an important cognitive dimension. Sensors are oriented to concrete information, evidence, and facts — what they can sense directly — whereas Intuitors tend to perceive abstract relationships and meaning, and rely more on their intuition than descriptive facts in understanding the world. Thinkers tend to think rationally, and attempt to be objective in assessing their actions, while Feelers choose a subjective approach, and are inclined to base decisions on their values rather than analysis. Judgers prefer order, structure, and predictability in their environment, whereas Perceivers tend to be spontaneous and to assess and respond to situations as they develop, rather than plan in detail.

Understanding the preferences of our clients along these dimensions is clearly very valuable in a broad range of contexts, including many aspects of relationship development and management. Many companies provide not only salespeople but also other staff with training in the MBTI to increase their awareness and ability to communicate effectively with people who have contrasting personality styles. Of the four dimensions in the MBTI, an understanding of Sensor/Intuitor is the most directly relevant in designing knowledge communication. However, the others are all valuable in developing richer communication and client relationships.

### Learning Style Inventory

The Learning Style Inventory (LSI) was developed on the basis of work by David Kolb on learning cycles, described in Chapter 10. It identifies how people prefer to learn. As such, it is directly relevant to our concerns of maximizing the utility of knowledge transfer. Understanding the diversity of different learning styles can be very valuable in adapting and tailoring our communication.

The LSI combines the four phases in the learning cycle of abstract conceptualization, active experimentation, concrete experience, and reflective observation into pairs of preferences. This results in four learning style types: converger, diverger, assimilator, and accommodator. In brief, convergers are best at identifying practical uses for ideas, divergers prefer to observe situations from many perspectives, assimilators are best at taking in diverse information and synthesizing it into a structured form, and accommodators learn mainly from direct experience and experimentation. Each style demonstrates different preferences in taking in information and developing their personal knowledge.[34]

This framework is probably more useful than the MBTI in constructing teams for, say, knowledge co-creation. The LSI is certainly a useful tool for people to develop greater awareness and thus flexibility in their own learning styles, but also very much for gaining insight into clients' preferences in dealing with information and learning in the course of professional service relationships, and using that to refine their approaches and interactions.

## Representational System Preference

We have seen that people use visual, auditory, and kinesthetic representations in their mental representations. Everyone uses each of these representational systems to some degree. However, most individuals will demonstrate a preference for one of these systems in any given situation. This concept, originally introduced by the field of NLP, has been taken and applied broadly in many contexts. In the context of knowledge transfer, it is most useful in designing interaction and the presentation of information.

It is also useful to contrast analogical and propositional representations, and to note that people not only demonstrate preferences among sensory representational systems, but also between these and propositional representations. Some people are heavily oriented to propositional representations, and almost only think in "language," whereas others favor visual or other sensory-based "thinking."

## Meta-programs

Meta-programs in general describe the perceptual or behavioral preferences or orientation of a person along a given dimension. For example, the four dimensions of the Myers-Briggs test can be considered meta-programs. The value of the concept is that it allows us to focus on and develop the meta-programs or dimensions that are of particular interest to us, in this case in effective knowledge communication and elicitation.

For example, one basic meta-program I have found to be of value in professional communication is that of Complexity/Simplicity. In communicating rich conceptual information, for example, research on international financial markets or emergent industries, people tend to show preferences for complexity or simplicity of the causal structures implicit in the presentation. Some people tend to accept only explanations or analyses that exceed a certain level of complexity, whereas others prefer frameworks that contain a limited number of elements and interrelationships. Considerably greater refinement is possible in understanding the diversity of people's preferences in taking in highly conceptual information. However, applying even this simple filter of cognitive preference can greatly enhance communication.

## Scenario Formation

As we have seen, people often think and make decisions on the basis of the possible scenarios for the future they have generated. Gaining insight into the structure of how clients form and work with mental scenarios in their analysis and decision making can be very valuable in tailoring communication. This is clearly challenging, as clients very rarely have any perception of this themselves. Still, it is possible to gain some understanding of these processes within an ongoing relationship.

This is an aspect of cognitive style, as people display different preferences for how they form scenarios in their analysis and decision making. Some of the key dimensions are the degree to which thinking is focused on a single central scenario, as opposed to several scenarios considered reasonably plausible; how much detail the central scenario is developed; to what degree secondary scenarios can be contradictory to the central scenario; and how flexible the central scenario is to change given new information. Another important preference is whether people form scenarios in analogical or propositional forms (or both). This will vary depending on the context. Situations involving personal experience such as social interaction are more likely to be constituted by images or conversations, while conceptual issues such as the state of the economy will tend more to be propositional. However, individuals will show markedly different individual preferences. Having even some idea of these aspects of how a client forms mental scenarios in making decisions can be very valuable in being able to present information and ideas more effectively, and in adding greater value.

## Applications of Cognitive Style

As we have seen, there are a wide variety of frames and perspectives on the diversity of cognitive styles. The broader study of personality styles assists us in the full scope of our interactions with others, while understanding cognitive styles is primarily valuable in enhancing the communication and development of knowledge with others.

The greatest value of the understanding of cognitive styles is in direct contact with clients, so front-line professionals need training and development in an appropriate model or models of cognitive style, selected to be relevant for the way in which they usually interact with their clients. This should be specifically framed to provide a starting point for professionals to develop their understanding on an ongoing basis as they apply what they learn in their client interactions.

The most obvious application of cognitive styles is in tailoring interaction with individuals and small groups so that there is the most effective flow of knowledge. These skills are basic ones in the toolkit of the facilitator, especially in knowledge creation projects.

On a broader level, understanding the diversity of cognitive styles means that all communication and interaction should be designed to be useful and accessible to all people, rather than a narrow group of people. The design of everything from documents to conferences should specifically consider these issues. Most people (and professionals are perhaps more guilty than most!) tend to communicate and interact in a way that suits their own cognitive style, on the implicit assumption that others think like they do. Educating professionals to communicate more effectively to a broader audience can result in substantial benefits.

## ELICITING MENTAL MODELS

It can be immensely valuable to help make an individual's or group's mental models explicit, as we saw in Chapter 4. Some of the benefits are that this allows clients to do the following.

- Understand better the basis on which they are making decisions, and their underlying assumptions
- Enrich and enhance the usefulness of their mental models for the situation
- Integrate individual mental models within a group
- Create a framework for constructive discussion
- Establish whether the actions they are taking are in fact consistent with their mental models

Over the last couple of decades a number of researchers have been developing and experimenting with approaches to making mental models explicit. As Eden points out, however, "the process of articulation is a significant influence on present and future cognition."[35] In other words, the process of making mental models explicit changes the mental models. For academic purposes, this is a significant problem in understanding the nature of people's mental models, and how they relate to their behavior. In professional services and consulting, this is not a significant issue, as virtually invariably the changes that happen in making mental models explicit result in richer and more useful mental models.

Gaining insight into how you think requires and provokes reflection and consideration that can only result in enhancements. As such, simply engaging in the process of making a client's mental models explicit can add very significant value in itself, by the knowledge development it evokes. Cossette and Audet write of the "emancipatory" properties of cognitive maps, and distinguish research in the field into the use of cognitive maps as decision-making tools and their application to personal development, in which self-examination facilitates the modification of attitudes and behavior.[36]

## Individual and Group Mental Models

The basic concept of mental models clearly refers to individuals. It is individuals who build mental models based on their experience, and use these to understand the world and decide how best to act effectively. While some scholars suggest that it is inappropriate to treat a group or organization as if it has a mental model in the same ways as that of an individual, it clearly can be done, and in a business context the issue is whether it is *useful* to do so, and if so how best to adapt approaches to suit groups.[37]

Certainly groups have at least some shared experiences and commonality of understanding of their environment, and use this to make decisions that reflect what is in effect an implicit group mental model. For a group to come to an effective decision, there must be some element of shared meaning.[38] As a group works together, there will be further shared experience, and in the ongoing discussion of the meaning and relevance of that experience the group's mental models will be reinforced, in terms of greater integration of the individual's mental models and ability to make effective decisions as a group.[39] This process of integrating individual mental models within a group and developing a useful and flexible group framework for making decisions is greatly facilitated by thinking in terms of the group's mental models, and working with the group at that level. The fundamental approaches of much strategy consulting work, for example, is based on an implicit assumption that the client's senior executives have collective mental models.

## Cognitive Mapping

*Cognitive mapping* covers a broad range of techniques for developing visual and sometimes data-based representations of a person or group's cognition of some part of their environment. Other terms, such as *concept mapping* and *causal mapping*, are sometimes used for related ideas. Here, our focus is cognitive maps that help to make explicit people's mental models, in the sense of their understanding of behavior and causality on which they base their decisions and actions in a particular domain.

There are a wide variety of approaches that have been developed and used for building cognitive maps.[40] These techniques can be used for capturing expertise and knowledge, studying organizational decision making, and a variety of other processes. However, we are primarily interested in using them as a practical tool for working with individuals and groups to enrich and integrate their mental models. This is most easily achieved in a facilitated process, which draws out people's perceptions of key concepts and the relationships between them and maps these visually so that people can iteratively refine their collective understanding through consideration and discussion. These can be mapped on whiteboards or paper, or alternatively software is available to represent the cognitive maps and analyze the resultant framework.[41] One of the valuable focuses for discussion is getting agreement on the meanings of the core concepts or units on which the map is based, which enables the building of a vocabulary that is truly shared across the group.

More structured approaches can sometimes be valuable. In these, individuals are commonly interviewed using consistent methodologies to uncover the key elements and causal relationships implicit in their mental models, and shown the resultant maps for feedback. The cognitive maps of the individuals can then be used as a basis for work as a group, or combined into composite maps.

A simple example of a basic style of cognitive map, mapping part of one professional's thinking, is shown in Figure A–4. A plus symbol on an arrow indicates that this relationship supports the target concept, while a minus symbol indicates that it erodes it. A preliminary glance at this simple map suggests an awareness of key business issues but a lack of strategic clarity on the part of the subject. Building a more complex map of existing thinking would usually be just the first step in developing an enhanced conception of the strategic direction of the organization in the context of a systemic understanding of the business environment.

## VISUAL KNOWLEDGE ACQUISITION

Since people to whatever degree think visually, it makes sense that showing people visual representations will help their understanding

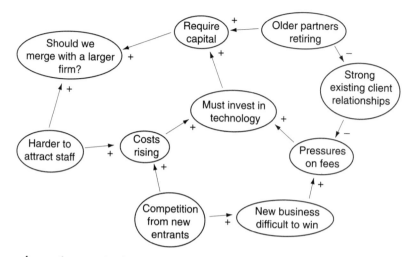

FIGURE A–4   *An example of a basic cognitive map.*

and acquisition of knowledge. Acquiring knowledge is largely about forming associations and relationships within and between concepts and domains, and visual representations implicitly allow the depiction of relationships in two and even three dimensions, with variables such as size, direction, type, and strength of relationship, and so on all readily represented.

The empirical evidence strongly supports the value of visual representations in knowledge acquisition. One researcher has stated "probably no other instructional device leads to more consistently beneficial results than does adding pictures to text," noting that those benefits have been shown to extend across a wide variety of tests, subjects, and types and functions of pictures.[42] In studies of the use of visual representations in the development of mental models in science education, researchers found evidence that visuals resulted in superior mental models, including better and more accurately organized concepts.[43] Interestingly, these and other studies have also shown that the addition of graphics can improve the performance of high-IQ students more than low-IQ students. Winn suggests that more able students are better able to handle and use the greater information load given by pictures supplementing text, which can overburden less able students.[44]

The key issue is that if people perceive and think visuospatially as well as propositionally, we need to present information and ideas to them both propositionally (in words and equations) and visually (in diagrams and illustrations). As such, visual representations will almost never stand alone, but are an incredibly valuable *complement* to text, especially for concepts difficult to verbalize. Text is still often used alone, limiting its ability to be effectively internalized as knowledge.

Cognitive load theory, developed by John Sweller, suggests that instruction will be more effective if it takes into account the limitations of working memory.[45] One of the techniques this implies is avoiding splitting the attention of learners. In situations in which text and visuals provide complementary messages, integrating these into a single representation that incorporates the necessary text into the diagram will facilitate learning.

On a very practical level, well-designed visual representations help cut through information overload in a number of ways. Visuals attract the eye, drawing clients' valuable attention. Not only do people tend to look at the diagrams in documents before text but the reduced time required to assimilate information using visuals means that people will consistently favor those documents, and have their information burden eased.

## SYMBOLS AND CONVENTIONS

There is a wide variety of symbols and conventions used, usually implicitly, in visual representations. Some of these reflect how people without preconceptions tend to understand diagrams, others are learned through convention, and some differ across cultures. Without trying to cover these conventions exhaustively, it is worth pointing out a few that represent the types of issues that can be useful in the design of visual representations of concepts.

- The size of the representation of a concept is perceived to be related to its importance.
- In a diagram that shows associated concepts, the physical proximity on the page or screen of the concepts is considered to show how closely related the concepts are.
- A number of boxes placed in a line below a single box are assumed to represent a hierarchy.
- A left-to-right string of tasks or events is perceived as representing a sequence occurring over time.

Using these types of conventions allows the implicit communication of conceptual relationships in easily assimilated representations. Many of these types of conventions are taken for granted when designing visuals, but it can also be useful to use them more deliberately in order to structure the communication of complex ideas.

## Summary: Mental Models and Knowledge Acquisition

To transfer knowledge effectively we must understand how people acquire knowledge and understanding. Cognitive science and related disciplines provide valuable lessons for business professionals. An understanding of these fields will become an increasingly important part of the core knowledge and expertise required by all professionals.

Our mental models are the foundation of how we understand our world and act in order to achieve the results we desire. Knowledge acquisition is about integrating new experiences and information into our existing mental models, and the breadth and richness of our existing mental models determines how easily and usefully we can internalize new experience. If we understand the *structure* of how people build mental models, and the *differences* in how they take in information and act on it, we are able to communicate far more effectively in allowing others to integrate it as their own personal knowledge.

There is much empirical evidence to help us to understand the fundamental nature of the structure of mental models, and a number of frameworks and tools we can use to gain an understanding of the cognitive styles of our clients. Cognitive mapping, which covers a broad range of approaches, is a powerful tool for eliciting, enriching, and integrating the mental models of individuals and groups, while the judicious use of visual representations can greatly assist effective knowledge acquisition.

These insights, tools, and techniques are potentially very useful and effective in the context of all knowledge-based client relationships, but are by no means simple to learn and apply. It is an ongoing journey to gain deeper insight into how the people you work and interact with acquire knowledge, and to refine the ways you interact with them so as to facilitate their ability to acquire and develop knowledge. The rewards, however, are immense, as the strong positive feedback loop of knowledge-based client relationships means that gaining even a slight edge over your competitors in your ability to develop richer knowledge-based interaction with your clients will result in ever-closer and more profitable relationships, with abundant value creation for both yourself and your clients.

## Notes

1   Ray Jackendoff, *Languages of the Mind: Essays on Mental Representation*, Cambridge, MA: The MIT Press, 1995, p. 18.

2   See, for example, Allan Paivio, *Mental Representations: A Dual-Coding Approach*, Oxford, U.K.: Oxford University Press, 1986.

3   See, for example, Allan Paivio, "The Empirical Case for Dual Coding," in *Imagery, Memory, and Cognition: Essays in Honor of Allan Paivio*, J. C. Yuille (ed.), Hillsdale, NJ: Lawrence Erlbaum Associates, 1983.

4   For a review of experimental evidence on the dual-coding theory, see Michael Eysenck and Mark Keane, *Cognitive Psychology: A Student's Handbook.*, 3rd ed., Hove, U.K.: Psychology Press, 1995.

5   For a detailed study of visuospatial cognition, see Manuel de Vega and Marc Marschark (eds.), *Models of Visuospatial Cognition*, New York: Oxford University Press, 1996.

[6] See, for example, Robert B. Dilts, Todd Epstein, and Robert W. Dilts, *Tools for Dreamers: Strategies for Creativity and the Structure of Innovation*, Capitola, CA: Meta Publications, 1991, p. 372.

[7] William James, *The Principles of Psychology*, 1890, chapter 18. James also described the principles of mental representations in his groundbreaking work, which is available on the Web at *www.yorku.ca/dept/psych/classics/James/Principles/index.htm*.

[8] See Noam Chomsky, *Aspects of the Theory of Syntax*, Cambridge, MA: The MIT Press, 1965.

[9] For an example of experimental confirmation of this, see Philip N. Johnson-Laird and R. Stevenson, "Memory for Syntax," *Nature*, vol. 227, 1970, p. 412.

[10] See, for example, Noam Chomsky, *Language and Problems of Knowledge: The Managua Lectures*, Cambridge, MA: The MIT Press, 1988.

[11] From Kenneth Craik, *The Nature of Explanation*, Cambridge, U.K.: Cambridge University Press, 1943, as quoted in Philip N. Johnson-Laird, *Mental Models: Towards a Cognitive Science of Language, Inference and Consciousness*, Cambridge, U.K.: Cambridge University Press, 1983.

[12] Johnson-Laird, p. 2.

[13] Gordon H. Bower and Ernest R. Hilgard, *Theories of Learning*, Englewood Cliffs, NJ: Prentice-Hall, 1981.

[14] Jerry A. Fodor, *Concepts: Where Cognitive Science Went Wrong*, Oxford, U.K.: Oxford University Press, 1998, p. 27.

[15] Alfred Korzybski, *Science and Sanity: An Introduction to Non-Aristotelian Systems and General Semantics*, 2nd ed., Lancaster, PA.: International Non-Aristotelian Library Publishing, 1941, p. 58.

[16] Johnson-Laird.

[17] Amos Tversky, "Features of Similarity," *Psychological Review*, vol. 84, 1977, pp. 327–352.

[18] Dedre Gentner, "Structure-Mapping: A Theoretical Framework for Analogy," *Cognitive Science* 7, 1983, pp. 155–170.

[19] See Hillel J. Einhorn and Robin M. Hogarth, "Judging Probable Cause," *Psychological Review*, vol. 99, no. 1, 1986, pp. 3–19.

[20] Amos Tversky and Daniel Kahneman, "Extensional Versus Intuitive Reasoning: The Conjunction Fallacy in Probability Judgment," *Psychological Review*, vol. 90, 1983, pp. 293–315.

[21] George A. Miller, "The Magic Number Seven, Plus or Minus Two," *Psychological Review* 63, 1956, pp. 81–93.

[22] Herbert A. Simon, "How Big Is a Chunk?," *Science* 183, 1974, pp. 482–488.

23 Miller, Galanter, and Pribram suggest that all intentional behavior is guided by hierarchical plans, driven by the attempt to use our limited memory capabilities. See George A. Miller, Eugene Galanter, and Karl H. Pribram, *Plans and the Structure of Behavior*, New York: Holt, 1960, pp. 130–132.

24 As described in Eysenck and Keane, from M. T. H. Chi, P. J. Feltovich, and R. Glaser, "Categorization and Representation of Physics Problems by Experts and Novices," *Cognitive Science* 5, 1981, pp. 121–152; and from M. T. H. Chi, R. Glaser, and E. Rees, "Expertise in Problem Solving," in *Advances in the Psychology of Human Intelligence, Volume 2*, R. J. Sternberg (ed.), Hillsdale, NJ: Lawrence Erlbaum Associates, 1983.

25 Douglas Hofstadter, *Gödel, Escher, Bach: An Eternal Golden Braid*, New York: Basic Books, 1979.

26 H. Maturana and F. Varela, *Autopoiesis and Cognition: The Realization of the Living*, Dordrecht, Netherlands/Boston: D. Reidel, 1980.

27 John D. W. Morecroft, "System Dynamics: Portraying Bounded Rationality," *Omega*, vol. 11, no. 2, 1983, pp. 131–142.

28 See, for example, Michel Bougon, Nancy Baird, John M. Komocar, and William Ross, "Identifying Strategic Loops: The Self-Q Interviews," in *Mapping Strategic Thought*, A. S. Huff (ed.), Chichester, U.K.: John Wiley & Sons, 1990; and Colin Eden and Fran Ackerman, "The Analysis of Cause Maps," *Journal of Management Studies*, vol. 29, no. 3, May 1992, pp. 309–323.

29 See Senge. See also Joseph O'Connor and Ian McDermott, *The Art of System Thinking: Essential Skills for Creativity and Problem Solving*, London, U.K.: Thorsons, 1997.

30 D. H. Ingvar, "'Memory of the Future': An Essay on the Temporal Organization of Conscious Awareness," *Human Neurobiology* 4, 1985, pp. 127–136.

31 Tversky and Kahnemann.

32 George Lakoff and Mark Johnson, *Metaphors We Live By*, Chicago: The University of Chicago Press, 1980.

33 Dorothy Leonard specifically suggests using the MBTI to design creative abrasion. See D. A. Leonard and S. Straus, "Putting Your Company's Whole Brain to Work," *Harvard Business Review*, vol. 75, no. 4, July/August 1997.

34 Kolb.

35 Colin Eden, "On the Nature of Cognitive Maps," *Journal of Management Studies*, vol. 29, no. 3, May 1992, pp. 261–265.

36 Pierre Cossette and Michel Audet, "Mapping of an Idiosyncratic Schema," *Journal of Management Studies*, vol. 29, no. 3, May 1992, pp. 325–347.

37 See, for example, Eden.

[38] For a good review of the relevant literature on consensus and shared meaning, see Choo, pp. 80–84.

[39] See Kees van der Heijden and Colin Eden, "The Theory and Praxis of Reflective Learning in Strategy Making," in *Managerial and Organizational Cognition: Theory, Methods and Research*, Colin Eden and J.-C. Spender (eds.), London, U.K.: Sage, 1998, pp. 58–75.

[40] Very useful reviews of a range of approaches to cognitive mapping are provided in Anne S. Huff (ed.), *Mapping Strategic Thought*, Chichester, U.K.: John Wiley & Sons, 1990; and in Colin Eden and J.-C. Spender (eds.), *Managerial and Organizational Cognition: Theory, Methods and Research*, London, U.K.: Sage, 1998.

[41] An example of cognitive mapping software is Decision Explorer (previously COPE), distributed by Banxia and Scolari.

[42] B. Weidermann, "When Good Pictures Fail," in *Knowledge Acquisition from Text and Pictures*, H. Mandl and J. R. Levin (eds.), Netherlands: Elsevier Science Publishers, 1989.

[43] W. D. Winn, "The Effect of Block-word Diagrams on the Structuring of Science Concepts as a Function of General Ability," *Journal of Research in Science Teaching* 17, 1980, pp. 201–211; and R. E. Mayer, J. L. Dyck, and L. K. Cook, "Techniques That Help Readers Build Mental Models from Scientific Text: Definitions, Pretraining and Signaling," *Journal of Educational Psychology* 76, 1984, pp. 1089–1105, as quoted in W. D. Winn, "Design and Use of Instructional Graphics," in *Knowledge Acquisition from Text and Pictures*, H. Mandl and J. R. Levin (eds.), Netherlands: Elsevier Science Publishers, 1989, p. 135.

[44] Winn (1989) again quotes Winn (1980), as well as P. E. Parkhurst and F. M. Dwyer, "An Experimental Assessment of Students' IQ Level and Their Ability to Profit from Visualized Instructions," *Journal of Instructional Psychology* 10, 1983, pp. 9–20.

[45] See, for example, P. Chandler and J. Sweller, "Cognitive Load Theory and the Format of Instruction," *Cognition and Instruction* 8, 1991, pp. 293–332.

# Bibliography

Abramson, Gary. "Their Pain, Your Gain," *CIO Enterprise*, October 15, 1998.

Anonymous. "Creative Agency of the Year: Mother," *Marketing*, December 12, 2002.

Argyris, Chris. "Single-Loop and Double-Loop Models in Research on Decision Making," *Administrative Science Quarterly*, vol. 21, September 1976, pp. 363–375.

Argyris, Chris. "Teaching Smart People How to Learn," *Harvard Business Review*, May/June 1991, pp. 99–109.

Arthur, Brian W. "Competing Technologies, Increasing Returns, and Lock-in by Historical Events," *The Economic Journal*, no. 99, March 1989, pp. 116–131.

Ashby, W. Ross. *An Introduction to Cybernetics*. London, U.K.: Chapman & Hall, 1956.

Badarraco, Joseph L. *The Knowledge Link: How Firms Compete Through Strategic Alliances*. Boston: Harvard Business School Press, 1991.

Bateson, Gregory. *Steps to an Ecology of Mind*. London, U.K.: Paladin, 1973.

Beach, Lee Roy. *The Psychology of Decision Making: People in Organizations*. Thousand Oaks, CA: Sage Publications, 1997.

Bougon, Michel, Nancy Baird, John M. Komocar, and William Ross. "Identifying Strategic Loops: The Self-Q Interviews," in *Mapping Strategic Thought*, A. S. Huff (ed.), Chichester, U.K.: John Wiley & Sons, 1990.

Bower, Gordon H., and Ernest R. Hilgard. *Theories of Learning*. Englewood Cliffs, NJ: Prentice-Hall, 1981.

Bresnahan, Jennifer. "The Latest in Suits," *CIO Enterprise*, October 15, 1998.

Brooking, Annie. *Intellectual Capital: Core Asset for the Third Millennium Enterprise*. London: International Thomson Business Press, 1996.

Brown, John Seely, and Estee Solomon Gray. "The People Are the Company," *Fast Company*, no. 1, November 1995, p. 78.

Capon, Noel. *Key Account Management and Planning: The Comprehensive Handbook for Managing Your Company's Most Important Strategic Asset.* New York: The Free Press, 2001.

Chandler, P., and J. Sweller. "Cognitive Load Theory and the Format of Instruction," *Cognition and Instruction* 8, 1991, pp. 293–332.

Chomsky, Noam. *Aspects of the Theory of Syntax.* Cambridge, MA: The MIT Press, 1965.

Chomsky, Noam. *Language and Problems of Knowledge: The Managua Lectures.* Cambridge, MA: The MIT Press, 1988.

Choo, Chun Wei. *The Knowing Organization: How Organizations Use Information to Construct Meaning, Create Knowledge, and Make Decisions.* New York: Oxford University Press, 1998.

Clarke, Thomas, and Stewart Clegg. *Changing Paradigms: The Transformation of Management Knowledge for the 21st Century.* London: HarperCollinsBusiness, 1998.

Cohen, Don, and Bruno Laporte. "The Evolution of the Knowledge Bank," *KM Magazine*, March 2004.

Cohen, Wesley M., and Daniel A. Levinthal. "Absorptive Capacity: A New Perspective on Learning and Innovation," *Administrative Science Quarterly* 35, 1990, pp. 128–152.

Cossette, Pierre, and Michel Audet. "Mapping of an Idiosyncratic Schema," *Journal of Management Studies*, vol. 29, no. 3, May 1992, pp. 325–347.

Cotterill, Brian. "*How Outsourcing Helped Shell Achieve World's Best Practice*," Competitive Advantage from Best Practice Outsourcing: The Untold Success Story Conference, University of Technology Sydney, Sydney, Australia, June 24, 2004 (unpublished).

Craik, Kenneth. *The Nature of Explanation.* Cambridge, U.K.: Cambridge University Press, 1943.

Daft, Richard L., and Robert H. Lengel. "Information Richness: A New Approach to Manager Information Processing and Organization Design," in *Research in Organizational Behaviour*, B. Staw and L. L. Cummings (eds.), vol. 6, Greenwich, CT: JAI Press, 1984.

Daft, Richard L., and Robert H. Lengel. "Organizational Information Requirements, Media Richness and Structural Design," *Management Science*, vol. 32, no. 5, May 1986, pp. 554–571.

Davenport, Thomas H. "The Fad that Forgot People," *Fast Company* 1, November 1995, p. 70.

Davenport, Thomas H., and Laurence Prusak. *Working Knowledge*. Boston: Harvard Business School Press, 1998.

Davenport, Thomas H., and John C. Beck. *The Attention Economy*. Boston: Harvard Business School Press, 2001.

Meyer, Davis, Stan, and Christopher. *Blur: The Speed of Change in the Connected Economy*. Reading, MA: Perseus, 1998.

Dawson, Ross. "Information Overload — Problem or Opportunity?," *Company Director*, October 1997, pp. 44–45.

Dawson, Ross. "Performance Management Strategies for Knowledge Organisations," *Reward Management Bulletin*, vol. 2, no. 3, February/March 1998, pp. 183–186.

Dawson, Ross. "Did You Forecast Asia? Scenario Planning in Portfolio and Risk Management," *The Australian Corporate Treasurer*, August 1998.

Dawson, Ross. *Living Networks: Leading Your Company, Customers, and Partners in the Hyper-Connected Economy*. Upper Saddle River, NJ: Financial Times/ Prentice-Hall, 2002.

Dawson, Ross. "The Five Key Frames for the Future of KM," *KM Review*, vol. 7, Issue 4, September/October 2004, p. 3.

Dembo, Ron S., and Andrew Freeman. *Seeing Tomorrow: Rewriting the Rules of Risk*. New York: John Wiley & Sons, 1998.

de Vega, Manuel, and Marc Marschark (eds.). *Models of Visuospatial Cognition*. New York: Oxford University Press, 1996.

Dilts, Robert B., Todd Epstein, and Robert W. Dilts. *Tools for Dreamers: Strategies for Creativity and the Structure of Innovation*. Capitola, CA: Meta Publications, 1991.

Drucker, Peter. *Managing for the Future*. Oxford, U.K.: Butterworth-Heinemann, 1992.

Drucker, Peter. *Post-Capitalist Society*. New York: HarperCollins, 1993.

Dunn, Paul, and Ron Baker. *The Firm of the Future: A Guide for Accountants, Lawyers, and Other Professional Services*. Hoboken, NJ: John Wiley & Sons, 2003.

Eccles, Robert G., and Dwight B. Crane. *Doing Deals: Investment Banks at Work*. Cambridge, MA: Harvard Business School Press, 1988.

Eden, Colin. "On the Nature of Cognitive Maps," *Journal of Management Studies*, vol. 29, no. 3, May 1992, pp. 261–265.

Eden, Colin, and Fran Ackerman. "The Analysis of Cause Maps," *Journal of Management Studies*, vol. 29, no. 3, May 1992, pp. 309–323.

Eden, Colin, and J.-C. Spender (eds.). *Managerial and Organizational Cognition: Theory, Methods and Research*. London: Sage, 1998.

Edvinsson, Leif, and Michael S. Malone. *Intellectual Capital: Realizing Your Company's True Value by Finding Its Hidden Roots*. New York: HarperBusiness, 1997.

Einhorn, Hillel J., and Robin M. Hogarth. "Judging Probable Cause," *Psychological Review*, vol. 99, no. 1, 1986, pp. 3–19.

Elliott, Susan. "Manpower Creates Customer Loyalty Through Shared 'Stories,' Information," *Knowledge Management in Practice*, Issue 13, 3Q 1998, American Productivity & Quality Center.

Ensor, Benjamin. "European Brokers Survey: Pulling Away from the Pack," *Euromoney*, November 1997.

Evans, Philip, and Thomas S. Wurster. *Blown to Bits: How the New Economics of Information Transforms Strategy*. Boston: Harvard Business School Press, 2000.

Eysenck, Michael, and Mark Keane. *Cognitive Psychology: A Student's Handbook* (3rd ed.). Hove, U.K.: Psychology Press, 1995.

Fischetti, Mark. "Masters of the (Information) Universe," *Fast Company*, August/September 1997, pp. 181–187.

Fisher, Lawrence M. "Technology Transfer at Stanford University," *Strategy & Business*, 4th Quarter 1998.

Fodor, Jerry A. *Concepts: Where Cognitive Science Went Wrong*. Oxford, U.K.: Oxford University Press, 1998.

Gentner, Dedre. "Structure-Mapping: A Theoretical Framework for Analogy," *Cognitive Science* 7, 1983, pp. 155–170.

Goldman, Steven L., Roger N. Nagel, and Kenneth Preiss. *Agile Competitors and Virtual Organizations: Strategies for Enriching the Customer*. New York: Van Nostrand Reinhold, 1995.

Gregg, Deidre. "Preferring Gradual Growth, Consulting Firm Point B Is Selective About Its Projects," *Puget Sound Business Journal*, May 21, 2004.

Hamel, Gary. "Competition for Competence and Interpartner Learning Within International Strategic Alliances," *Strategic Management Journal* 12, 1991, pp. 83–103.

Hatfield, Stefano. "Mother Loves Your," *Creativity*, March 2002, pp. 30–31.

Hofstadter, Douglas. *Gödel, Escher, Bach: An Eternal Golden Braid*. New York: Basic Books, 1979.

Huff, Anne S. (ed.). *Mapping Strategic Thought*. Chichester, U.K.: John Wiley & Sons, 1990.

Ingvar, D. H. "'Memory of the Future': An Essay on the Temporal Organization of Conscious Awareness," *Human Neurobiology* 4, 1985, pp. 127–136.

Isenberg, Daniel J. "How Senior Managers Think," *Harvard Business Review*, November/December 1984.

Jackendoff, Ray. *Languages of the Mind: Essays on Mental Representation*. Cambridge, MA: The MIT Press, 1995.

James, Geoffrey. "Methods of Payment," *CIO Enterprise*, October 15, 1998.

James, William. *The Principles of Psychology*, 1890, available at *http://psychclassics. yorku.ca/James/Principles*.

Janis, Irving L. *Groupthink: Psychological Studies of Policy Decisions and Fiascoes*. Boston: Houghton-Mifflin, 1982.

Johnson-Laird, Philip N. *Mental Models: Towards a Cognitive Science of Language, Inference and Consciousness*. Cambridge, U.K.: Cambridge University Press, 1983.

Johnson-Laird, Philip N., and R. Stevenson. "Memory for Syntax," *Nature* 227, 1970.

Kelly, Kevin. *New Rules for the New Economy: 10 Radical Strategies for a Connected World*. New York: Viking, 1998.

Kintsch, Walter. "The Role of Knowledge in Discourse Comprehension: A Construction-Integration Model," *Psychological Review*, vol. 95, no. 2, 1988, pp. 163–182.

Koestler, Arthur. *The Act of Creation*. London: Hutchinson, 1964.

Kolb, David A. *Experiential Learning: Experience as the Source of Learning and Development*. Englewood Cliffs, NJ: Prentice-Hall, 1984.

Korzybski, Alfred. *Science and Sanity: An Introduction to Non-Aristotelian Systems and General Semantics* (2nd ed.). Lancaster, PA: International Non-Aristotelian Library Publishing, 1941.

Kuhn, Thomas S. *The Structure of Scientific Revolutions*. Chicago: University of Chicago Press, 1970.

Lakoff, George, and Mark Johnson. *Metaphors We Live By*. Chicago: University of Chicago Press, 1980.

Lane, Peter J., and Michael Lubatkin. "Relative Absorptive Capacity and Interorganizational Learning," *Strategic Management Journal* 19, 1998, pp. 461–477.

Leonard, Dorothy. *Wellsprings of Knowledge: Building and Sustaining the Sources of Innovation*. Boston, MA: Harvard Business School Press, 1995.

Leonard, D. A., and S. Straus. "Putting Your Company's Whole Brain to Work," *Harvard Business Review*, vol. 75, no. 4, July/August 1997.

Liedtka, Jeanne M., Mark E. Haskins, John W. Rosenblum, and Jack Weber. "The Generative Cycle: Linking Knowledge and Relationships," *Sloan Management Review*, Fall 1997, pp. 47–58.

Liedtka, Jeanne M., and John W. Rosenblum. "Shaping Conversations: Making Strategy, Managing Change," *California Management Review*, vol. 39, no. 1, Fall 1996, pp. 141–157.

Lovik, Terje. "Meeting the Challenges of SAM in a Service Environment," *Focus: Europe*, vol. 3, no. 2, 2nd Quarter 2003, pp. 12–15.

Maister, David H. *Managing the Professional Service Firm*. New York: The Free Press, 1997.

Mandl, H., and J. R. Levin (eds.). *Knowledge Acquisition from Text and Pictures*. Amsterdam, Holland: Elsevier Science Publishers B. V., 1989.

March, James. *A Primer on Decision Making: How Decisions Happen*. New York: Harvard Business School Press, 1994.

Markides, Constantinos. "Strategic Innovation," *Sloan Management Review*, Spring 1997, pp. 9–23.

Mathias, Peter, and Juergen Fitschen. "Managing Global Client Relationships at Deutsche Bank: Mangement Discipline, Process and Technology," *Focus: Europe*, vol. 1, no. 1, 1st Quarter 2001, pp. 1–5.

Maturana, H., and F. Varela. *Autopoiesis and Cognition: The Realization of the Living*. Dordrecht, Netherlands/Boston: D. Reidel, 1980.

Meyer, Chris. "What's the Matter?," *Business 2.0*, April 1999, p. 88.

Mieszkowski, Katharine. "Opposites Attract," *Fast Company*, Issue 12, December 1997, p. 42.

Miller, George A. "The Magic Number Seven, Plus or Minus Two," *Psychological Review* 63, 1956, pp. 81–93.

Miller, George A., Eugene Galanter, and Karl H. Pribram. *Plans and the Structure of Behavior*. New York: Holt, 1960.

Minto, Barbara. *The Minto Pyramid Principle: Logic in Writing, Thinking and Problem Solving*. London: Minto International, 1996.

Mintzberg, Henry. *The Nature of Managerial Work*. New York: Harper & Row, 1973.

Mintzberg, Henry. *Mintzberg on Management: Inside Our Strange World of Organizations*. New York: Free Press, 1989.

Morecroft, John D. W. "System Dynamics: Portraying Bounded Rationality," *Omega*, vol. 11, no. 2, 1983, pp. 131–142.

Negroponte, Nicholas. *Being Digital*. New York: Knopf, 1995.

Newbold, Tim. "More Clients Ride Lovells' 'Mexican Wave'," *Legal Week*, September 16, 2004.

Nicou, Monica, Christine Ribbing, and Eva Åding. *Sell Your Knowledge: The Professional's Guide to Winning More Business*. London: Kogan Page, 1994.

Nonaka, Ikujiro, and Hirotaka Takeuchi. *The Knowledge-Creating Company*. New York: Oxford University Press, 1995.

Normann, Richard, and Rafael Ramírez. "From Value Chain to Value Constellation: Designing Interactive Strategy," *Harvard Business Review*, July/August 1993, pp. 65–77.

O'Connor, Joseph, and Ian McDermott. *The Art of System Thinking: Essential Skills for Creativity and Problem Solving*. London: Thorsons, 1997.

O'Hara-Devereaux, Mary, and Robert Johansen. *GlobalWork: Bridging Distance, Culture, and Time*. San Francisco: Jossey-Bass, 1994.

Osborn, Alex F. *Applied Imagination* (3rd rev. ed.). New York: Charles Scribner's Sons, 1963.

Ozzie, Ray. "Ray Ozzie Looks Back, Looks Ahead," *ZDNet*, December 6, 2004, at *news.zdnet.com/2100-9589_22-5479624.html*.

Paivio, Allan. "The Empirical Case for Dual Coding," in *Imagery, Memory, and Cognition: Essays in Honor of Allan Paivio*. J. C. Yuille (ed.), Hillsdale, NJ: Lawrence Erlbaum Associates, 1983.

Paivio, Allan. *Mental Representations: A Dual-Coding Approach*. Oxford, U.K.: Oxford University Press, 1986.

Peppers, Don, and Martha Rogers. *The One-to-One Future: Building Relationships One Customer at a Time*. New York: Currency Doubleday, 1993.

Peppers, Don, and Martha Rogers. *Enterprise One to One: Tools for Competing in the Interactive Age*. New York: Currency Doubleday, 1997.

Peters, Tom. *Liberation Management: Necessary Disorganization for the Nanosecond Nineties*. New York: Fawcett Columbine, 1992.

Polanyi, Michael. *The Tacit Dimension*. London: Routledge & Kegan Paul, 1967.

Prahalad, C. K., and Gary Hamel. "The Core Competence of the Corporation," *Harvard Business Review*, May/June 1990.

Prokesh, Steven E. "Unleashing the Power of Learning: An Interview with British Petroleum's John Browne," *Harvard Business Review*, September/October 1997.

Quinn, James Brian, Philip Anderson, and Sydney Finkelstein. "Managing Professional Intellect: Making the Most of the Best," *Harvard Business Review*, March/April 1996, pp. 71–80.

Ransdell, Eric. "Redesigning the Design Business," *Fast Company*, Issue 16, August 1998, pp. 36–38.

Rempel, John K., John G. Holmes, and Mark P. Zanna. "Trust in Close Relationships," *Journal of Personality and Social Psychology*, vol. 49, no. 1, 1985, pp. 95–112.

Reuters. *Dying for Information?*. Reuters, 1996.

Ring, Peter S., and Andrew H. Van de Ven. "Structuring Cooperative Relationships Between Organizations," *Strategic Management Journal* 13, 1992, pp. 482–498.

Ring, Peter S., and Andrew H. Van de Ven. "Developmental Processes of Cooperative Interorganizational Relationships," *Academy of Management Review*, vol. 19, no. 1, 1994, pp. 90–118.

Roos, Johan, Göran Roos, Leif Edvinsson, and Nicola Dragnetti. *Intellectual Capital*. Basingstoke, U.K.: Macmillan Press, 1997.

Rosenberg, Geanne. "Big Four Auditors' Legal Services Hit by Sarbanes-Oxley," *New York Lawyer*, January 5, 2004.

Santangelo, Charles J., and William G. Johnston. "Tale of Compensation: Even in the Best of Times, Partner Compensation Isn't Easy," *Legal Management*, vol. 19, Issue 1, January/February 2000.

Schön, Donald A. *The Reflective Practitioner: How Professionals Think in Action*. New York: Basic Books, 1983.

Schwartz, Peter. *The Art of The Long View: Planning for the Future in an Uncertain World*. New York: Doubleday Currency, 1991.

Senge, Peter M. *The Fifth Discipline: The Art and Practice of the Learning Organization*. New York: Doubleday Currency, 1994.

Shapiro, Carl, and Hal Varian. *Information Rules: A Strategic Guide to the Network Economy*. Boston: Harvard Business School Press, 1998.

Shaw, Gordon, Robert Brown, and Philip Bromiley. "Strategic Stories: How 3M Is Rewriting Business Planning," *Harvard Business Review*, May/June 1998.

Shelley, G. C. "Dealing with Smart Clients," *Ivey Business Quarterly*, Autumn 1997, pp. 50–55.

Simon, Herbert A. "How Big Is a Chunk?," *Science* 183, 1974, pp. 482–488.

Simon, Herbert A. *Administrative Behavior: A Study of Decision-Making Processes in Administrative Organizations* (4th ed.). New York: The Free Press, 1997.

Sperry, Joseph. "Turning Innovative Account Management into Dollars: The Satyam-Caterpillar Story," *Velocity*, Q4 2003, pp. 31–34.

Stata, Ray. "Organizational Learning — The Key to Management Innovation," *Sloan Management Review*, Spring 1989, pp. 63–74.

Stewart, Thomas A. "Your Company's Most Valuable Asset: Intellectual Capital," *Fortune*, vol. 130, no. 7, October 3, 1994.

Stewart, Thomas A. "The Dance Steps Get Trickier All the Time," *Fortune*, May 26, 1997.

Stewart, Thomas A. *Intellectual Capital: The New Wealth of Organizations*. New York: Doubleday, 1997.

Stratford, Sherman. "Bringing Sears into the New World," *Fortune*, October 13, 1997.

Sutton, Robert I., and Andrew Hargadon. "Brainstorming Groups in Context: Effectiveness in a Product Design Firm," *Administrative Science Quarterly* 41, 1996, pp. 685–718.

Sveiby, Karl-Erik. *The New Organizational Wealth: Managing and Measuring Knowledge-Based Assets*. San Francisco: Berrett-Koehler, 1997.

Treat, John E., George E. Thibault, and Amy Asin. "Dynamic Competitive Simulation: Wargaming as a Strategic Tool," *Strategy & Business*, 2nd Quarter 1996.

Tufte, Edward. *The Visual Display of Quantitative Information*. Cheshire, CT: Graphics Press, 1983.

Tufte, Edward. *Envisioning Information*. Cheshire, CT: Graphics Press, 1990.

Turner, Arthur N. "Consulting Is More Than Giving Advice," *Harvard Business Review*, September/October 1982.

Tversky, Amos. "Features of Similarity," *Psychological Review* 84, 1977, pp. 327–352.

Tversky, Amos, and Daniel Kahneman. "Extensional Versus Intuitive Reasoning: The Conjunction Fallacy in Probability Judgment," *Psychological Review* 90, 1983, pp. 293–315.

van der Heijden, Kees. *Scenarios: The Art of Strategic Conversation*. London: John Wiley & Sons, 1996.

van der Heijden, Kees, and Colin Eden. "The Theory and Praxis of Reflective Learning in Strategy Making," in *Managerial and Organizational Cognition: Theory, Methods and Research.* Colin Eden and J.-C. Spender (eds.), London: Sage, 1998, pp. 58–75.

Vitrano, Paul, and Helen Bertelli. "B-School for Lawyers," *Legal Times,* May 10, 2004, p. 24.

Violino, Bob, and Bruce Caldwell. "Analyzing the Integrators," *Information Week,* November 16, 1998.

Wack, Pierre. "Scenarios: Uncharted Waters Ahead," *Harvard Business Review,* vol. 63, no. 5, September/October 1985, pp. 71–90.

Wack, Pierre. "Scenarios: Shooting the Rapids," *Harvard Business Review,* vol. 63, no. 6, November/December 1985, pp. 131–142.

Wathne, Kenneth, Johan Roos, and Georg von Krogh. "Towards a Theory of Knowledge Transfer in a Cooperative Context," in *Managing Knowledge: Perspectives on Cooperation and Competition,* Georg von Krogh and Johan Roos (eds.), London: Sage Publications, 1996, pp. 55–81.

Webber, Alan M. "What's So New About the New Economy?," *Harvard Business Review,* January/February 1993.

Weidermann, B. "When Good Pictures Fail," in *Knowledge Acquisition from Text and Pictures,* H. Mandl and J. R. Levin (eds.), Netherlands: Elsevier Science Publishers B. V., 1989.

Winn, W. D. "Design and Use of Instructional Graphics," in *Knowledge Acquisition from Text and Pictures,* H. Mandl and J. R. Levin (eds.), Netherlands: Elsevier Science Publishers B. V., 1989.

Wolfe, Tom. *The Bonfire of the Vanities.* New York: Bantam, 1988.

Wriston, Walter B. "Dumb Networks and Smart Capital," *The Cato Journal,* vol. 17, no. 3, Winter 1998.

Wurman, Richard Saul. *Information Architects.* New York: Graphis, 1997.

# Index

Page numbers with "t" denote tables; those with "f" denote figures

**Ross Dawson** is CEO of Advanced Human Technologies, a boutique international consulting firm that works with major professional services, financial services, and technology firms to enhance their strategic and client relationship capabilities. His reputation as a global business thought leader was firmly established by his bestselling first edition of *Developing Knowledge-Based Client Relationships,* and consolidated by his highly acclaimed second book *Living Networks*. He has also published over 60 articles, including the highly influential Microsoft Strategic White Paper, *How to Lock-in Your Clients*.

Ross is in strong demand worldwide as a keynote speaker, consultant, and workshop leader, having delivered speeches and workshops across five continents, with global media appearances including CNN, Bloomberg TV, SkyNews, European Business Network, and Channel

News Asia. Clients for Ross's speaking, workshops, and consulting include many of the world's most prestigious organizations, such as ABN AMRO, American Express, AXA, Deloitte, Deutsche Bank, IBM, KPMG, Microsoft, and Morgan Stanley. He is one of a few external faculty selected to run executive programs at the Australian Graduate School of Management, which is rated #1 in Asia and Australasia for executive programs by Financial Times, and has run executive programs and lectured at numerous academic institutions around the world.

Prior to establishing Advanced Human Technologies in 1996 Ross's positions included working for Thomson Financial in London as Global Director — Capital Markets, in Tokyo as Asian Director — Capital Markets, and in relationship management roles for Merrill Lynch and NCR. He holds a B.Sc.(Hons) from Bristol University, UK, and is certified as a Master Practitioner of Neuro-Linguistic Programming (NLP). He has extensive international business experience, and speaks five languages.

Ross Dawson
Advanced Human Technologies Inc.
Web: www.ahtgroup.com
Email: rossd@ahtgroup.com
Tel (US): +1-415 439 4890
Tel (Australia) +61-2 9994 8066